The World Book of

# HAPPINESS.

*edited by*
**Leo Bormans**

# The World Book of
# HAPPINESS.

**mc** **Marshall Cavendish**
Editions

Copyright © 2012, Marshall Cavendish International
For the English edition (world rights excluding Asia and North America).

Copyright © 2010, Uitgeverij Lannoo nv. For the original edition.
Original title: Geluk. The world book of happiness. Translated from the Dutch language.
www.lannoo.com

This edition published in English in 2012 by Marshall Cavendish Editions
An imprint of Marshall Cavendish International

PO Box 65829
London EC1P 1NY
United Kingdom
info@marshallcavendish.co.uk

and

1 New Industrial Road
Singapore 536196
genrefsales@sg.marshallcavendish.com
www.marshallcavendish.com/genref

Marshall Cavendish is a trademark of Times Publishing Limited.

**Other Marshall Cavendish offices:**
Marshall Cavendish International (Asia) Private Limited, 1 New Industrial Road, Singapore 536196 • Marshall
Cavendish Corporation. 99 White Plains Road, Tarrytown NY 10591-9001, USA • Marshall Cavendish International
(Thailand) Co Ltd. 253 Asoke, 12th Floor, Sukhumvit 21 Road, Klongtoey Nua, Wattana, Bangkok 10110, Thailand •
Marshall Cavendish (Malaysia) Sdn Bhd, Times Subang, Lot 46, Subang Hi-Tech Industrial Park, Batu Tiga, 40000
Shah Alam, Selangor Darul Ehsan, Malaysia.

A CIP record for this book is available from the British Library.

ISBN 978-981-434-632-0

Printed and bound in Slovenia by DZS.

Marshall Cavendish publishes an exciting range of books
on business, management and self-development.

If you would like to:
• Find out more about our titles
• Take advantage of our special offers
• Sign up to our e-newsletter

Please visit our
special website at: www.business-bookshop.co.uk

## A lot of fun

Work on subjective well-being has brought together researchers from the fields of economics, sociology, psychology, political science, brain sciences, and so on. Encouraging **dialogue** between different kinds of researchers is difficult but essential, and I am very glad that happiness research has helped to play this role. Although we have an idea about how some things work, we shouldn't underestimate how **little** we actually know. Anyone who pretends otherwise is probably a charlatan. Most of our scientific knowledge about happiness relates to rich countries, and may not be applicable to the **majority** of the world's population: once again, at the moment we simply do not know. There is so much more work to be done before we can be sure, and I am certain that it will be a lot of fun doing it.

**Professor Andrew Clark** (France)


## No duty

How ought we to live? This has been a central question in the ethical playground of philosophers throughout the centuries. It has been customary for these philosophers to use a **top-down approach** when addressing the issue of what a good life really means; unfortunately, their assessments do not incorporate information about how people actually experience this life. Therefore, the philosophical approach has been more prescriptive than descriptive, and philosophers' proposals about how we ought to live carry with them a sense of **duty**, and are usually accompanied by sanctions for those who fail to comply. Happiness research is based on the study of **how people assess their own lives** and the identification of those factors that systematically show up as fostering or deterring people's satisfaction with life. Like philosophy, happiness research also leads to proposals about how we can live a satisfactory life. However, these proposals carry the status of **recommendations** rather than of duty: you are not obliged to follow them. In fact, it is not even possible for everyone to follow them. Moreover, there are no sanctions in the case of failure to comply – although such failure is usually accompanied by regret.

**Professor Mariano Rojas** (Mexico)

*'Where is the **wisdom** we have lost in **knowledge**?*

*Where is the knowledge we have lost in **information**?'*

T.S. Eliot, Nobel Prize-winner for Literature, 1948

# Welcome in The World Book of Happiness

My friends tell me that I am a life-expert in optimism. And so I decided to write a book about it: *100% Positivo*. In this book I went in search of the secret of optimism, both in myself and in the world around me. In the course of this search, I discovered that thousands of studies have already been carried out into optimism and happiness. And new ones are being conducted every day. **The beginning of the 21st century is therefore not only shrouded in bad news.** Worldwide, thousands of researchers are throwing themselves wholeheartedly into the relatively new discipline of positive psychology. Positive psychology does not take faults, failures and negative syndromes as its starting point, but is based on the positive power of people. If we have a better understanding of the things that make us healthy, happy and successful, then we can make better use of these mechanisms to create our own happiness and happiness in the world around us. After a lecture, I was once approached by a 17-year-old boy. He said: "Now I know what to answer when people ask me what I want to be. I am going to be an optimist. I understand now that this is also something you can learn."

The first questions that journalists ask to people who specialise in optimism and happiness are always full of suspicion. "Are you some sort of idealist? Can you not see what a sad and terrible place the world really is?" These questions are often tinged with cynicism. **Cynics are not often happy, but they are very pleased with themselves. They are effectively saying: "Look how clever and intelligent I am! In just a few minutes I can extinguish all the passion, fire and hope that burns within you!"** This is the easiest – but not the most rewarding – philosophy of life. Others try to play down optimism with trite formulas. "I am neither an optimist nor a pessimist, I am a realist." So-called realists are really pessimists who won't admit it. Of course, there are times when things go wrong and everyone has the right to feel sad on these occasions. Even so, there is an immeasurable positive force in each of us. And we can develop and strengthen this force. In Nepal I learnt the meaning of the daily greeting which says so much: Namasté ("I bow to the god in you").

For this book I have read miles and miles of scientific reports and research results. But I was always surprised that none of my friends had ever heard anything about all of this. "Positive psychology? What's that?" And so I decided to contact **100 of the most prominent experts in the field** and asked them to sum up their work in **a maximum of 1,000 words,** as a message for the world. I discovered that positive psychologists are also nice people in real life. They were almost all happy to agree to my request. Because this was almost too easy, I decided to give myself an extra challenge. I wanted to bring insights from all over the world into contact with each other. I wanted to find specialists from **50 different countries**, the number of countries I have been fortunate enough to visit myself. They would tell us (I hoped) how to make a difference in our lives by focussing on four key elements. Firstly, I only wanted **insights founded on research-based knowledge**: I wasn't interested in spiritual philosophy. Secondly, their conclusions should **not only concentrate on individual happiness**, but also on the happiness of groups, biotopes, organisations and countries. Moreover, these conclusions should enable a cross-fertilisation of ideas within **a global vision** for universal happiness. Finally, the texts needed to be written i**n a language that ordinary people can understand**: in our search for happiness we don't want to trip over the stumbling block of academic jargon. All the professors I contacted found this an original and testing challenge. But they rose to that challenge brilliantly. They succeeded in transforming information into knowledge, and knowledge into wisdom. I thank them all from the bottom of my heart and I hope that this book, in one way or another, will contribute to the happiness of every person in the world, so that we will not allow ourselves to be paralysed by the fatalism of fear, but will be inspired by the dynamic of hope – in spite of everything… and precisely for that reason.

**Leo Bormans**
Author & Editor-in-Chief

*I dedicate this book*
*to all the people in the world*
*who will never read it*

With special thanks to Riet, Ine, Kasper,
my friends, Ruut Veenhoven,
De Heerlijckyt van Elsmeren
and all other collaborators
in this wonderful project.

For further background, a short film,
updates, reactions and contact:
**www.theworldbookofhappiness.com**

While there are subtle differences in
the meanings of the terms 'subjective well-being',
'life satisfaction' and 'happiness', we will understand them to mean the same thing in this book.

# Contents

# *Discover the 'other' in yourself*

→ **Quite alone on top of the mountain. Happy?**

→ **You're at home, but you keep your doors and windows shut. Happy?**

→ **'I'll manage by myself'. Happy?**

Could someone on their own be completely happy? **Christopher Peterson** thinks not. In his opinion, we get our greatest happiness from others. Peterson laid the foundations of positive psychology. Would he succeed in summarizing his knowledge and findings in twenty lines? 'Three words are enough', he says. Fortunately, he adds twenty lines to explain those three words.

## Other People Matter

Positive psychology is the scientific study of what makes life most worth living. The topics of concern to this new field of investigation range from the biochemical bases of joy to the well-being of nations. However, a three-word summary suffices: other people matter. There is not a finding or theory in positive psychology that does not underscore the importance of other people for our happiness and health.

Money can buy happiness on others spend it if we

The best way to savour pleasure is in the company of others. The most important determinants of a satisfied life are social. Indeed, good relationships with others may be a necessary condition for a happy life. Money can buy happiness – if we spend it on others. Achievement results not just from our own genius and perseverance but also from teaching and nurture by those who care. Character is learned from our parents and teachers. A good friend at work matters more than salary or status. People with close relationships are healthier than those without, despite – we assume – greater exposure to germs.

The Beatles told us that all we need is love. Positive psychology explains why. The good life follows in the wake of loving relationships with friends, neighbours, colleagues, family members, and spouses.

Other people matter. And we are all other people to someone else.

## The keys

→ **Don't look for happiness within yourself but in your involvement with others.**

→ **Cherish the people who are important to you: your parents, teachers, family, colleagues and friends.**

→ **Realise that you too are always someone else's 'other'.**

---

Christopher Peterson is Professor of Psychology at the University of Michigan (usa). He is often called the founding father of positive psychology. He is a member of the Positive Psychology Steering Committee and Science Director of the via Institute on Character. Christopher Peterson is appreciated worldwide for his work on character, health, optimism and well-being.

*'Ambition makes people happy but envy makes them unhappy.'*

# Go for ambition

Two groups of students have to solve a puzzle in separate rooms. Both groups can do so in about ten minutes. Yet group A is much happier with the result than group B. Why is that? Group A has been told that the others needed a quarter of an hour to solve the problem. Group B heard that the others had solved it in five minutes.
In reality both groups took the same time: they solved the puzzle in ten minutes. But their feelings of happiness have nothing to do with the reality of the situation.

## Comparison spoils your happiness

Adaptation and comparisons generally spoil the welfare benefit of income and growth. But comparisons can sometimes make people happy: this happens when people can learn about their own prospects by looking at those they compare with. Positive expectations and prospects for improvement also make people happy. It seems that people have a taste for increasing income profiles, i.e. for progression per se. In summary, ambition makes people happy but envy makes them unhappy.

So my recommendation is this: turn away from comparison benchmarks and focus on your own projects. This will make you happy and will preserve the welfare benefit that you derive from what you have.

## The keys

→ **Don't compare yourself with others.**
→ **If you do compare, look at what you can learn from the comparison.**
→ **Banish envy. Make room for ambition.**

Claudia Senik is a professor at the University of Paris-Sorbonne (France). Her main research interest is the micro-economic analysis of income distribution and subjective well-being. She frequently appeals to a comparative approach, based on the different environments in Western versus Eastern Europe. Claudia Senik is in charge of several international scientific cooperation programs.

# *Reframe your failures*

**Robert Biswas-Diener** is widely known as the 'Indiana Jones of positive psychology' because his research on the emotional good life has taken him to such far flung-places as Kenya, India, Greenland, Spain and Israel. He is the son of Ed Diener, the world's foremost expert on happiness.

*'My fascination with people began in the third grade, when my parents took me out of school to travel down the Amazon in a dugout canoe. Seeing tribal people living in wooden houses on stilts beside the river set a foundation for a lifelong curiosity about culture. This interest ultimately led me to a career travelling the world and studying happiness. In each of these countries I have gained a little more insight into what makes people happy, and I try to apply these lessons in my own life, teaching and coaching. When I sat down to write my contribution to The World Book of Happiness, something very unexpected jumped on to my computer screen! I had a great time writing this but I am not sure if it fits with what you are looking for...'*

Robert Biswas-Diener

# Failure, flexibility and happiness

As a happiness researcher, I pride myself on the fact that I get out of the research laboratory, off the university campus and out into the field to conduct my studies. Critics have long charged psychologists with relying too heavily on college student samples for their research insights about human nature. It is, of course, sometimes necessary to use the controlled environment of the laboratory for scientific purposes. As for myself, I think it is simply more fun to venture out into the wide world in search of happiness. And venture I have! I have been fortunate to travel to many beautiful places and conduct research with fascinating people. I have worked with Amish farmers in the American Midwest, seal hunters in Northern Greenland, tribal people in East Africa and sex workers in the slums of Kolkata (Calcutta). With all this international research experience under my belt, you might think that the greatest lessons I have learned about happiness have something to do with cultural differences or similarities. If so, you would be wrong: the most important lessons I have learned about happiness are not to be gleaned in the results of my published studies, but are rather to be found in the failures and hardships of conducting the research itself.

The first failure I experienced was in 2002, while I was conducting research on happiness with the Inuit people of Northern Greenland. I was interested, in part, in collecting data with the locals while they engaged in traditional hunting and fishing activities. It is the only place where I have ever had to hunt for my own dinner and – while I was terrible at it – I could see the immense satisfaction that can be gained through this activity. Greenland is a dramatic, empty landscape and I wanted to do a little adventuring outside my scientific duties, so I decided to hike approximately 40 kilometres from a fishing camp to the nearest settlement. I set out under the midnight sun and walked along the coast, being trailed by a family of seals. As an American, I confess that I think in a somewhat Hollywood manner, and I could easily imagine myself as the triumphant hero strolling into town after an epic hike through polar bear filled territory. I could even imagine the soundtrack! However, after 7 or 8 hours I found my path blocked by a massive glacier headwall. I had the choice: I could try to scale and traverse the glacier – a very dangerous feat – or I could turn around and walk the 7 or 8 hours back to camp in defeat, and hope that my companions had not already left (in which case I would likely die of hypothermia). My goal was to reach town and I *really* wanted to succeed. Nevertheless, I ultimately decided to take the more cautious path, and so I turned around and headed back to camp. As I walked, my feet aching and my body temperature dropping, **I realised that I had merely replaced one goal with another.** My new goal was to return safely, to be careful so that I could stay alive to return home to my wife and children – a goal no less worthy than my original one. By thinking flexibly, I was able to reframe a perceived failure in new terms and re-envision my hike as a success.

## '*I had been using my goal as a bludgeon, to hit people and to get my way.*'

A similar failure happened when I went to conduct happiness research with the Amish. The Amish are a religious sect that eschews modern technologies, such as television sets and automobiles. Because they purposefully try to distance themselves from the larger social world, it can be very difficult to gain an entrée into their society. I spent months visiting with families, just to make myself more familiar and to earn their trust. Even so, I felt frustrated time and again when people backed out of my research, often at the last minute (they don't have phones, so they could never 'call ahead'). My explicit goal was to get as many Amish to participate in my happiness study as possible, and I felt as if I were failing. I am known for being able to work with hard-to-access groups and my failure with the Amish was a disappointment with myself as much as it was frustration with them. After a number of cancellations, I stepped back and re-evaluated my goal. I realized that my goal was not necessarily the goal of the Amish people with whom I was working. I had been using my goal as a bludgeon, to hit people and to get my way. I began thinking about what the Amish people might want, and about what I might have to offer them. I realised that instead of just collecting happiness data, as if I were a phlebotomist taking blood, it would be more mutually beneficial to have an information exchange. Starting the very next week I began giving talks about daily life in other cultures at Amish grade schools. The local community flocked to these presentations and I realised that by giving as much information as I was taking, I felt better about myself and was more successful in my research goal. My response rate went up dramatically.

In both cases – working with the Amish and with the Inuit – I was presented with the same hard truth: **sometimes your most treasured goals run up against serious obstacles.** Sometimes these obstacles are outside circumstances and sometimes they are related to how we have framed the goal in the first place. When this happens we tend to react with frustration and disappointment. But by learning to think flexibly about our goals and to adjust them in the face of failure, we can end up feeling happier. If you imagine your life as a narrative, a story that unfolds like a book, then you can also imagine yourself as the author of this story. It is possible to revise the tale even as it happens; making small edits that improve the story of your life and increase your happiness. I didn't fail to hike to a distant settlement in Greenland, I succeeded in wandering through a barren landscape unharmed and made a tough but smart choice that probably saved my life. I didn't fail to get a huge number of Amish people to participate in my research, I succeeded in giving the Amish something they wanted – news about other cultures. Maintaining flexible thinking about your failures can help you learn from them, grow from them, and even transform them into successes. I have never published any papers on this topic, but I think there are folk in Borneo, Mongolia or Madagascar who might want to participate in the research!

## The keys

→ **Sometimes obstacles are related to how we have framed the goal in the first place. Set your goals clearly: for yourself and for others.**

→ **Don't be ashamed to step back and re-evaluate your goal. Learn to think flexibly. Try to reframe a perceived failure in terms of success.**

→ **Imagine your life as a story that unfolds like a book, with yourself as the author.**

Robert Biswas-Diener has published more than two dozen books and chapters on happiness and is on the editorial board of the 'Journal of Happiness Studies' and the 'Journal of Positive Psychology'. He is the founder of Positive Psychology Services (USA) and a programme director at the Centre for Applied Positive Psychology (UK). He is author of 'Happiness: Unlocking the Mysteries of Psychological Wealth'. In an effort to make sure that the benefits of positive psychology are available to everyone, he co-founded a positive psychology humanitarian organisation called The Strengths Project.

*'More and more income*
*does not lead to*
*more and more happiness.'*

# The Paradox

A study by Ed Diener demonstrated that the richest Americans, earning more than $10 million annually, report levels of personal happiness only slightly greater than the people who work for them. And why is it that people in some developing countries are happier than people in rich countries? This phenomenon is called the 'Happiness Paradox'. Professor **Stavros Drakopoulos** is currently researching the effect of money on happiness. His advice?

## The link between income and happiness

One of the interesting findings that many economists have uncovered is the relationship between the level of income and overall reported levels of happiness. In particular, the results from many national studies indicate that the level of income is very important for how happy many people feel. However, it seems that this effect is very strong when income is quite low, but not so strong when income is high. Experts have called this relationship the 'Happiness Paradox'. In other words, income is very important for people's happiness when they are poor but much less so when they are financially comfortable or well-off. This not only seems to be true within individual countries but also when different countries are compared. For example, some developing countries report higher levels of happiness than in many of their developed high-income neighbours. One might explain this by arguing that, in general, humans feel very unhappy if their basic needs such as food and shelter are not met. Once they can meet these needs, different factors become important. This means that having an adequate income to cover important needs (as they are defined in a modern society) is crucial. However, further increases of income do not

seem to provide analogous increases in happiness. Consequently, other factors such as freedom, quality of life, trust and personal and social relationships all affect happiness more than income, once the level of income is sufficient to cover socially-determined material needs.

The theoretical basis of this explanation is the hierarchical structure of human needs. It therefore seems that income is important for happiness, but that more and more income does not lead to more and more happiness. Another point relating to the effect of income on happiness is what economists describe as 'comparison income'. This means that we tend to compare our income level with people who are in the same job, with similar qualifications and similar years of experience. In particular, we tend to feel unhappy when we discover that our income is lagging behind, when compared to the income of our equivalent contemporaries. As a result, we might not be happier when we get a pay rise, if our peers receive an even bigger pay increase.

Overall, it might be beneficial for our happiness if we put more emphasis on non-income factors, once our income is more than adequate to cover our basic needs.

## The keys

→ **Income is important for happiness, but more and more income does not lead to more and more happiness.**

→ **Don't compare your own income with the income of your colleagues or other people.**

→ **Put greater emphasis on freedom, quality of life, trust and relationships. They all affect happiness more than income.**

Stavros A. Drakopoulos is Professor of Economics at the University of Athens (Greece). He has been a lecturer at the Aberdeen and Glasgow Universities in Scotland. One of his many publications is 'Values and Economic Theory: The Case of Hedonism'. His research interest focuses on the relationship between happiness and economics.

*'In the long run*
*only happy societies*
*survive.'*

# Let's learn happiness

'The first impact of the new possibility to produce greater happiness by experimentally tested social policies is emerging in many fields: in education as in the economy, in healthcare as in housing, in churches as in sport clubs,' says specialist **Ernst Gehmacher**. There are good and bad forms of happiness. But can we learn the good ones without training?

## Fit, friends and fun

My involvement as a social scientist in happiness research during the last forty years has taught me two fundamental natural laws:

→ In the long run, only happy societies survive – they are the winners in the process of cultural evolution. Throughout history, human happiness was the crucial test of success for civilizations, cultures, communities and economies – as it is today. It is also the universal criterion for social cohesion in any social unit, from the simple family to humanity as a whole.

→ Progress is dependent on knowledge, knowledge is dependent on objective observation, and objective observation is dependent on accurate measurement. We have learned to measure atoms and the extent of the cosmos, the activity of neurones in the brain,

the cycles of economic demand and supply – but we have no generally accepted metric of happiness. A good functioning objective measure of 'Gross National Happiness Product' is a high priority for our new global world order, if we wish to avoid future catastrophes.

But happiness is not easy to find – and even harder to hold. There are good, long-lasting forms of 'sustainable' happiness: there is fun in do-it-yourself, love and friendship, health and fitness, gaining friends and improving society. But there are also bad forms of 'addictive' happiness: drink and drugs, the hunt for success and status, boring entertainment and lonely socialising. In the long run, these addictions will ruin you, the environment and society. The good forms of happiness have to be learned and trained. People are easily seduced by the bad forms, particularly in situations of stress and deprivation. But good happiness is not only good for your friends, your neighbours and society – even for mankind as a whole. It is also good for you! Happiness is essentially democratic – nobody can be happy without personal commitment, but personal commitment cannot make you happy without social help.

Happiness research gives a clear message: happiness can be found and can even increase with age, if three fundamental elements are in place: fitness, friends and fun.

→ **Fit?** Chronic diseases hit more than 80 percent of people above the age of 50 with a lonely and unhealthy life style. They hit only 5 percent of people with good 'social capital' (community life), fun in their work or active hobbies.

→ **Friends?** The best chance for 'social' happiness occurs when people have at least four, but not more than twelve, tight relationships of 'full trust' and 'reliable help' within their circle of family and friends. At the same time, they are engaged in at least fifteen (with no upper limit) other friendly and co-operative relationships with persons who they know well and they also have a strong sense of belonging to a larger social body (the criteria of 'optimal social capital').

→ **Fun?** Wealth (the amount of income and material possessions) makes the poor happier and the rich unhappier. Growth of wealth (wins, gains, career, wage increases, general economic growth) makes people happier for a short time, but not lastingly so. Great inequality of wealth fosters aggression and unhappiness for all. Aim to achieve good and sustainable forms of happiness.

Happiness has to be learned. Happiness can even be taught in school. The first experiments with 'happiness lessons' in secondary schools have been shown to be successful.

## The keys

→ **Drop bad, addictive forms of happiness and choose good, sustainable forms.**

→ **Your happiness will increase if three fundamentals are in place: fit, friends and fun.**

→ **Happiness can and must be learned. So let's get learning right away!**

'Contributing my message to The World Book of Happiness has contributed to my own happiness,' says Prof. Ernst Gehmacher from the Club of Rome and BoaS (Büro für die Organisation angewandter Sozialforschung) in Vienna (Austria). He is closely involved with the Organisation for Economic Cooperation and Development (OECD). The OECD programme 'Measuring Social Capital' is initiating happiness research as a first step towards providing global policy-making with an instrument for the 'pursuit of happiness'.

# *The Mexican Wave*

Mexico's per capita income is about 7,000 US dollars. Australia's is five times this amount. Nevertheless, we find Mexico higher in the ranking of the happiest countries than Australia. 'Once you reach a reasonable standard of living, about the level of Mexico today, further growth in wealth doesn't add to happiness,' says the 'Journal of Happiness Studies'. Dr. **José de Jesus Garcia Vega** lives and works in Monterrey (Mexico). During the sixties this place was probably the origin of the famous Mexican Wave.
So let's raise our arms and swing to the rhythm!

## The ultimate goal

They say that happiness is a journey, and not a destination. And indeed, this is what the study of happiness has meant for me: a truly wonderful journey! But even before I realised that you can actually study happiness, I felt that happiness was the most important thing in my life. When I re-discovered Aristotle – who told me that most things we do are intended to make us happier – it became clear to me that happiness was the ultimate goal.

Since then, I have found plenty of other ideas which have made my life easier and happier. I have also developed a feeling that it is my task to spread the word, to preach the gospel of happiness. I often think that ignorance is our greatest obstacle to becoming happy. There are many tools, procedures and ideas which can help people to become happier. And they have been proven to work! We just need to make them accessible for everybody.

Let's begin at the beginning. Once you start to think about the possibility of becoming happier, you are on your way already. It is amazing how many of us spend our lives working hard and trying to reach new pinnacle of success, whilst at the same time forgetting our need to be happy. We are constantly striving for material things, but when we try to enjoy them we find that it is already too late. It is often said that people spend the best years of their life trying to make money and sacrificing their health and their family in the process,

only to spend the rest of their days paying out that same money in an attempt to recover their lost health and their estranged family!

I have also learned that it is a great help if we can accept things as they are. I recall an old prayer which says: *Lord, give me patience to accept the things I cannot change; give me strength to change the things that can be changed; and give me wisdom to recognise one from the other.* We spend a lot of time complaining about the things that happen to us, but this is simply a waste of time and effort. We can always complain and we can always want more, but it will never get us anywhere. To be happy, we need to enjoy what we have.

In addition, I now realise that I always have the freedom to choose the manner in which I approach any given situation. After a setback or a disappointment, it is for me to decide whether I sit down and cry or whether I cheer up and try to do something about it. I have used this creed regularly and I have tried to promote its use in others. In the end, my happiness depends solely on me and my attitude. All the rest is of secondary importance.

To me, life is like a great party to which we have all been invited. Our only task is to enjoy it, and to be happy. And the only fee we have to pay is a responsibility to help others to be happy as well, and to leave the room in the same condition as we found it, or perhaps even better. Those before us have worked hard to give us this wonderful stage on which to play, and it is only fair that we should do the same for those who will follow once we have gone.

## The keys

→ **Don't forget to be happy. A lot of people spend their best years trying to make money, sacrificing their health and their family in the process. Later, they spend that same money trying to recover their lost health and estranged family.**

→ **Accept things as they come. To be happy, we need to enjoy what we have.**

→ **You always have the freedom to choose the manner in which you wish to approach any given situation.**

Dr. José de Jesús García Vega works in the 'Centro de Estudios sobre el Bienestar' at the University of Monterrey (Mexico). 'Perhaps the greatest thing I have acquired from the study of happiness is the number of friends I have made amongst researchers all over the world. They are always willing to help me to become happier and to learn more about what makes others happy. They are wonderful people and they have assisted me and many of my colleagues to advance the study of happiness.'

# *Guanxi in China*

Western societies tend to focus on individual happiness. In other countries society plays a more dominant role. This relationship is often difficult to grasp and to translate. In Middle Eastern countries it is called *wasta*. A similar concept exists in the Philippines, known as utang na loob ('debt of gratitude'). Professor **Ying-yi Hong** studied in Hong Kong and New York and points out the importance of Guanxi in Chinese culture.

## The two forces of happiness in Chinese culture

Research has shown that Chinese culture (in comparison to Western cultures) is characterized by a stronger interconnectedness among people. For many Chinese people, the fulfilling of their social obligations is often a higher priority than asserting their individual rights, when the two are in conflict. This means that Chinese people would not feel happy if they attained their own aspirations at the expense of their duties and obligations. The two need to go together. While the former – personal – type of happiness is associated with excitement and ecstasy, the latter – social – type of happiness is associated with feelings of relief, calmness and harmony.

This being said, Chinese societies are not monolithic entities. The population is diverse in ethnicity and religion, and is influenced by foreign cultural exposure and rapid economic development. In modern China, on the one hand people face demands arising from the market economy and the need to compete with others, in order to achieve upward social mobility. On the other hand, people, as in old days, still depend on their social relationship networks for both instrumental and emotional support. These two forces give rise to the formation of *guanxi* (relationship) networks, through which people attain their personal interests, whilst at the same time being constrained by and abiding by their social obligations. Successful navigation among these complicated social matrices is a prerequisite for happiness in modern China.

Moreover, to make matters more complicated, various philosophies and religious beliefs are competing with the dominance of communist ideologies. Apart from the long tradition of Buddhism, Taoism and Confucianism, the influences of Christianity and Islam are on the rise. People holding different philosophies and religious beliefs have different and alternative ways to seek happiness, and are therefore less likely than before to rely solely on fulfilling the duties prescribed by the communist party to gain happiness.

## The keys

→ **Happiness is not only a matter of individual endeavour.**
→ **It is also about fulfilling your social duties and obligations.**
→ **Feelings of happiness can be expressed through excitement and ecstasy, as well as through calm and serenity.**

Professor Ying-yi Hong studied in Hong Kong and New York. She now works at the Nanyang Technological University (Singapore) and in the Department of Psychology at the University of Illinois (Urbana-Champaign, USA). Ying-yi is a member of the International Academy for Intercultural Research and editor of the journal 'Advances in Culture and Psychology'.

*'Happiness is more than the individual.'*

*'Human beings are social animals.'*

# The Russian tunnel

'Since the beginning of the 1990s the Russian ideas on success, common life values and even 'normal' behaviour have been updated. As this transformation process has progressed, an unusual phenomenon appeared in Russia: the presence of the so called *tunnel effect*,' reports **Ekaterina Selezneva**, whose research is concentrated on the impact on happiness of reference groups and social norms, particularly in the tumultuous setting of the Russian economic transition.

## 'We are in the other lane'

When the structure of society and economy changed in Russia, people realised that the possibility of 'social lift' – upward social mobility – had appeared. They had all seen the 'American dream' in films: with a bit of luck, even a poor but talented person can have a meteoric career. This dream now became a possible reality, available to all (and not only to communist party functionaries, as had been the case in the past). But how do you evaluate your own chances in these constantly changing conditions? You could get additional information by observing what is achieved by those who represent your reference group (similar people living in the same area). They are in the same 'tunnel' with you, in the same traffic jam, but in another lane. What do you feel if they are lucky, successful, and moving forward in their lane? I imagine that you would be happy, since you hope to do precisely the same thing behind them! Your turn is next, just relax and be patient. Dame Fortune will soon be knocking at your door. This kind of social fluidity rarely happens in a stable country, where the 'rules of the game' have been fixed for a long time. But it happened in Russia.

My research showed me that even though Russia achieved the status of a country with a market economy in 2002, the transitional process was not yet completed in the minds of the people. Those who were getting less than the others in their reference group still hoped to change their situation for better – even 15 years after the start of the transition.

'Human beings are social animals.' Even if most people agree with this statement, it is not always readily perceived in ordinary life how deeply the impact of societal settings affects our actions, our satisfaction with these actions and our lives as a whole. Being inserted into a system of relationships, direct or indirect, not only with people we know but also with strangers, implies continuous comparisons with all the people of the world.

## The keys

→ **Always look forward with optimism and hope for some good luck.**
→ **Meanwhile, don't just wait until your turn comes. You have to act positively and improve your skills.**
→ **The world is changing constantly. Do not blindly stick to 'the old rules of the game'.**

Dr. Ekaterina Selezneva studied at St. Petersburg State University (Russia) and at the University of Turin (Italy). She is now a researcher at the Osteuropa Institut in Regensburg (Germany). Her interests include the relationship between economics, the labour market, gender and subjective well-being.

*'Happiness is also a matter of history.'*

# Lessons from the Sahara

Deep in the Sahara people live in difficult conditions. Yet they often have a smile on their faces. Are they happy? And what is the impact of the progressive changes in their happiness? In Algeria, there is a sharp contrast between the more 'modern' north and the more traditional south. Professor **Habib Tiliouine** and his team have for years been researching their feelings of happiness. Every eighteen months they interview more than 10,000 people. From north to south. The Sahara teaches us a lesson.

## Taking the risk of change?

In an increasingly shrinking world, developing countries have no choice but to face modernity and adapt themselves to its requirements. It is true that such a process can be painful, at both the individual level and at social levels. For instance, the unprecedented multi-faceted crisis which has shaken my country, Algeria, since the beginning of the 1990s could be viewed in this wider perspective.

Satisfaction with life and subjective well-being are lower in Algeria than in developed countries. This cannot be explained solely by the low standard of living. Data collected in the southern parts of the country (Adrar District, *Wilaya*), deep in the Sahara desert, contradict such an interpretation. Unexpectedly, people from these locations are found to be happier than their counterparts in the more developed and modern – i.e., richer – north (Oran District). But how should we best interpret such a paradox?

Apparently, the traditional structure of the *Sahraoui* society has remained intact across time: strong family relationships, higher inter-individual trust, strong religious brotherhoods (*Zaouias*), lower security problems…. The community networks continue to function properly and social roles are pre-defined within that 'traditional' social system. In contrast, communities in the north have lost the strength of traditional social cohesion and hence have weaker homogeneity. This has a negative effect on the happiness of the individual. We also found that the differences between *Sahraoui* men and *Sahraoui* women in satisfaction with life and happiness were much smaller than that of their counterparts in the more modern north.

Historically speaking, the Algerian south (Sahara) has been isolated from direct foreign influences, mainly French colonialism. The heavy colonial presence in the north disrupted almost all aspects of individual and social life. This would suggest, therefore, that happiness is also a matter of history.

Fortunately, human societies have inherent resilience mechanisms which help them to face such traumas. Our research provided evidence that as the spectre of the recent social turmoil in Algeria has been slowly dissipating and the country's economy improving, so the well-being of the population has gradually increased. But this should not hide the fact that within this society there are varying degrees of happiness amongst the different social groups. For instance, people with higher education, when compared with those of lower education levels, perceive themselves as happier. The same trend is registered in other social groupings: married people compared to single people, religious people compared to less religious people and healthier people compared to ill people. This is mostly true of similar comparisons elsewhere. Nonetheless, a word of caution needs to be sounded.

Some international research has already proven that equating Islam with extremism is totally wrong. The finding that Islamic religiosity, like other forms of religiosity, is linked to higher levels of happiness has also been confirmed. The possible explanation – which we have empirically verified – is that Islam provides its followers with meaning in life. The link between having meaning in your life and being happy has already been established in previous research.

There are, of course, numerous ways to interpret these results, but at least they indicate that some degree of stability in the individuals' life is a prerequisite for human well-being. For this reason, it almost goes without saying that having a good level of education, a partner, a religious/spiritual life and being in good health are all associated with happiness.

One specific lesson could, however, be drawn from our research. Each human society accepts change at its own pace. But if accelerated change is necessary, one should be wise enough not to brutalize people, not to destroy their 'social capital'. This can be a good lesson for rulers and decision-makers at all levels in developing countries in general. How to modernise a country while maintaining its basic equilibrium must be their greatest concern – and their greatest challenge. In this respect, social research should continue to provide guidance and the study of happiness remains a noble enterprise.

## The keys

→ **Happiness is also a matter of history. Each society accepts change at its own pace.**

→ **Poor people in traditional areas can be happier than richer people in more modern areas.**

→ **Some stability in the individual's life is a prerequisite for human well-being.**

Professor Habib Tiliouine (University of Oran, Algeria) is founder of the Laboratory of Educational Processes and Social Context in Algeria. He has built up expertise in quality of life in Islamic countries, well-being studies, development and educational policies. He is also member of the editorial board of 'The Journal of Happiness Studies'.

**Michael Eid**

# *Pride and Modesty*

'It is very important to experience positive emotions in life. The feelings of joy, pride, attachment, love and satisfaction are major ingredients of a happy life.' But Michael Eid has learnt that it is important that these emotions are embedded in a social context.

It is not only important to know that social relationships are amongst the most powerful sources of positive emotions and that positive emotions can be more easily maintained when we are with others, but it is equally important to realise that the quality of positive emotions and their impact on happiness changes when the social context comes into play. Take pride, for example. Pride is an important emotion in Western cultures, because it shows that you are successful, that you have been able to reach your goals, and that your self-esteem is high. As a result, people who often feel pride will be happier. However, **success is almost never the result of a single person acting alone** – it depends on the contribution of other people and also on good luck. People can often be proud of their success without realising that it depends to some extent, either in an obvious or less obvious way, on the contribution of others (even if this contribution was long ago – such as the influence of parents, teachers or colleagues). Realising that you live a happy and successful life because of the help of others and by virtue of fortunate circumstances seems to me to be an important condition for real happiness. Why? Because it links pride to modesty and gratitude. Pride without gratitude is a much weaker source of long-lasting happiness than pride embedded in gratitude. In fact without gratitude there may even be a risk of narcissism. A strong feeling of gratitude towards life in general and towards others in particular is a major source of happiness. This is not only true for pride, but also for many other positive emotions. **If individual emotions such as pride are paired with social emotions such as gratitude, they will have a much more powerful effect on our happiness.** Consequently, by regularly thinking about the positive things in your life and by activating a deep feeling of gratitude, you can find the road to true happiness.

Michael Eid, PhD has been engaged in research on subjective well-being for the last 20 years. He is Professor of Psychology at the Freie Universität in Berlin (Germany) and is co-editor (with Randy Larsen) of the book 'The Science of Subjective Well-being'.

*'Begin with a good oven.'*

# The recipe

'There is no recipe for happiness,' say the sceptics. 'What would you put in the pots and pans?' Yet **Dubravka Miljkovic & Majda Rijavec's** have come up with a recipe which comes reasonably close to proving the sceptics wrong. They have established which ingredients are really essential and which could improve the taste still further. The proportions will vary according to individual likes and dislikes. But, most importantly, don't wait until you have a big party to try the recipe out. This is a recipe for an everyday dish of happiness.

## Six essential and five optional ingredients

Begin with a good oven (the one that has been in your family's possession for a long time), some proper cooking skills, an adequate temperature and sufficient baking time.

*Six essential ingredients:* A few good, reliable friends (and possibly one bad, just to be aware of the difference). One (at a time!) stable loving relationship. The challenge of a job that is matched to your skills. Enough money to satisfy your basic needs (and some non-basic ones – from time to time). At least three good things on a daily basis. Gratitude for having all of the above.

*Five optional ingredients:* One or more kids (with an additional amount of gratitude). (Mostly) one god and several saints. Several additional years of education. Physical and (more or less) mental health. A few disappointments.

Mix everything with raw opinions. Serve with more positive than negative emotions. Worry sometimes, but be happy(ier). And do not stop being curious, learning new things and growing as a person.

## The keys

→ **Your personal history and skills are the basics.**

→ **Make a personal mix with all the essential and some of the optional ingredients.**

→ **It is the positive sauce that gives your dish of happiness its final taste.**

---

Dubravka Miljkovic & Majda Rijavec are authors of several successful books on aspirations and life satisfaction. They are involved in teacher training and have introduced a programme of positive psychology in secondary schools. As psychologists and university professors in Zagreb (Croatia) they frequently work together: 'Happiness? Happiness is discovering and using your talent. For ourselves, we can say that we are best at writing and teaching, and that we are best when doing it together. Sharing is the vital component of happiness. And we enjoy it very much.'

*'It is the combination of strong individualism and high trust that does the trick.'*

# *The secret of the Viking World*

**Christian Bjørnskov** lives and works in Denmark, one of the happiest countries in the world. What is the reason for this success? And how did Christian himself, a professor of economics, get into the study of happiness? The importance of an ice cream.

## It started with an ice cream

I got into happiness research by accident. Finding it hard to concentrate on writing a paper on social capital and economic development while the Danish summer was at its magical best outside my window, my mind began to wander. Somehow, it connected the new concept of social capital with the equally recent interest for happiness in economics. I eventually left my office for a walk in the sunshine and an ice cream, to let my unconscious work while I was doing something else.

Two weeks later, my mind had sorted things out and I had written what was to be my first contribution to the literature in happiness studies. The paper was called 'The Happy Few' and outlined part of the explanation for why a small group of countries, including my own country, Denmark, come out on top in most surveys as the happiest places in the world. The secret is not the Scandinavian welfare state, government services, democracy or other political explanations. Virtually everything that the welfare state does is something to which people adapt very quickly, making it irrelevant to happiness. Instead, Danes trust each other more than anyone else to behave honestly – and, in general, they are indeed surprisingly honest.

Inadvertently, my own behaviour in leaving my office to do something else other than I was supposed to be doing, reflects another characteristic that seems to contribute to Danish happiness: believing in your personal freedom, and acting upon that belief. In other words, the strong sense of individualist freedom works the last little bit of magic to move the world's oldest kingdom into first place. People in Denmark and Iceland – another top five country – tend to share the belief with inhabitants of a number of particularly (and surprisingly) happy Latin American countries that if something is wrong in your life, you can change it yourself. This purely subjective belief does not characterize Swedes and Norwegians – the other half of the former Viking world – to the same extent as Danes and Icelanders, and is probably one of the main reasons why they lag behind in happiness. It is the Danish combination of strong individualism and high trust in your fellow human beings that does the trick.

Meeting other social scientists in happiness research taught me the first and most important lesson in our field: at the end of the day, happiness studies have given us a number of surprising insights and we have to accept that many objectively good things do not contribute to subjective well-being. Children are not the way to a happy life (quite the contrary in most cases), 'good' things like democracy, gender and income equality are either entirely unimportant or only matter to the richest countries, and people adapt to both good and bad economic and political changes surprisingly quickly. So when it comes to providing happy advice, we need venture no further than the ancient Romans: *Carpe Diem*. Take control of your own life, assume responsibility and know that you can change it yourself – even if it may not always be what you were 'supposed' to do. I certainly didn't that summer's day when I strayed into happiness research, but it turned out right in the end. And as Julius Caesar once said: 'It is better to die once than to live in fear of death all the time.' Enjoy your life while you are living it.

## The keys

→ **Believe strongly in yourself and give a high degree of trust to your fellow human beings.**
→ **Take control of your own life, assume responsibility and know that you can change it yourself.**
→ **Dare to eat an ice cream. Don't always do what you are supposed to do. Enjoy your life while you live it.**

Christian Bjørnskov is Professor of Economics at Aarhus University (Denmark). He has published a great deal of work on social trust, subjective well-being and life satisfaction. As a swimmingcoach, he was responsible for talent development.

# The medicine

For more than 20 years, Finland has been following over 20,000 persons from the Finnish Twin Cohort, aged between 18 and 64 years old, measuring their life satisfaction and happiness ratings. Researcher Heli Koivumaa-Honkanen has come to the conclusion that healthy people are not happier. The inverse is true: happy people are healthier. Three ingredients of the powerful medicine of happiness.

An analysis of our statistics over 20 years show that, at the end of the day, it doesn't really matter whether people are healthy or sick and it doesn't really matter what happens with their health in later years (even if they become disabled): those who are satisfied with their life are always better off – are happier – than those who are dissatisfied. Their life satisfaction is based on four factors (happiness, loneliness, interests and living standards). This satisfaction is a potent indicator and predictor of health at all ages. Satisfied people live longer and commit suicide less.

In terms of both depression and schizophrenia, the possession of good social support networks is a predictor of better life satisfaction and better treatment outcome.

Throughout history, people have always strived to achieve happiness and peace of mind, without ever really knowing that life satisfaction and happiness could benefit their health. Now we know this for certain. Positive mental health has long-lasting benefits. The most important factors are the ability to enjoy yourself and your life; the ability to respect, need and love others; and the ability to create and maintain good relationships. These abilities do not flourish by themselves. They need support and nurture right from the very beginning of human life. Positive mental health can and should be built, preserved and promoted across different sectors of society. Failure to do this now simply means passing the bill to future generations. I hope that this book will gather worldwide attention to the importance of happiness and subjective well-being as a means to assess mental health in the general population and to promote physical and mental health prevention at an early stage.

Heli Koivumaa-Honkanen is a professor in the Department of Psychiatry at the University of Oulu, the Lapland Hospital District and Kuopio University Hospital (Finland). She believes that enjoying the evening sunset after a sauna in a quiet Finnish summer cottage is especially good for mental health.

# *The health factor*

Three out of every four Swedish men and women report that they are satisfied
or very satisfied with life as a whole. In other words, they are happy. Four factors
have a major impact on their level of happiness, in the following order of priority:
relationships (partner, family life, sexual life), health (somatic and psychological
health), leisure (contacts with friends, leisure activities) and standard of living (job,
economy). In particular, the closeness of relationships has a powerful positive
influence. This influence is significantly (and unavoidably) associated with partner
status (and is therefore lower for singles). Perceived vocational and financial status,
much less than good health, are associated with a relatively lower level of happiness.

But what about people who suffer serious injury or illness? A wide range of
subjects with chronic disease or injury sequelae have been investigated by us
and by others researchers. Among samples of subjects who had survived complete
spinal cord injury or severe multi-trauma or chronic vocationally disabling back-
pain or stroke or multiple sclerosis, considerably fewer (about 35-45%) reported
that they were happy. Some minorities (22-41%) derived satisfaction from the areas
of leisure and sexual life. In particular, former stroke victims reported low levels
for most satisfaction items. Hence, from a medico-social point of view, the victims
of these ailments are severely punished in terms of the meaningfulness of their life.

It is our contention that happiness and domain-specific aspects of life satisfaction
are very important issues for interpreting extent to which medical intervention can
lead to improvement in social life-adaptation and, hence, to increased levels of
happiness. Unfortunately, this dimension is often neglected in medical practice.
We believe that the inclusion of the happiness and satisfaction dimension would
enhance the efficacy of our clinical endeavours, since it reflects the meaningfulness
of life as seen in a 'goal achievement' mirror. In order to broaden and deepen
the concept of happiness within the medico-social world much more attention
should be focused on happiness research.

> Axel R. Fugl-Meyer is a specialist on life satisfaction. He is Professor Emeritus
> at the Department of Neuroscience & Rehabilitation at the University of Uppsala
> (Sweden). His wife, Kerstin S. Fugl-Meyer, designed the checklist and is
> associate professor of sexual medicine at the Karolinska Institute in Stockholm.

*'Strive for a job*
*which is meaningful*
*both to you and to society.'*

# Money in the box

What would you do if you suddenly came into money?
Save it, buy something, or give it to a good cause? And which
of these three possibilities would make you happiest?
**Erich Kirchler** has carried out experiments in social and economic
psychology. For a year he also closely followed the day-to-day
decisions (including financial ones) of forty western couples.
Does he know if money makes people happy?

## The glitter of gold soon dims

Happiness is perhaps the most important topic of study in economic psychology.

Economics is the science that studies decisions about the allocation of scarce resources, with the aim of meeting the greatest possible proportion of human needs. The satisfaction of these needs (as opposed to their frustration) should therefore make individuals and nations happy. Money and material possessions are often said to hold the key to happiness. But can money really buy everything, even happiness? Surprising but compelling research has concluded that money has little capacity to make us happy, and that happiness gained through material wealth fades quickly.

Economic psychological experiments show, for instance, that instead of rationally maximising their own profit, people prefer to act altruistically by giving to charity, and also derive happiness from volunteering.

Psychology teaches us that happiness originates from satisfying, loving relationships and reliable and trustworthy friends; from the ability to enjoy the pleasures of life; and from a meaningful and socially relevant job.

My advice is, therefore, as follows. Strive for an enduring, intimate relationship and invest strongly in the stability of that relationship. Put effort into friendships and share your personal experiences of pleasure and pain, laughing together and supporting each other. Allow yourself to enjoy the pleasures of everyday life, to appreciate the small things as well as the important ones. Be suspicious of any ideology that preaches guilt over enjoyment. My last piece of advice is to find a job which pays you a decent wage without necessarily making you rich, but which also demands responsibility and offers you autonomy in return. In short, a job which is meaningful both to you and to society; a job with which you can identify, both when working and while enjoying the fruits of your labours.

Simple? Perhaps, but not as easy as you might think!

## The keys

→ **Don't imagine that you can buy happiness with money.
  Happiness bought with money soon melts away.**

→ **Instead, invest in relationships and friendships – and enjoy them.**

→ **Look for a job which is meaningful both for you and for society.**

Erich Kirchler is Professor of Psychology at the University of Vienna (Austria). He is author of 'Love, Money and Everyday Life' and other publications dealing with economic psychology, behavioural economics, conflicts in close relationships, etc. In 'The Economic Psychology of Tax Behaviour' he reveals that not everybody feels sad about paying taxes. It depends, for instance, on the country in which you live. 'It works if tax authorities have legal and expert powers, and treat taxpayers as fair partners, rather than inferiors unwilling to pay their share.'

*'Those who feel good, do good.'*

# The Ten Commandments of Happiness

Imagine you have been a specialist in happiness studies for more than fifteen years and you have written more than seventeen books. Then 'The World Book of Happiness' dares to ask you to summarize your research in something like twenty lines. **David G. Myers** sighs and tries to do so with a smile in The Ten Commandments of Happiness.

## Want a happier life?

**Realise that enduring happiness doesn't come from success.** People adapt to changing circumstances – even to wealth or disability. Thus, wealth is like health: its utter absence breeds misery, but having it (or any other circumstance we long for) doesn't guarantee happiness. **Give priority to close relationships.** Intimate friendships with those who care deeply about you can help you to weather the difficult times. Confiding in someone is good for both soul and body. Resolve to nurture your closest relationship by *not* taking your loved ones for granted, by displaying to them the sort of kindness you display to others, by affirming them, by playing together and sharing together. To rejuvenate your affections, resolve to *act* lovingly. **Seek work and leisure that engage your skills.** Happy people often are in a zone called 'flow', absorbed in tasks that challenge but don't overwhelm them. The most expensive forms of leisure (sitting on a yacht) often provide less flow experience than gardening, socialising or craft work. **Take control of your time.** Happy people feel in control of their lives. To master your use of time, set goals and break them down into daily aims. Although we often overestimate how much we will accomplish in any given day (leaving us frustrated), we generally underestimate how much we can accomplish in a year, given just a little progress every day.

**Act happy.** We can sometimes act ourselves into a happier frame of mind. Manipulated into a smiling expression, people feel better; when they scowl, the whole world seems to scowl back. So put on a happy face. Talk *as if* you feel positive self-esteem, are optimistic, and are outgoing. Going through the motions can trigger the emotions. **Join the 'movement' movement.** An avalanche of research reveals that aerobic exercise can relieve mild depression and anxiety, whilst at the same time promoting health and energy. Sound minds reside in sound bodies. So get off your bums, couch potatoes! **Give your body the sleep it wants.** Happy people live active vigorous lives yet reserve time for renewing sleep and solitude. Many people suffer from a sleep debt, with resulting fatigue, diminished alertness, and gloomy moods. **Focus beyond the self.** Reach out to those in need. Happiness increases helpfulness (those who feel good, do good). But doing good also makes you feel even better. **Nurture your spiritual self.** For many people, faith provides a support community, a reason to focus beyond self, and a sense of purpose and hope. Study after study finds that actively religious people are happier, and that they cope better with crises. **Keep a gratitude journal.** Those who pause each day to reflect on some positive aspect of their lives (their health, friends, family, freedom, education, senses, natural surroundings, and so on) experience heightened well-being.

## The keys

→ **Give priority to close relationships instead of success.
Engage your skills, control your time.**

→ **Smile. Move enough and sleep enough.**

→ **Do good to others, nurture your spiritual self and keep a gratitude journal.**

Social psychologist Professor David G. Myers has written specialized articles and popular books including 'The Pursuit of Happiness: Who Is Happy and Why'. The ten commandments are a summary of the ideas in this book. His scientific writings have been recognized by the award of the Gordon Allport Prize. David G. Myers is an all-weather bicyclist and works in a university with a perfect name for happiness research: Hope College (Michigan, USA).

*'It's about freedom of choice and control over choice.'*

# The universal law of choice

Two students both only expected a maximum of 7 out of 10, but they got an 8. The first one is happy ('My effort!'), the other one is not ('Fate!'). The reality is the same for both students, but their reaction is not. And why don't we become happier when the choice of products in the supermarket doubles? **Paolo Verme** has visited more than eighty countries and reveals the universal law of choice.

## Who or what determines the outcome of your choice?

Happiness is about freedom of choice and control over choice. People who feel freer to choose also feel happier, but only if they believe that they can control the outcome of their own choices. More freedom of choice does not invariably lead to more happiness. We have to appreciate freedom of choice and trust that choice is a valuable asset, in order to be able to derive happiness from it.

There is evidence that such trust depends on an aspect of personality known as the *locus of control*. People who believe that the outcome of their own choices derives from their own abilities and efforts (internal locus of control) tend to appreciate freedom of choice more than people who believe that the outcome of their own choices derives from fate and destiny (external locus of control).

Research in psychology and economics has shown that such beliefs are not simply a genetic gift but the result of social upbringing, including learning in families and in schools.

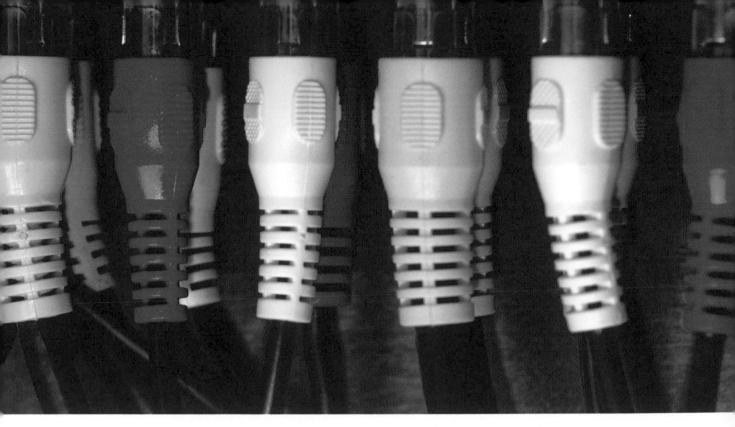

Both parents and teachers have a role to play in the happiness of future adults. Equipping children with more trust in their own capacity to determine the outcome of their own choices is an invaluable asset for the happiness of individuals and societies alike.

## The keys

→ **Freedom of choice only makes us feel happy when we believe
that we can control the outcome of our choice.**

→ **We are happier when we believe more strongly in our own abilities
and efforts than in fate and destiny.**

→ **This attitude can be learned. Parents and teachers should equip children with
more trust in their own capacity to determine the outcome of their choices.**

Paolo Verme has worked, lived and travelled in over eighty countries. He initiated his career as a volunteer for a NGO in Africa and has served as a senior policy advisor in transitional and developing economies for governments, international organisations and private companies, including the European Union, Unicef and Unesco.
He is currently Contract Professor of Economics at the University of Turin and at Bocconi University in Milan (Italy) and a consultant of the World Bank.

*'A surprising 40% is in our own hands.'*

# *What about genetics?*

You have two good friends. Let's call them John and Michael. They have no real problems and are living in nearly the same conditions. Nevertheless, John is chronically unhappy and Michael is remarkably happy. What makes these men so different? Professor **Sonja Lyubormirsky** has been doing research on cases like this for more than 20 years. She has advice for John (and for Michael!) that can make a 40% change.

## We don't have to obey the directives of our genes

Growing research with identical and fraternal twins suggests that each person is born with a particular 'happiness set point'. This is a baseline or potential for happiness, to which he or she is bound to return, even after major setbacks or triumphs. The set point for happiness is similar to the set point for weight. Some people are blessed with a 'skinny disposition'. They can easily maintain their weight, without even trying. By contrast, others have to work extraordinarily hard to keep their weight at the desired level, and the moment they slack off, the pounds creep back on. Much the same principle applies to John and Michael. Michael may simply possess a higher set point for happiness, a higher potential for well-being. He doesn't have to work hard at it – he just *is* happy.

So if Michael's happiness is due to genetics, what can poor old John do? Are we all doomed to obey the directives of our genes? The answer is 'no'. I am an experimental social psychologist who has conducted the first controlled experimental intervention studies to increase and maintain a person's happiness level **over and above his or her set point**. In broadest terms, this research suggests that sustainable happiness is attainable **regardless** of genetics, *if* one is prepared to do the work. Much like permanent weight loss and fitness, becoming lastingly happier demands some permanent changes, requiring effort and commitment every day of one's life: commit yourself to your goals, avoid over-thinking, invest in relationships, learn to forgive, use your body, take care of your soul, practice acts of kindness, savour life's joys and count your blessings.

My two colleagues (Ken Sheldon at the University of Missouri and David Schkade at UC San Diego) and I have developed a theory that describes the most important factors determining happiness. In sum, we argue that the set point determines just 50% of happiness, while a mere 10% can be attributed to differences in people's life circumstances – whether they are rich or poor, healthy or unhealthy, married or divorced, etc. This leaves a surprising 40% of our capacity for happiness within our own power to change. This means that John *can* be a great deal happier – and Michael could be even happier than he already is!

## The keys

→ **50% of our capacity for happiness is determined by our starting set point. We have to accept this.**

→ **10% can be attributed to our life circumstances. Don't focus too much on this.**

→ **40% is within our own power to change. Like weight loss, this demands some permanent changes, requiring effort and commitment every day of our lives.**

Professor Sonja Lyubomirsky is an experimental social psychologist. She has been doing research on happiness for more than 20 years and is a worldwide authority, writer and speaker on this topic. She studied at Harvard and Stanford University and is working at the Department of Psychology, University of California (USA). She is the author of the popular book The How of Happiness, a scientific approach to getting the life you want.

# *The dream holiday*

Having the time of our life in an extraordinary holiday resort:
does that make us happy? And if so, why can't we bring that feeling
back home? 'I used to be a travel writer and tourism researcher,
meeting all sort of folks on wonderful locations around the globe.
They were relaxing, enjoying themselves, taking advantage of their
holidays. But they were not happy,' reports **Elena Pruvli**.
How people transfer the lie of a 'dream holiday' to their supposed
'dream life' – and forget what really matters.

## Front and backstage positions

The first lesson about happiness I learnt from tourists was that marvellous surroundings,
luxurious conditions, beautiful nature and outstanding companionship are not necessarily
sources of pleasure and contentment. That a 'dream holiday' is in fact a widely spread
cliché, which imposes on them a socially-shaped stereotype to shape their own dreams.
Surroundings and external well-being are important, but not crucial for happiness.
Similarly, many people are trying to live a 'dream life', doing things which are intended
to create an impression in the eyes of their real or imagined audience that they are living
a happy existence. The gap between the real image of how one's life should be and
the imposed stereotype approved by society is huge – and this increases the distance
to real peace of mind and happiness.

When I later decided to augment my diverse international practical experience with a theoretical base, I soon discovered that there are *front* and *backstage* positions in every culture. There are, perhaps, no happy or unhappy cultures as such, but in some cultures the impact of the showy, loud, pretentious front stage is so strong that the representatives of these cultures are losing the ability to learn what they personally want from their lives. In other words, how to be truly themselves.

In the last decade, I have earned my living by teaching intercultural communications and training people how to be happier in foreign settings and during international exchanges. From every audience with whom I've had a long-term commitment – engineers or film-makers, entrepreneurs or executives, Chinese or Indians – I've learned how to be happier in return. It's all about change, humour and children.

We are not talking here about the shepherd's happiness: sharing picturesque sunsets in the virgin mountains with just your herd at your side. No, we are talking about busy modern people, whether they live in big mega cities or small villages. So the ability to accept change and to find positive and 'closer-to-my skin' motivation is definitely useful, if you want to be a happier person. If you are eager to learn, keen to experience something new and not ready to rest on your laurels, you will see change as a challenge. And this is the way to improve your life internally and externally. Never regret the past. Remember, you are now stronger, smarter, wiser, and have more memories and more experience to share with your loved ones.

Next in importance I would place humour. Self-deprecation goes hand in hand with self-respect. Don't take yourself too seriously. See the joy and the funny side of every situation. Read good books, watch happy movies, listen to kind jokes, communicate with positive people, but avoid and ignore everything sarcastic and full of poison. Don't support mocking, teasing or the making of humiliating jokes at the expense of other cultures you are not familiar with. Instead, remind yourself of the funny and happy moments of your life.

*'Living a dream life for the eyes*
*of an imagined audience.'*

Equally crucial is the way we were treated in the earlier stages of our own lives and the way we are now treating our children. We are not able to analyse our own culture critically but surely we can help our children to be happy by giving them the opportunity to understand themselves, to learn their real needs and wants, to have a sense of a valuable personality. I would strongly recommend parents to create an environment where their children are encouraged to construct their own opinions. All children's thoughts and opinions should be respected and taken seriously, regardless of their lack of experience. There may be friendly discussion in this respect but always coupled to positive dialogue. This will encourage an open-minded attitude to life in the future.

## The keys

→ **Accept changes. Take them as a challenge and learn.**
→ **Don't take yourself too seriously. See the joy and the funny side of every situation.**
→ **Take your children seriously and encourage them to construct their own opinions.**

Elena Pruvli, MA Westminster (United Kingdom), graduated in communication and is now a lecturer and intercultural trainer. She has travelled a great deal and conducted intercultural communication courses for entrepreneurs and students all over Europe, also for Chinese masters students at the Institute of Management in the Estonian Business School, Tallinn (Estonia), where she is working now.

*'We hold happiness within a fairly narrow range of values.'*

# *Measure the temperature*

You can measure your happiness level.

Professor **Robert A. Cummins** does that in Australia every year with a random selection of 2,000 people. How happy do they feel? Does that happiness differ from year to year? And how much does it vary? Is the happiness meter more like a barometer (from stormy to calm) than the thermometer to measure your body temperature (mainly constant)? Robert has found a system.

## The system that controls happiness

Happiness, like so many English words, is bothersome in having more than one meaning. To most people it means a fleeting emotion attached to a nice experience. Like a cup of tea on a hot day, or resting after a job well done. But most current research concerns something different: a mood, rather than an emotion. Whereas emotions are fleeting, moods are more stable. They represent a deep feeling state which is constantly present, even if we lose contact with it sometimes.

The reason why this feeling state has become such a popular area of study is that it exhibits some very interesting characteristics. Perhaps the most important of these is the fact is that the state is positive. Because of this, people normally feel good about themselves. Moreover, their feelings of positivity are so remarkably stable that it has led to the idea that people have a 'set point' for their level of happiness, which is genetically determined.

This stability has been amply demonstrated by the Australian Unity Well-being Index. This project has regularly measured the happiness of the Australian population since April 2001. Each survey involves 2,000 randomly invited people, who record their happiness using our standard measurement instrument, the Personal Well-being Index. We have now conducted 21 such surveys.

The most remarkable statistic to emerge is that, between these different surveys, the average level of population happiness has varied by only three percentage points. How can this be so? We propose that happiness is controlled by a management system called Subjective Well-being Homeostasis. This draws an analogy with the control of physiological systems, such as body temperature, to suggest that we hold happiness within a fairly narrow range of values. The precise width of this range is uncertain but my guess is about 12 percentage points, or 6 points on either side of the set point.

This homeostatic system is also resilient. When unusually good or bad experiences happen, the system is briefly defeated, but it then bounces back to restore happiness to within the normal range. At least, that is what normally happens. However, all homeostatic systems have a limited capacity to absorb challenges to their authority. If negative experiences become too strong, for too long, the system cannot recover. Then, happiness lies persistently below its normal range, with a consequential high risk of depression.

So how can people increase their homeostatic resilience? They need resources, and we characterise these as external or internal. The two major external resources are relationships and money. **Having an emotionally intimate relationship is the most powerful defence.** A confidant may help to avoid negative challenges. Moreover, when negative experiences do occur, they are available to talk through the problem; an age-old and effective remedy to the loss of happiness.

The other major external resource is money. Its primary importance is, of course, to provide the necessities of life. But beyond this, it allows defences to be purchased. You don't like cleaning your house? No problem, if you have the money. Just pay someone else to do it. But note: this is the defence of mood-happiness. It is not 'buying' happiness through the purchase of luxury goods. Such purchases yield only emotional happiness, which adapts quickly, ensuring that such pleasant joys will be fleeting.

So is more always better? We believe that it is. Evolution has supplied a highly developed 'on' button that drives us to seek more and more resources. This is a useful strategy in a resource-poor environment but is not well adapted to modern life. We particularly fall

foul of this old programming when it comes to money. How much homeostatic defence can one buy? The answer, averaged across Australia, is that happiness rises only marginally beyond a gross household income of about $100,000, and after $150,000 there is no further reliable increase. The reason for this phenomenon is that some sources of challenge demand more than money. The problems of having a bad marriage or unpleasant children are not solved by earning more. An alternative strategy is to invest more time in personal relationships. This may not only solve your interpersonal problems, but is also a hot strategy for increasing resilience.

When these external defences fail, as occasionally they must, all is not lost. The processes of thinking now get to work, with the aim of trivialising the bad event. You got fired from work? You soon convince yourself that it was a lousy, dead-end job and that you are lucky to have escaped. Such 'cognitive restructuring' empowers us to rationalise the situation to our own advantage and to feel normally positive again.

Together, these external and internal resources allow us to meet most of the challenges we face. To feel positive about life is normal. It is our genes' way of telling us we are okay.

## The keys

→ **Distinguish between your general mood (fairly stable) and your emotions (fairly volatile). For greater happiness, concentrate on the former.**

→ **Look for someone you can confide in, someone you can talk to in good times and bad. This will strengthen your resilience.**

→ **Regard your feeling of happiness as something like your body temperature: sometimes it goes up, sometimes it goes down, but usually it comes back to its normal level.**

Professor Robert A. Cummins is Doctor of Psychology in the School of Psychology at Deakin University (Australia) and editor-in-chief of the 'Journal of Happiness Studies'. He has collaborated to produce a large number of tests, indexes and reports on the quality of life. Robert A. Cummins is designated 'Expert of International Standing in Quality of Life Research'.

*'Anything can make*
*people happy, if they want it to.'*

# Find your own Quastenflosser

In Paramaribo, the capital of Surinam, men walk about the streets holding their wife with one hand, and a birdcage with the other. 'If he was as pleased to see me as that damned bird, I'd be happy,' said a woman. How can someone be perfectly happy just by seeing or hearing a bird? And why should people in one country be much happier than in another? Professor **Wolfgang Glatzer** has spent a lifetime researching this. Everyone has a right to his own Quastenflosser.

## From your own experience to the happiness of a country

I should start by saying that I have never tried to gain happiness by applying my own research results to myself. My expectation of happiness was built on inner feelings, developed spontaneously. However, once when I was attending a major happiness conference in South Africa, I accidentally gained a very deep insight. This actually happened outside the meeting. I was in my hotel and a man told me he was completely happy that day: he had been to the ocean and had finally seen something that he had been trying to see for many years: the Quastenflosser. The Quastenflosser is a very old, rare fish living deep in the sea, similar to a coelocanth. The chances of meeting one is almost zero. I wondered why this had made him so happy and so I began to regard him as an interesting object of happiness research. I asked myself if I could make anyone else happy by suggesting they look for a Quastenflosser. Of course, the answer is 'yes': anything can make people

happy if they want it to. Each human being can have – symbolically speaking – their own personal Quastenflosser. What makes you happy depends on you, your needs, your social development and your lifestyle. For a long time sociology has taught: 'If we define something as real, then it is real in its consequences.'

I very much like the terms 'having, loving, being' to describe our world of happiness. We have to secure a basic living standard, we have to take care of friendly social relations and we may also choose distinctive characteristics that make us happy beyond that.

Happiness and unhappiness are both structural features of the world and they exist in different dimensions. On the one hand, there are aspects of positive well-being, such as happiness, satisfaction, pleasure, health and joy; and on the other hand, there are negative aspects like anxiety, alienation, fear, sadness, depression and others. Positive and negative aspects of well-being are positively correlated but not very strongly. So it is likely that you will contribute something towards your happiness if you are successful in reducing your unhappiness. But increasing your positive well-being is something different to decreasing your negative well-being. Just as we experience our positive well-being in contrast to our negative well-being, so it is a paradox that our negative well-being contributes in a certain sense to our positive well-being.

**Happiness depends not only on present conditions but also on future perspectives.** How people see the future is decisive for their overall well-being. Bad present conditions combined with a good outlook are perhaps better than good present conditions combined with a bad outlook. In general, most individuals are characterized by inconsistent conditions and ambivalent outlooks.

These observations are made in respect of individuals. But happiness is also a question of collective social units, such as cities, regions, countries, societies and continents. There are procedures to find out scientifically which nation is at the top of the world happiness rankings. These levels of happiness sometimes change, in response to significant events, but the main impression is one of continuity. There are always ups and downs, but in the end they all add up to zero. In developing countries we find the highest increase in happiness if beyond a certain amount of money is spent.

The key question is whether or not there is a factor which explains different levels of happiness between nations. Many factors seem to play a part, but a few of the most interesting ones should be mentioned. The relatively small countries in the north of Europe are all among the happiest countries in the world. Small countries seem to provide better conditions to enable people to live happily, perhaps because of a heightened feeling of belonging. In Northern Europe there is also another factor which could explain the exceptional happiness status of these countries, namely the welfare state of the social democratic type. Perhaps people like social security so much that the welfare state has become an important generator of happiness. But in countries such as the United States people seem to prefer more liberal conditions. This leads us to the question of inequality. Until recently, inequalities were defined in terms of income, wealth, education and life chances. Now, however, new dimensions of subjectively perceived inequality are being investigated: **societies are divided into satisfied and dissatisfied strata.** Various mixed constellations of perceived inequalities exist.

Generally, it can be said that people look at their personal conditions with more concern than their collective conditions, and that they cherish public good less than private good. This is a problem for modern societies. Is individualism to be our future? The same conditions of living do not necessarily generate equal levels of happiness. The most important clue to happiness is simply to be aware of the beautiful things in life – whether they are private or collective.

## The keys

- → **There are three steps to happiness: having (a basic living standard), loving (family, friends) and being (what goes beyond).**
- → **Increasing your positive well-being is something different to decreasing your negative well-being.**
- → **Happiness depends not only on present conditions but also on future perspectives. Bad conditions with a good outlook make us happier than good conditions with a bad outlook. Think positive.**

And remember; countries differ. The same living conditions do not necessarily generate equal levels of happiness.

Wolfgang Glatzer (Professor of Sociology at the Goethe University, Frankfurt am Main, Germany) has published many books on social, structural and cultural change and the quality of life, such as 'Challenges for Quality of Life in the Contemporary World'. He is a founding member of the international research group Comparative Charting of Social Change and has been president of the International Society for Quality of Life Studies. Wolfgang Glatzer is a member of the editorial board of the 'Journal of Happiness Studies'.

# *A Quantum Leap in Happiness*

Animals do not search for happiness. Their behaviour is determined by the four F's. Professor **Yew-Kwang Ng** now adds his own 4 F's to the recipe for human happiness. But he also goes a big step further. In recent years we have been able to stimulate our brains artificially to make them experience happiness. Why don't we invest massively in this? It would immediately take us forward in a quantum leap.

## Put the emphasis on the 4 F's

Some research (including studies of twins) has shown that the happiness of an individual has a genetically determined set point, around which fluctuations occur. However, at least to some extent, one can become much happier just by adopting a more positive attitude. Think less about sad things, and more about happy things; spend more time doing things you enjoy (without harming your health), even if it means you make less money. Except for the unfortunate minority still threatened by starvation and malnutrition, money is not really an important factor for happiness. This is particularly true if you put less emphasis on material things and relative competition, and more on the things that are really important for happiness. In this respect, I believe in the importance of the 4 F's of happiness: faith (religious or otherwise), form (health), family, and friends. These 4 F's mirror the well-known 4 F's of animal behaviour: feeding, fighting, fleeing, and mating. (Please don't ask me to explain why the last one doesn't start with an 'f'!).

In the long term, however, society can only break away from the genetic set points by making use of science and technology, especially with regard to brain stimulation and genetic engineering. We normally acquire pleasures through the stimulation of our peripheral nervous systems: through touch, sight, taste, etc. Such pleasures have very serious limits due to the processes of habituation (diminishing marginal returns in the short term) and adaptation (diminishing marginal returns in the long term).

A little girl asks her mum: 'Is it true that an apple a day keeps the doctor away?' 'Yes,' replies the mother, 'This week I have kept seven doctors away like that, but I think I need one now!" In other words, diminishing returns help us to avoid excessive consumption. However, in the four billion years of life on Earth, no species had managed to stimulate its brain directly until 1954, when Homo sapiens was accidentally responsible for the electrical stimulation of the cerebral pleasure centres of rats. The returns from this direct stimulation do not diminish, either in the short or long term. This means that such stimulation can induce intense and prolonged pleasure. Many people regard this as unnatural. Nevertheless, if we had told people three hundred years ago that people today would spend hours each evening watching shadows in a box for their entertainment, they would also have said that it was unnatural. All civilised things are 'unnatural'. Perhaps, instead, we should be asking government why no funding for the development of a safe method for the stimulation of our pleasure centres has been provided during the past half a century.

True, we need to be very careful, especially with regard to the genetic engineering of our own capability for happiness, in order to avoid counter-productive outcomes. However, in the long term, genetic engineering has the potential to far surpass brain stimulation in terms of providing quantum leaps in our happiness. With appropriate safeguards, the risk involved is much less than our current 'business-as-usual' attitude towards global warming. Why can people tolerate such unnecessary and unrewarding risks, yet refuse to accept a far smaller risk which promises to increase world happiness possibly a thousand fold? There is only one answer: irrational fear of the unknown.

## The keys

→ **Concentrate on the 4 F's of happiness: faith, form, family and friends.**
→ **Don't focus too much on sensory pleasures. Such pleasures have serious limits.**
→ **Why shouldn't we invest in the artificial and direct stimulation of our brains to raise our levels of happiness? This would provide a quantum leap in world happiness.**

Professor Yew-Kwang Ng was born in Malaysia. He has received high awards in recognition of his work at the Monash University in Melbourne (Australia). Yew-Kwang Ng is renowned for his life-long work in welfare economics and welfare biology. He has written more than one hundred refereed papers and books, such as 'Economics and Happiness' and 'The Unparalleled Mystery'. The motto of his university is Ancora imparo ('I am still learning').

*'The laws of inner happiness are not the same as the laws for outer achievement.'*

# The Happiness Detective

Do all these researchers on happiness apply their discoveries to themselves? Let's put that question to a Professor Emeritus who has studied happiness for a life time. The story of an adrenaline junkie who turned into a happiness detective.

## Making progress in achieving the life you want

From my years of research on happiness I have not only made various discoveries, but I have actually applied those discoveries to become happier myself. Some writers claim that 'happiness only comes if it is not pursued', but scientists have applied science to pursue the laws of happiness with considerable success. I learned that if I want to be happy I must make an effort to nurture and encourage happiness in my life. I now read books and articles on happiness research. I try applying to myself the exercises that work for others, and then monitor whether they are working for me. Each night, I fill out a 3-minute 'happiness diary', rating how happy I was during the day, how hopeful, how energetic, and which practices seemed to help. I can see how my happiness increases over time as I use the 'three blessings' exercise in gratefulness: the meditation practice so that I get to know myself better; the practice of forgiveness so that I am not consumed with bitterness; the practice of mature optimism so that I can persevere; and the practice of setting goals that I can be proud of.

Another important lesson I have learned is that the laws of inner happiness are not the same as the laws for outer achievement. To achieve things in the outer world, we can often use 'brute force' and adrenaline-charged action to succeed – for example, to save our child from danger, or even just to finish a report for the boss. Adrenaline-charged methods work well during periods of danger, because they allow us to temporarily ignore 'how we feel'. But if we persistently ignore how we feel in order to achieve outer goals, we are in danger of hollow achievements, chronic stress, and an unsatisfying life. As a lifelong 'adrenaline junkie', I have learned to resist applying these methods when I am not in danger. Instead, I have become a 'happiness detective', always unobtrusively observing my feeling tone, taking care to nurture the good times, experimenting with new ways to act that increase happiness in me and in others. Perhaps there is less drama in my life, but more consistent progress towards achieving the life I really want.

## The keys

→ **Don't believe the old adage that happiness only comes when it is not pursued. You *can* successfully pursue the laws of happiness.**

→ **Don't use the laws for outer achievement ('brute force and adrenaline-charged action') to achieve inner happiness.**

→ **Become a happiness detective, always observing your own feeling tone and nurturing the good times.**

Michael Hagerty started with computer science and psychology. He was once elected as Teacher of the Year in the Graduate School of Management. Afterwards, many honours and awards followed, including one for the best paper published in the 'Journal of Happiness Studies'. He is a consultant to organisations and nations on measuring the quality of life and is a keynote speaker on Changes in Life Quality. Michael Hagerty is Professor Emeritus at the University of California, Davis (usa).

*'There are many different ways*
*for many different people.'*

# The treasury

'I'll give you everything money can buy, if you open the treasury
of real happiness for me,' says an old king in an ancient fairy tale.
He is looking for three golden keys to this magic treasury.
Professor **Alec C. Michalos** might be the right magician
to show him where they are. He has spent a lifetime on happiness
research. But should the old king accept his keys?
And would they work for him?

## Three golden keys

I would like to send three main messages about what I have learned in over 40 years of
research on happiness. The word, of course, has several somewhat different meanings
to different people, running from something very close to pure pleasurable experience to
a very robust array of constituents and determinants of a good life. My own preference
is for the latter sort of definition.

First, people today are not very different from people living in ancient Greece in the fifth
century BC, at least not in terms of what they need and want for a good life. From then until
now, people have needed and wanted much the same thing: good mental and physical health
in the most basic sense of well-functioning organic systems; nourishing food, adequate
shelter and clothes; someone who cares about them, usually friends and relatives;
means of financial security; adequate voice in the governance of their communities;
personal and communal security; fresh air, drinking water and land; aesthetic expression
and opportunities for aesthetic experience; justice and fairness in personal and political
relations; opportunities for personal and public exploration of the natural world and
its inhabitants; and good luck.

Second, the most important lesson we have learned about what makes people happy over the past 40 years is that there are many different ways for many different people. The list of things in the previous paragraph is a good start, but one might also mention genetic inheritance of certain temperaments and native abilities of one sort or another; developed virtues like patience, persistence, courage, compassion, temperance, wisdom and justice; personal and social standards of evaluation that are reasonable and moral; and choices, purposes, goals, aims, projects and activities that tend to produce and reproduce all the things mentioned so far.

Third, the most dangerous feature of research and publication (both by scholars and the popular press) in this area is the human tendency to oversimplify human beings and the human condition. Researchers tend to use a minimum number of variables to describe and explain people, their motives and actions. If we are not prone to search for a 'silver bullet', we are at least prone to select relatively few. Too often, human agency in the form of personal evaluations, choices, purposes, goals and motives are neglected in favour of simple and simple-minded economic, materialistic, deterministic explanations. So, the guiding principle for happiness researchers and for those in search of happiness should be this: remember that all human beings are very complicated organisms; that life itself is complex; and be suspicious of simple descriptions and explanations of what makes anyone happy. In short, there are no golden keys. The king will have to unlock the door himself.

## The keys

→ **Our search for happiness is universal. What we need and want for a good life has changed little in the past 2000 years.**

→ **There are many different ways to happiness for many different people. Make your own choice.**

→ **There are no golden keys. Human beings and life itself are too complex for that.**

→ **Be suspicious of simple explanations.**

Alex C. Michalos is Professor Emeritus in Political Science at the University of Northern British Columbia (Canada). He has published 22 books and over 90 refereed articles, and founded or co-founded six scholarly journals. He is past president of the International Society for Quality of Life Studies and was awarded the Gold Medal for Achievement in Research from the Social Sciences and Humanities Research Council of Canada.

*'There is no one word in our language for happiness.'*

# *Don't neglect the soul*

Malaysia is a multi-ethnic society with Malays, Chinese, Indians and others. Each group has its own separate language, culture and religion based on animism, Hinduism, Buddhism and Islam. Professor **Noraini M. Noor** works at the International Islamic University of Malaysia in Kuala Lumpur. Most of her Malay students find it difficult to grasp the concept 'happiness'. She looks for an answer in the culture and religion of the Malays.

## Why do we focus on mind, matter and body?

While everyone talks about happiness, the concept itself remains elusive. At present, there is still no agreed definition of what it actually means. In many cultures, most people believe that happiness is achieved when one becomes successful, rich, or popular. In psychology, numerous measures of happiness have been developed which emphasise the experience of joy, satisfaction, and the absence of negative feelings. Even so, happiness is still hard to pin down.

I would like to argue that 'happiness', as defined in the West, is limited and arises out of the need to counter the negative associations of human nature and behaviour with mental illness, such as depression. The new field of positive psychology, with its emphasis on the positive side of human nature, has helped to increase the profile of research into happiness or subjective well-being. Since **secularisation marginalised religion as a private personal matter, the West no longer devotes sufficient attention to the soul of the person.** For example, psychology – the scientific study of a person's cognition and behaviour – focuses exclusively on mind and matter – or in other words, the body. Thus, while the body is given plenty of attention, the soul is neglected.

For a Muslim, the way to happiness is to submit to the one and only God: 'Truly, in remembering God do hearts find rest' (Quran 13:28). Happiness is therefore a feeling that resides in the heart and is characterised by contentment and being at peace with oneself and the world at large.

How does submitting to the one and only God help a person to achieve happiness? In Islam, a person is only one of God's creatures, created by Him to manage the affairs of the world according to His directives – with justice for the prosperity and well-being of all His creations. To do so, God empowers men with body (mind/intellect and matter/physical) and soul (spirit). To be content and happy, these components must be nurtured, so that a balance is achieved between the body and the soul. If this balance is not maintained – for example, if people only focus on the advancement of their intellectual and physical selves (through worldly pursuits) without heed of their spiritual needs – they may experience feelings of emptiness, restlessness and recklessness, as if something is still missing. Likewise, a **swing to extreme spirituality is also unhealthy, for this will lead to spiritual fanaticism.** Islam provides guidelines on how to address and attend to the needs the body and soul, so that a person can be content and at peace.

When Islam spread out of Arabia to other parts of the world, it quickly became conflated with the prevalent local culture of the time, so that the Islamic meaning of happiness is infused within the local traditions and customs. For example, when I asked my Malay students, who are Muslims, what is happiness in the Malay language, their definition included the Islamic conception of happiness (contentment, aspects of spirituality, having a balance in worldly pursuits and the Hereafter), Western ideas of happiness (experiences of joy or elation, satisfaction, and the absence of negative affects), as well as the cultural understanding of what it means to be happy (such as one's role obligations in the social structure). In other words, the Western definition of happiness, which does not include aspects of religion and the influence of culture, is insufficient to capture

the full essence of happiness as understood by the Malays. That is why there is no one word in the Malay language that is able to comprehensively convey the meaning of happiness. While the need to be happy is universal, the striving for and the expression of this need may be culture bound.

## The keys

→   **Happiness is characterised by contentment and being at peace with oneself and the world at large.**

→   **To be content and happy, it is necessary that a balance is achieved between body and soul.**

→   **While the need to be happy is universal, the striving for and the expression of this need may be culture bound.**

Noraini Mohd Noor is Professor of Psychology and coordinator of the Women for Progress Research Unit at the International Islamic University of Malaysia in Kuala Lumpur. She has published numerous articles and books on well-being, work stress, women's work and family roles. She has worked and studied in Australia, New Zealand and England. Noraini is a member of the editorial board of the 'Asian Journal of Social Psychology'.

*'Paradise is definitely
not a place to go,
if nobody is there'.*

# *The party temperament*

War is not the best condition for happiness. The Lebanese people have suffered much from the conflicts of recent years. 'We have had to pay a heavy price,' reports Professor **Elie G. Karam** from Beirut. But he has discovered a secret strength in his fellow countrymen: their temperament. It helps them to manage their lives in a way which allows them to cope with their difficult situation. In fact, they show that life can be a constant, collective party – if we want it to be.

## Know yourself

We recently carried out a unique research project, measuring the affective temperament of a representative sample of Lebanese citizens from all over the country. We found that a large proportion of them possess what is referred to as a hyperthymic temperament. Individuals with a hyperthymic temperament are often seen as strong, energetic, productive and well-respected. They are self confident, risk-taking, generous, cheerful and warm. This type of temperament is also characterised by high levels of energy and fun seeking. The next most frequent temperament was the anxious temperament, which involves a greater tendency to worry about human affairs. Moreover, we also found that the anxious temperament was the most important predictor of mental disorders, whereas the hyperthymic temperament was a protector against most of them (except possibly and interestingly *substance use* and *separation anxiety disorder in adults*). These findings for the hyperthymics might explain the high frequency of celebrations amongst the Lebanese, usually with quite stable groups of friends and/or family members.

Since we found that particular types of temperament are linked to mental disorders, this means that it might be potentially possible to manage one's own temperament (which defines our emotional reactions to life experiences) in order to avoid unnecessary pain and suffering. And if a mental disorder does set in, it will help us be aware of it and allow us to pursue the best available, yet personalised, method of dealing with that disorder – if necessary, with professional help.

We believe that the well-known adage 'know yourself' is the key to problem-solving, and also the best way to assist the individual's quest for 'happiness'. **Knowing your temperament and your character will therefore help you to manage yourself and your life in a more predictable manner.** For example, if idleness creates stress for a person, this is a clear signal that they need to work seriously to develop activities (including hobbies) which carry a low risk of harm to themselves or others. Similarly, if sociability is a 'need', then the remedial activities should be planned to include others (including the younger generations for older people).

The Lebanese engage in collective partying at all ages, and during the summer months the country receives an influx of visitors equal to half of its population. This creates a unique atmosphere – that of an on-going party. It is a lifestyle for which the Lebanese and the Mediterranean peoples are well-known and of which they are rightly proud. In fact, a Lebanese proverb summarises this lifestyle perfectly: 'Paradise is definitely not a place to go, if nobody is there'. This might in part explain why this tiny republic on the shore of the Mediterranean continues to amaze its own inhabitants and the rest of the world, with its own special brand of fun, always mixed with a good dose of caution. It is easy to see how, on a collective basis, this satisfies hyperthymic temperaments and minimises the worries of those with a more anxious disposition. And as for the few Lebanese with the third type of temperament – the cyclothymic, which is characterised by ups ad downs – the intensity of social life may help to reduce their panic about the downs within bounds, since the ups will be coming thick and fast. Moreover, the cyclothymics are inherently creative, and there are plenty of hyperthymics around, ready and waiting to explore and exploit new possibilities…

This is a truncated look at happiness, and our ability to manage our own brain will no doubt improve as more knowledge is accumulated with time. Greater happiness probably depends on the balance between your own make-up (at any given point in time) and your shaping of your life's possibilities. This needs to be based on a serious and continuous self-evaluation and an assessment of what can work for you, in the ever-evolving process of cultivating one's garden by picking the best ingredients and remedies, with lots of helps from family, friends and… specialists.

## The keys

→ **An anxious temperament is the most important predictor of mental disorders.**

→ **An energetic, cheerful and warm (hyperthymic) temperament is a protector against most mental disorders.**

→ **Learn to know your own temperament and character, and try to manage yourself.**

Professor Elie G. Karam is head of the Department of Psychiatry and Clinical Psychology at the Balamand University School of Medicine in Beirut (Lebanon). He has studied mental disorders and the effects on women and children of the long years of war in Lebanon. The Lebanese Epidemiologic Burden Assessment of the Needs Of the Nation survey (L.E.B.A.N.O.N) carried out by his group is the first ever such survey in the Arab world. It continues to shed light on a variety of dimensions, such as education, income, dating, marriage, exposure to stressors, health and a very detailed look at mental health and how this affects our lives.

**Vahid Sari-Saraf**

# *The power of sports*

'There is a common saying in Iran : laughter is a cure for every pain,'
says Dr. Vahid Sari-Saraf. He focuses on the immune system of happy people
and discovers the secret power of sports.

No Rooz (the first day of the New Year) is as ancient as Iranian history itself, and
is traditionally the day when people open the gates of their hearts to happiness.
Happiness has a valued and valuable position in our culture. I work in the field
of exercise physiology. There is no way to discuss physiology without studying
its relationship with psychology. Happy persons have a high-functioning immune
system and vice versa: unhappy people have a low one.
Sports are a major source of happiness. They provide the social satisfaction which
comes from belonging to clubs and teams and from the close personal interaction
involved in most active games. Sports are also of particular interest, because their
selection is a matter of individual choice and they are more under personal control
than many other sources of satisfaction. Happiness is related to stable extraversion
and easy sociability, combined with a natural and pleasant interaction with other
people. Similarly, numerous studies have shown that instability and neuroticism
are connected to unhappiness. Research with Iranian students has shown that
athletes have more extrovert personalities and are happier, when compared with
non-athletes. There is also a higher relationship between extraversion and
happiness in non-athletes as a group. On the other side of the coin, the neurotic
aspects in athletes are at a lower level than in non-athletes. This means that we can
predict someone's happiness by measuring the extraversion traits of his personality.
Regular participation in favourable sports, as a pleasant and highly social activity,
can improve your personality and your happiness. The emerging consensus of
research suggests that there is no significant difference between the happiness
effect of team and individual sport activities.

Dr. Vahid Sari-Saraf is an associate professor in exercise physiology at
the Tabriz University in Iran. His main topics of interest are immune systems
and the relationship between happiness and personality (especially for athletes).
He combines these activities with his role as the leading investigator in his country
for the Australian Centre on Quality of Life. He and his wife have called their
daughter Shadi – which means 'happy' in the Persian (Farsi) language.

*'The good news is that we compare
the unpleasant outcomes as well.'*

# The social circle

How honest is our answer to the question: 'Are you happy?'
Most people will give you the impression that they believe the answer
to this question lies deep in themselves. But the reality is slightly
different: we primarily look at the people around us. The importance
of the social circle.

## We always compare

My work in the field of happiness has examined thousands (or tens, or even hundreds
of thousands) of individual replies to questions about life satisfaction, job satisfaction or
other measures of subjective well-being. I have particularly been interested in whether
our happiness is determined by what happens to other people around us: in other words,
is there a social context to happiness?

The results of this research have convinced me that there is. And the results are perhaps
depressing: many aspects of life seem to be evaluated relatively. For example, I am happier
when I earn more income, but less happy when others earn more income. This implies that
a general increase in income, where we all become richer, may not make us any happier.
The good news, perhaps, is that these types of comparisons can also be found for more
unpleasant outcomes as well. Unemployment is one of the most dissatisfying or
unpleasant experiences that we have identified. But it seems to hurt individuals less in
high-unemployment areas, where presumably the stigma of unemployment is lower.

Happiness is therefore social as well as individual: other people matter for your own well-being. They matter via their income, via what they are doing on the labour market, and probably via many of the other things that they do. They also matter in some general social sense. The quality of interactions between individuals, and between individuals and institutions, is likely a key component of well-being. Some recent work looked at the quality of the relationship between individuals and their place of work. Specifically, individuals were asked whether they were '*willing to work harder than I have to, in order to help the firm or organisation I work for to succeed*'. Out of the 17 different countries for which we had information, people in the USA and Canada were most likely to agree with this statement; those in France were the least likely. I think that this kind of distrustful relationship at work, and with institutions in general, is unlikely to make people happy. The difficult question, of course, is how to change it...

## The keys

→ **Happiness is social. We compare our pleasant and unpleasant experiences with the people around us.**

→ **The quality of interactions between individuals is a key component of well-being.**

→ **A trustful relationship at work and with institutions is likely to make people happy.**

Professor Andrew Clark (Paris School of Economics, France) has worked in the UK and the USA. His research interests (170 conference presentations and 130 articles in 53 specialised journals) are job and life satisfaction, social interactions and social learning. He even studied the effect of lottery prizes. Andrew Clark has written reports for the OECD and the UK government. He is a member of the United Nations Well-Being Group.

*'We survive because we are experiencing.'*

# The nine experiences

Walking through China's Forbidden City in Bejing, the guide
illustrates the importance of the number 9 in Chinese history:
nine stairs to each platform, nine times nine buttons on the emperor's
doors, nine statues on the roofs of the 9,999 rooms.
Professor **Xing Zhanjun** works with other kinds of numbers:
the statistics of happiness, reflecting the subjective well-being of
people in China. His final conclusion to improve our happiness?
The nine experiences.

## Happiness is your experience

If you ask me what is happiness or where it can be found, I would tell you that happiness
is your experience. In a sense, we could also say that life is experience. We survive because
we are experiencing. Although there is much suffering in our real life, we can still keep up
our spirits. With this attitude of mind and with our best endeavours, we can make our life
better and better. In our research into the subjective well-being of the Chinese people,
we have found that some experiences are particularly important to people's happiness.
The basic experience is one of **satisfaction and abundance**. Although money is not
a panacea, life becomes totally unacceptable if there is no money. When a person lacks
a basic material guarantee, happiness is naturally out of the question. Therefore, the basic
premise of happiness is at least to be able to make enough money to live comfortably,
thereby avoiding the pressure of economic conditions. Of course, a contented person is
happy with what he has. When you have more abundant material resources, and your
expectations are appropriate, happiness will be within your reach. Nine experiences
will help you to improve this happiness.

**Experience of mental health.** Happiness is a positive psychological experience, which means possessing psychological health, a good attitude, an open mind and a cheerful character. If a person has such a positive psychological attitude, he can often feel more energetic, and can deal with his daily work and his life issues more smoothly. Even if facing difficulty, he can deal with it calmly.

**Experience of physical health.** Physical health is also an experience. In some ways it is a question of good fortune – and therefore happiness – if you can avoid major illnesses. But there is also happiness when a person can still enjoy life when suffering from a disease, even if it is a serious one. If you are satisfied with your health, if you feel comfortable with your body and if you are not troubled by serious illness, then you will be more likely to be happy. But bodily disease is not necessarily a source of unhappiness; rather it is your positive mental attitude which is a source of happiness.

**Experience of psychological balance.** Envying other people's success; laughing at someone else's misfortune; being wise in your own conceit; having grandiose plans but few abilities… If a person possesses this kind of mental attitude, he will almost certainly not feel much happiness. Happiness is the ability to readily accept your own state of life, and to face your own life experiences with honesty and without complaint. You must certainly seize the opportunities which life presents, but you must approach them in a pragmatic manner.

**Experience of adaptation to interpersonal relations.** Do you have a harmonious and sincere relationship with your soul mates? Do you have intimate friends with whom you can reach mutual understanding and agreement? Establishing good social interaction will help you to become a truly social being. This can help you to avoid mistakes and bitterness. Of course, it will also lead to happiness.

**Experience of family atmosphere.** Family is very important for everyone, everywhere. For Chinese people, 'home' has a special significance. Even in our modern society, the family's emotional function has not been weakened. Within the family circle, people are better able to cope with pressure and can relax more freely. If a person can feel the warmth of his family, it allows him to reach mutual understanding and agreement. If the atmosphere in the family is harmonious and relaxed, he will always experience pleasurable feelings.

**Experience of confidence towards society.** People cannot leave the social environment and survive. This means that a person's experience of social development similarly affects his happiness. When a person lives in a society which is relatively good for everyone's best

interests and when he is confident that society's development trends benefit the individual, he will experience more happiness.

**Experience of self-acceptance.** Being able to recognise your own advantages and tolerate your own disadvantages, and being able to adopt a positive attitude towards yourself: this is a mature attitude of self. Such a mature attitude can in many cases help people to transcend themselves. They get a sense of satisfaction and happiness, which leads to self-confidence and self-restraint.

**Experience of goals and personal values.** If a person holds clear convictions, it will help him to define his position and direction in life. He will know what he wants, and will know the value and meaning of what he is doing. He will always feel full and contented. He will take delight in routine duties and be more likely to greet the new day with confidence.

**Experience of growth and progress.** Those who seek progress are able to face life positively and regard it as a continuous learning process. They usually find themselves moving forward in life and are aware of their goals. This helps them to overcome the obstacles between them and their objectives. Such a spirit of enterprise not only brings real practical benefits, but also gives people happiness.

## The keys

- → **Experience mental and physical health, and psychological balance.**
- → **Experience interpersonal relations, family atmosphere and confidence towards society.**
- → **Experience self-acceptance, goals and personal values, growth and progress.**

Xing Zhanjun is a professor at Shandong University in Jinan (China). He is a post-graduate doctor of the Institute of Sociology in the Chinese Academy of Social Sciences in Bejing and director of the Research Base in Shandong Province for the National Bureau of Statistics in China. His main interests are quality of life and social policy, combined with the measurement of subjective well-being.

*'People who lose their friends would have to be compensated, in material terms, with six times their income, in order to relieve the pain of their loss.'*

# *The price of a friend*

'Happiness depends on things as varied as the circumstances and problems which each of us face and the personal aspirations which each of us has. This makes it is impossible to propose a standard formula for happiness,' says **Eduardo Lora**. In his studies based on polls of over 40,000 people in Latin America and the Caribbean, he has discovered something remarkable and surprising: the price of a friend.

## The value of friends, a job and the things that money can buy

My studies support what we already know about the things which most influence our satisfaction with life: having friends in times of need, good health, strong religious beliefs, maintaining a stable relationship with your partner, and having a job and an income which is sufficient to cover basic needs. None of this is likely to surprise anyone. What is surprising, at least for an economist like me, is finding that income is worth so little in relation to happiness. People who lose their friends, for example, would have to be compensated, in material terms, with six times their income in order to relieve the pain of their loss. For people who lose their job, it is not enough simply to give them the same level of income, in order to make them feel good again. They need 60% more, because their job is not just a source of income but also a means of fulfilling or relating to important aspects of their life. For many it may seem grotesque to put a value on friends or a job, but that is not the purpose of these calculations. Instead, they are designed to show how little money is worth in comparison with the important things in life.

But I have learned something else from the study of the polls. Namely this: comparing yourself with others in terms of the material aspects of life makes money worth even less, and makes happiness dependent on obtaining even more money. People who live in very difficult economic conditions often feel more satisfied with a much lower income than people who have far more money, but can compare their car or job with those who live around them. For most people the effect of comparing the material aspects of life with others is very harmful. No matter how much more they earn, their level of satisfaction does not change, because they always know someone else who has more than they do.

Consequently, one of the keys to happiness is to enjoy the money you have, without worrying about what others have. If you can achieve this, you will quickly discover that you have more than enough money for your needs, and that it is better to look inside yourself and devote more energy to the things that really bring happiness.

## The keys

→ **A job or a friend cannot easily be replaced.**
→ **Money and income are worth little in comparison with the important things in life.**
→ **For most people the effect of comparing their material wealth with others is very harmful.**

Eduardo Lora is the manager of the Research Department of the Inter-American Development Bank in Washington, DC (USA). He is a native Colombian, who has devoted his professional career to the understanding of Latin American development problems. He has recently edited two books on happiness and the quality of life: 'Paradox and Perception' and 'Beyond Facts: Understanding Quality of Life'.

# *The experiment game*

Give people who don't know each other some money and start an experiment. Some of them can 'spend' money by giving it to others. Some of them have to wait until they receive. However, the game offers the possibility of gain on both sides. Two Italian professors conducted this experiment with their students and measured their levels of happiness. What makes us happier: giving or receiving? And what important lessons can we draw from the experiment for social welfare policy?

## What makes us happier: giving or receiving?

We investigated this issue by combining a survey with a happiness question and data collected in an experimental game, where players obtained varying material pay-offs as a consequence of their anonymous interactions during the game. The surprising thing – at least in the light of the standard economic assumption that people are motivated only by the pursuit of their own self-interest – is that contributing to social welfare increases people's happiness, even when it reduces their individual monetary pay-off.

Our experimental research involved 368 students from three different Italian universities. They were randomly paired and anonymously played the 'investment game'. In this game, people are endowed with a certain amount of money (in our case 10 tokens, where 1 token is equivalent to 0.50 euros). While one player (the 'trustee') cannot use his/her endowment,

## 'Contributing to social welfare increases people's happiness, even when it reduces their individual monetary pay-off.'

the other player (the 'trustor') must decide how much to send to the trustee. The amount sent, which may vary between zero and the total amount received, is tripled by the experimenter and is delivered to the trustee. Finally, the trustee must decide how much of this tripled amount to send back to the trustor. Obviously, both the trustor's and trustee's decision affect the game's outcome and final pay-offs. Moreover, the trustor has a value creating power, since the amount sent is tripled by the experimenter, and this is the only way to increase the total pay-off of the game (the 'social welfare').

According to the most frequently used happiness questions, we measured the self-declared happiness of the players involved in the experiment by asking: 'Taking all things into consideration, how happy do you consider yourself to be, on a sliding scale from 1 to 10, where 1 = completely unhappy and 10 = completely happy'. The question was randomly answered by participants: a) at the end of the game or b) before they even knew the rules of the game.

Our results clearly show that happiness declarations after the game are not affected by the personal pay-off obtained by the players. On the contrary, trustors' happiness is positively correlated with the amounts sent to the other player. In other words, people who decide to send money to the other person feel happier than people who do not. Moreover – and perhaps this is the most interesting result – people who give more are happier, even though their final monetary gain is lower. In fact, trustees tend not to reward trustors who send positive amounts, and their decision to send money is actually harmful in terms of the trustors' final payoff. We can exclude the possibility that our results depend on the fact that happier people are 'more generous'. In fact, there is no correlation between the amount sent by trustors and their happiness declarations before playing.

On further point should be stressed before we give our concluding remarks. We asked people about their overall happiness. **But how can their overall happiness be affected by the playing of a simple game?** A distinction made by the 2006 Nobel Prize winners, Daniel Kahneman and Alan Krueger, helps to shed light on this issue. Kahneman and

Kreuger distinguish between *experienced utility* and *remembered utility*: the first is the way people feel about experiences in real-time and the second is the way they recall their experiences after they have ended. It has been proven that retrospective evaluations of past experiences are subject to systematic biases with regard to real-time reports. Essentially, remembered utility seems to be a sort of average, where the importance of experienced utilities are not equal and more importance is attributed to end of period experiences. Our results essentially support the idea that recent experiences may significantly affect declarations on overall happiness. In particular, we consider the effect on the trustors' self-declared happiness in our experiment as the effect of a recent (with respect to the answer to the happiness question) pleasure experience which affected trustors' utility.

The investment game has never been used before to study the effect of the pay-offs on players and/or the effects of their behaviour in the game on their happiness levels. This methodology allowed us to point out an interesting effect of peoples' behaviour in relation to their happiness, which is robust (at least in our experimental setting) and which may be translated into an important suggestion for politicians and economists alike. To care for other people's welfare, even to the detriment of our own material advantage, may make us happier than only thinking about ourselves.

## The keys

→ **Our happiness is not affected by the personal pay-off obtained.**

→ **Happier people are not more generous. More generous people are happier.**

→ **To care for other people's welfare, even to the detriment of our own material advantage, may make us happier than only thinking about ourselves.**

Leonardo Becchetti is Professor of Economics at the University of Rome Tor Vergata (Italy). He is president of the ethical committee of Banca Popolare Etica and an executive member of Econometica, a consortium of more than 20 Italian universities engaged in research on the relationship between ethics and economics. Giacomo Degli Antoni is a research fellow at the interuniversity centre EconomEtica – University of Milano Bicocca, with a special interest in the relationship between happiness and economics.
The investment game was introduced by Berg, Dickhaut and Mc Cabe in 1995.

*'The revolution made things much better but not for interpersonal relations.'*

# The revolutionary experience

The non-violent Velvet Revolution in Czechoslovakia overthrew the communist government in 1989. One year later the country held its first democratic elections for more than forty years. Since then, two professors in Prague have kept an eye on the effect of social changes on the quality of life. They have discovered a shift in the value orientation of people and also a new conflict: between values. A revolutionary experience.

## The effects of a revolution

The transition from a totalitarian to a pluralistic political system in the Czech Republic in 1989 was accompanied by many social and economic changes. The impact of these profound changes on quality of life was investigated in a survey with a large sample of the Czech population in 2000-2001. More than ten years after the political change, Czechs were in general more satisfied than unsatisfied. When respondents compared their current life quality with that before 1989, most of them (65%) indicated that their life was better now.

Only twelve percent perceived their quality of life as worse. The only area that had, according to a majority of the respondents, deteriorated during the post-socialist period was 'interpersonal relations'. Although Czechs expressed high satisfaction with their friends and family life, they did not regard the development of relations in society as a whole as being good. **Women evaluated the changes connected to the new era less positively than men.** Men appreciated in particular their increased chance to achieve a better position at work. It seems that the market economy and its competition-related workings created more opportunities for men in the new era than for women. These new societal attributes therefore appear to be more in keeping with the male concept of a good life.

One of the main dimensions of the recent changes in the Czech Republic is the growth of individualism. Individualism is – by its inner logic – connected with the free market. And the progressive free market needs people to think of money and material wealth as important life values. However – and ironically – the more individuals are indoctrinated by the culture of materialism, the less they are satisfied with their lives. These findings from existing consumer research are not new, but were recently replicated in an investigation with a sample of Czech students. The results confirmed that the more materialist the students become, the less they are satisfied with their lives. This relation was quite strong, even when the possible effects of self-esteem, neuroticism and extraversion were eliminated.

It seems that one of the reasons why materialism creates such undesirable consequences is that materialists usually shift the life values which are beneficial for healthy personal growth – especially autonomy and love/interpersonal relationships – to lower and less significant positions in their value hierarchies. Moreover, their value choices are often conflicting. **Is autonomy really compatible with a deep commitment to love and friendship?** Is it possible, for example, to spend sufficient time with a loved one and at the same time build up a successful professional career?

How does this work in everyday life? In a study with Czech university students, it was found that the most frequent pair of conflicting values are 'love' and 'self-determination' (i.e. the right to freely pursue one's own goals). A significant number (35%) of respondents placed these two values in the first two positions of their value hierarchy. In comparison with the other students, this 35% were significantly less satisfied with their lives, and had experienced positive emotions, such as pleasure, happiness, and excitement, less often during the two weeks before the study. Additionally, their lifestyle was less healthy. They smoke more cigarettes per day, and drink alcohol more often. The health-risk behaviour of these respondents can be related to the psychic tension and imbalances which they experience as a result of an ongoing conflict between their value choices.

It seems that to achieve general happiness and mental tranquillity it is essential to be satisfied with your given life conditions, without placing undue emphasis on their material aspects. The setting of life priorities and preferences that are not contradictory, but complementary and mutually reinforcing, is an important condition for preserving mental equilibrium and personal integrity.

## The keys

→ **The more materialist we are, the less we are satisfied with our lives.**

→ **Values such as autonomy and love/personal relationships need to be placed high in the value hierarchy for healthy personal growth.**

→ **Set life priorities and preferences that are not contradictory, in order to find good mental equilibrium (e.g. between love and self-determination).**

Helena Hnilicova (Faculty of Medicine) participates in research projects on health and quality of life, and patient satisfaction. The research interests of Karel Hnilica (Faculty of Arts) include values, stereotypes, prejudice, discrimination and quality of life. They are assistant professors and colleagues at the Charles University in Prague (Czech Republic) and have a special interest in the effect of the country's revolution on how people feel.

# *City lights*

For the first time in human history, the world's population is now mostly urban. More than three billion people are living in towns and cities, and their number is increasing day by day. But will this help them in their search for happiness? Are people happier in urban or rural areas? It is certainly true that towns and cities offer an abundance of opportunities. But do they offer us a happier life? Working, living and driving in a busy Italian city like Milan, Professor **Giampaolo Nuvolati** tries to find the key to successful urban living.

## Abundant opportunities but…

One specific thing that I have learned from my empirical research and theoretical studies on the quality of life in the cities is that it is not only related to the quantity of the collective resources and services available in an urban area, but also to the opportunities and abilities of people to use such resources.

This approach entails a shift from 'commodities' to 'functions' and 'capabilities', means a move from simple 'having' to the more important 'being' or 'doing'. Let me give you an example. We 'have' a car, but we 'are' very slow in travelling around cities because of the traffic. We 'have' many theatres in our cities but only few of us 'are' habitual spectators. We would like to attend theatres but we have no time, or the tickets are very expensive, or the theatres are not easily accessible in temporal or spatial terms. The result is that the transformation of abundant urban resources into real quality of life becomes more and more complicated, especially in the large cities where many different urban populations (residents, commuters, city users, tourists) are concentrated. The result is that modern metropolitan life is nowadays strongly polarised, with some groups of residents and non-residents able to access numerous services, while many others are marginalised. In small and medium sized towns there are probably fewer resources but these resources are more easily accessible and directly usable, thereby improving the living conditions of the inhabitants. On the other hand, if the level of initial resources and services is too limited, even if they are readily available, the quality of life will most likely be negative.

To summarise, quality of life is the result of the easy accessibility for each individual citizen of the full set of urban resources and services available in a city, allowing use of those services and resources in a manner that can be concretely transformed into better personal conditions. This transformation is not only based on the improvement of personal wealth or the multiplication of public infrastructures, but also requires personal competence, social capital, education and information. Public policies which aim to increase sustainable mobility and accessibility to the available set of resources and services are also welcome. The relationship between objective quality of life and subjective happiness still needs to be investigated more fully, but we can reasonably assume that several relationships exist.

A specific piece of advice that I would offer to people all over the world, in order to improve their happiness, relates to their ability to 'play' with the so-called 'dis-embedding' and 're-embedding' continuities. This means – if possible – that they should travel, have international relationships, and use new technology for communications, whilst at the same time continuing to reinforce local networks, personal or community identities and direct contacts. Do not avoid post-modern complexities but try to deal with them, both in your every day life as well in long terms projects. On the one hand, this means that it is necessary to exploit all available opportunities. On the other, it also means that you must have respect for personal, familiar and local values. Sometimes it can be a hard balance to find.

## The keys

→ **Quality of life is the result of the easy accessibility and usability for each individual of the available set of urban resources and services.**

→ **Public policy should focus on education, information, mobility and accessibility.**

→ **Do not avoid post-modern complexities but try to deal with them: reinforce local networks while building up international relationships.**

Professor Giampaolo Nuvolati teaches Urban Sociology at the University of Milan-Bicocca (Italy). He is an international expert in studies on urban indicators for the quality of life. In his book 'Lo sguardo vagabondo' he analyses the old and the new 'flâneurs': 'urban animals trained at the difficult school of metropolitan existence'.

*'The 21st century will be the most religious century ever.'*

# Love of life

It's true. People who say that they 'believe' also claim to be happier. Religion offers social contacts, support by others, consolation, a goal in life and connection with something outside yourself. All things that can make you happier. Professor **Ahmed M. Adbel-Khalek** summarises more than twenty of his books in two crucial terms: Religion and Love of Life.

## The motivating force

My research in Arab countries, ranging from Egypt to Kuwait, focused on two specific aspects: studies on the new concept of love of life and the relationship between happiness and religiosity (or spirituality). The results show a positive correlation between these two concepts.

Love of life is defined as a generally positive attitude towards one's own life. It denotes a pleasurable attachment to and an appreciation for life. Love of life and the search for happiness are of paramount importance to human beings. They are positively correlated. Researchers have also shown conclusively that happiness can be taught. In the same vein, every person is able to learn how to love life, as long as he or she does not violate the social laws and complies with religious teachings. All of us have to learn how to enjoy life, depending on the resources available to us, while at the same time striving to achieve the best for ourselves and others. In this respect, the term 'enjoyment' incorporates both materialistic needs as well as moral obligations and religious principles.

Religion has been one of the major forces throughout history. However, there is also reason to believe that modern-day religion is returning to this previous high status. Some recent authors have indicated that the 21st century will be 'the most religious century' ever. For example, 95% of adults in the United States express a belief in God. A series of Gallup Polls indicated that 86% said that religion is important or very important to them. It has also been established that people in the Middle East are more religious than in any other part of the world. Perhaps this is not surprising. It was in this region that the three most important divine revelations – Judaism, Christianity and Islam – all originated. These three religions share a belief in one God as the main common element. A large body of research all over the world, including our own modest project, indicates that religious affiliation and commitment are beneficial to a sense of personal well-being, happiness, self-esteem and overall adjustment. Several studies have documented a positive association between religiosity (excluding extremists) and happiness, including physical and mental health.

To recapitulate, human beings are advised to learn how to love life without violating legal or moral rules, which also means complying with religious or spiritual principles. This religiosity is associated with better health, more happiness and greater satisfaction with life. Furthermore, religious beliefs are a strong motivating force in the search for – and attainment of – happiness.

## The keys

→ **Learn to love, enjoy and appreciate life, while striving to achieve the best for yourself and others.**

→ **Religious affiliation and commitment are beneficial to a sense of personal well-being, happiness, self-esteem and overall adjustment.**

→ **Religious beliefs (excluding extremism) are a strong motivating force and lead to better physical and mental health.**

Ahmed M. Abdel-Khalek is an Egyptian citizen, working at Kuwait University as Professor of Psychology. He has published 21 books in Arabic, eight psychological tests and 295 research papers in Arabic or English. His research interest is focused on personality structure and assessment, cross-cultural comparisons, death attitudes, childhood depression and sleep disorders. In the last decade he became interested in optimism, hope, happiness, love of life and religiosity.

# *Yin and Yang*

'One-fifth of the world's population lives in China. This means that any theory which claims to be universally applicable must include relevant data from China. With particular reference to the question of general applicability of happiness theories based on research findings generated from Western contexts, studies in different Chinese contexts are indispensable,' reports Professor **Daniel T.L. Shek** from Hong Kong.

## A more holistic approach

The conceptions and cultural manifestations of happiness in Chinese culture are different from those in Western culture. With a history of more than 5,000 years, traditional Chinese cultural values, closely related to Confucian, Buddhist and Taoist thought, constitute the fundamental building blocks of these Chinese conceptions and manifestations of happiness. For example, while positive feelings and open expression are important components of happiness in American culture, Chinese people emphasise contending feelings and a reserved expression of happiness. As such, it is important to conduct more studies on Chinese culture, in order to better understand cross-cultural differences in the conceptions of happiness and its manifestation. Obviously, Chinese philosophies, cultural values and traditional beliefs on happiness provide food for thought for happiness

researchers in the West. The happiness of the Chinese people is commonly studied at the individual level. With the growing popularity of ecological models asserting that human behaviour is embedded in different ecological systems (e.g., the family system or the macro socio-cultural system), it is obvious that a more holistic understanding of the concept of happiness and its related phenomena with reference to these different systems is called for. While there are some studies supporting the applicability of Western theories of happiness to the Chinese people, there are still many issues unresolved.

It is important to examine how the happiness of Chinese people, families, communities and cities has been transformed in the recent decades, following the establishment of a socialist political system in 1949, the changes wrought by the Cultural Revolution in the mid-1960s, and the adoption of an open-door policy and economic reforms since the late 1970s. With the intensification of economic reforms, the Chinese people have become more susceptible to the influences of economic change. Although economic reforms have brought a higher level of quality of living (which may promote happiness), **individual, family and social problems have also increased as a result of these economic reforms** (which may hinder happiness). Furthermore, issues of unemployment and economic disadvantage, which are theoretically non-existent in socialist systems, have become more prevalent in contemporary China.

The wisdom contained in Chinese philosophies and religions may have relevance to non-Chinese people who wish to 'promote' their own happiness. However, they must first undergo a 'paradigm shift' in their conception of what happiness means. In Confucian thought, while happiness is not necessarily regarded as bad, the expression of intense

*'Confucian, Buddhist and Taoist ideas provide food for thought.'*

emotional feeling is not encouraged under the 'doctrine of the mean'. Furthermore, self-cultivation is a precursor of happiness in Confucianism. In Buddhist thought, the notions of 'letting go' and a contending mentality are important precursors of real happiness in life. In fact, happiness in the hedonistic sense is regarded as an illusion that might actually block one's realisation of true happiness. In Taoist thought, the focus of happiness is on harmony with self, nature and the universe. Such emphases are in line with the existential and humanistic thoughts that one should have inner peace and a good relationship with the environment. Finally, the balance between 'yin' and 'yang' is upheld in traditional Chinese medicine an ideal form of human existence. Through the use of Chinese herbal medicines, meditation and the practice of Chinese marital arts, such as 'tai chi', one can attain a state of inner harmony which eventually promotes a sense of happiness in the self.

## The keys

→   **While positive feelings and open expression are important components of happiness in American culture, Chinese people emphasize contending feelings and reserved expressions of happiness.**

→   **We need a 'paradigm shift' in the accepted conception of happiness to make the wisdom contained in Chinese philosophies and religions relevant to non-Chinese people.**

→   **Through the balance between 'yin' and 'yang' one can attain a state of inner harmony which eventually promotes the sense of happiness in the self.**

Professor Daniel T. L. Shek (The Hong Kong Polytechnic University, China) is consulting editor of the 'Journal of Clinical Psychology' and a member of the editorial board of 'Research on Social Work Practice'. He has published more than 100 articles in international journals on adolescents, holistic health, social welfare and quality of life research in Chinese, Western and global contexts.

# *Hamba Kahle!*

'Actually, I found it a pretty daunting task, summarising my insights for *The World Book of Happiness*. If you had asked me for a "scientific" article, it would have been much less trouble,' reports Professor **D.J.W Strümpfer** from South Africa. For the last 20 years, he has been involved with Antonovsky's sense of coherence, resilience, and Keyes' psychosocial health continuum. 'I tried to convey some thoughts from all this in a practical way, without letting the theory come through.' Professor Strümpfer is 80 and offers us a lifetime's advice, accompanied by the Zulu greeting 'Hamba kahle' (meaning 'go well!').

## Flourishing

Life is brimming with health, beauty, joy, loving relationships and so much more. These are the fountains of our strength. When we lean into them, emphasise, explore and exploit them, we begin to *flourish* joyously.

Some of our strengths are in our genes, influencing our mental and emotional functioning. Some grow out of experience and personal learning, some out of education. Numerous strengths flow from our relationships, from our communities, and from the places where we live. The times we live in also determine numerous specific and general strengths. But like physical strength, one also has to work at developing psychological strengths. Developing some strengths demands arduous work, but so much also comes through actively going in search of joyous experiences.

How do we succeed? Allow yourself to *feel*. Smile! Laugh! **But also cry when you feel like crying – it will bring relief.** Keep your eyes and ears open to the beauty around you. Seek out beauty. One can gain great happiness from *listening* to birds singing and *watching* their flight, from intently *seeing* trees, plants and flowers, flowing water, clouds, sunrise and sunset. Listen to nature: water, rain, wind, thunder – but also to nature's silences. Attend carefully to what you touch, taste and smell – and *experience* those joys. Listen to music. Sing, whether you can or not.

Appreciate who you are and what you are. Believe in your own abilities. (Remember the little choo-choo train from the children's song: 'I think I can, I think I can…!') Do your best to remain optimistic and to find satisfaction and meaning in whatever you have to do, including your daily tasks. Guard your health: eat, drink and exercise sensibly. Search for insight: through discussion, listening, reading – but then think as well! What does it all mean to *you*?

Anticipate and open yourself up to support from your family, friends, strangers, your doctor, a police officer, the company, the union, your religious community – everyone around you. Anticipate spiritual support, too. However, this support will not always come without asking: seek it actively when you need it and continue asking until you receive it. Provide support to others too, wherever and however you can – strangely, it will strengthen yourself in turn.

Undeniably, life is also brimming with *negatives*: acute and chronic disease, disability, sorrow, death, disaster, bleak family, social, economic, and political conditions – an uninterrupted flow of demands, from bearable to devastating. Sometimes we languish there. However, we are *resilient* beings: we are able to 'bounce back' – returning to where we were before – but also to 'bounce forward' – going beyond where we were at first. The very overcoming of inordinate demands is often a source of growth and of new strength for future hardships. Our strengths help us to bear up, to overcome, and eventually to *flourish* again.

## The keys

→ **Allow yourself to feel, to listen, to taste, to see, to smell and to experience the joys of life.**

→ **Appreciate who you are and what you are, believe in your own abilities and search for insight.**

→ **Anticipate and open yourself up to support from everyone around you, seek it actively and provide support to others, too.**

D.J.W. Strümpfer is Professor Emeritus of Psychology at the University of Cape Town, South Africa. He is respected worldwide for his methodological studies on subjective well-being, thriving/flourishing and the quest for meaning. He even added a new word to the lexicon of psychology: fortigenesis. It refers to a process of developing strengths.

*'There is an important distinction between feeling happy and being happy.'*

# Behind the smiley

**:-)** (smile)

**:-D** (laughter)

**(^_^)** (Japanese smiley)

Texts on mobile phones and computers don't show our body language or intonation. That's why we use emoticons. The smiley ☺ is a world success. The sign expresses a feeling of joy and happiness. It's as easy as that: a circle, two dots and a bow. Its colour? Yellow. This colour does indeed seem to be connected worldwide with a joyful feeling. Nevertheless, we have been looking for the real meaning of happiness for thousands of years. Professor **Doh C. Shin** makes a survey and discovers three key elements, hiding always and everywhere behind the smiley.

## The three universal components of happiness

The first use of the term 'happy' refers to a feeling, which is usually of short duration. When Homer and Herodotus equated happiness with physical pleasure, and more recent philosophers thought of it as an affective state of mind, they were referring to short-term moods of gaiety and elation, which is fundamentally different from the core meaning of satisfaction. Such happy feelings are often termed euphoria: the presence of pleasure and the absence of pain. Viewed from this perspective, happiness is a hedonistic concept.

A second use is one in which a person is 'happy with' or 'happy about' something, and these expressions mean 'being satisfied with' or 'contented with' the state of ones well being, and do not imply that one has any particular feeling. Referring to happiness in this way refers to more than simple emotional pleasantry. The word is used exclusively to describe the welfare aspect of a life experience.

Thirdly, the term 'happy' is often used to characterize the quality of a human life as a whole, rather than making a statement about a particular aspect of it, as in the case with the second usage. In this sense, when a person says that he is happy, he means living a happy life; one in which the seeking of all of his objectives form a harmonious and satisfying whole. When he makes such a holistic judgment in the context of the concept of happiness, he takes into account various aspects of his condition and circumstances, as well as how he feels about them. In this case, a person's sense of happiness represents the highest assessment of his whole life.

Unlike the first two segmented views of happiness, this third conception encompasses the whole scope of human needs, desires, interests, tastes and demands, and seeks to determine whether they constitute a harmonious whole. Unlike pleasure, therefore, happiness is neither episodic nor subject to momentary moods. Feelings of pleasure and pain can occur both in the context of a happy life and in the context of an unhappy life. This distinction between *feeling* happy and *being* happy should always be considered in systematic accounts of happiness.

**If happiness refers to an overall quality of life, the essential question still remains: of what does happiness consist?** Philosophers and social scientists have examined a variety of life experiences in search for the constituents of happiness. In particular, they focus on three well-known explanations of the 'happy life'. The first of these is called the Epicurean ideals. These ideals hold that happiness consists in having (as opposed to doing) certain things that give one passive pleasure. For example, one might get pleasure from the enjoyment of beautiful paintings and good company. For an Epicurean individual, happiness is a matter of enjoying life by having enough of these pleasure-producing things.

The second ideal for a happy life is to be found in the writings of the utilitarian philosophers, who argued that happiness is derived from the satisfaction of desires.

In such a view, happiness is essentially contentedness – an equilibrium between needs on the one hand and satisfaction on the other. The prompt satisfaction of needs produces happiness, while the persistence of unfulfilled needs causes unhappiness. A utilitarian person's happy life would be one in which as many of his needs and desires as possible are met.

A third account of the happy life sees happiness neither in terms of passive pleasure, nor in the possession of property or the satisfaction of needs. This view, expressed in Aristotle's concept of *eudaimonia,* equates happiness with creative activity. Happiness derives from the fulfilment of one's capacities, from doing what one enjoys. In this view, happiness is a sense of *achievement* brought about by man's inner productiveness, and it is the accompaniment of all productive human activity.

Having considered all three of these philosophical accounts of happiness, I suggest that the three positive life experiences of *enjoyment, satisfaction,* and *achievement* constitute the three main components of happiness. I would also suggest that the particular combinations of these three components – which together shape a person's overall judgment of happiness – vary across culturally different societies. How do they vary exactly? This is an important question for the next generation of positive psychology researchers.

## The keys

→ **There are three main components of happiness. The first component is enjoyment: possessing certain things that give one (passive) pleasure.**

→ **The second component is contentedness: the equilibrium between needs and satisfaction.**

→ **Third component is achievement. Happiness derives from the fulfilment of one's capacities, by doing what one enjoys. The combinations of these three elements vary across cultures.**

Doh Chull Shin is chair professor of political science at the University of Missouri in Columbia (USA). He is the founder of the Korea Barometer and co-founder of the Asian Barometer (a systematic survey of attitudes and values). For the past two decades, he has conducted comparative research on democratization and quality of life. His latest publications include 'The Quality of Life in Confucian Asia'.

# *The right to sadness*

**Are we ready for some fun?**

**You and me and everyone**

**This is the happy, happy, happy song.**

**We gonna sing it all night long.**

**This is the happy, happy, happy song.**

**So let's smile.**

**This is the happiest song**

**in the world…**

These are the lyrics of the so-called 'happiest song in the world' on the Internet. But 'The Journal of Happiness Studies' has published a report on 230,000 songs composed since 1960. The result: songs have become sadder and sadder. Life is not a party and a day-long smile might hurt your cheeks. Even reading books on happiness might make you feel sad. Social scientist **Grant Duncan** examines whether we have a right to – or even a duty for – happiness. Are we allowed to feel sad?

## Happiness: no right and no duty

I suggest we drop the political idea that there may be a *right* to happiness. My research has mainly been about the political uses of happiness, and about the idea that governments may have an obligation to maximise the happiness of the people. My conclusions about that idea have been sceptical, but, like other people, I am still interested in how we can improve our own happiness and well-being as individuals. Certainly governments bear a responsibility to provide some goods and services – such as public education and protection of human rights – that are vital to our well-being. But, being subjective, happiness is the concern of each of us individually, and of those close to us. This also means that we can relieve ourselves of any idea that there may be some social obligation to be happy. Sometimes I wonder if people feel an expectation that they *ought* to be happy, and that there is something wrong with them, in other people's eyes, if they are not happy. Well, happiness is desirable, but not compulsory.

Melancholy and sadness are normal and healthy emotions. Sure, deep and prolonged sadness that appears to be unrelated to any life-event may be a sign of genuine depression and may require help. But **let's accept the creative and healthy side of ordinary sadness,** and even some forms of hardship. Our greatest achievements in life, especially when they involve creativity or care for others, often mean sacrificing some of the things that may have made us feel good in the meantime. We can accept a level of sadness and suffering in life as necessary or sometimes even worthwhile.

To return to happiness, simply to stop doing the things that make us miserable would be a good start. Sometimes it's as simple as getting more sleep. That alone can boost a person's happiness. But sometimes we need to ask ourselves some tougher questions, such as: Am I drinking too much? Am I desperately seeking love and approval? Do I bully others to get my own way? Set some goals to change such behaviours. Another thing to stop doing, if you want to be happy, is comparing yourself with others. Sure, it's natural to want to fit in to a social group. Belonging is an important aspect of well-being. And we benefit from positive role-models who set an example for us. But envy and resentment are corrosive feelings that really damage personal happiness. Take stock of yourself and appreciate the goods things that you have and the things you have achieved. **Celebrate other people's successes, and give yourself some credit for your own.**

Finally, I suggest that we put aside thinking about our own happiness for a while. Reach out and help someone else. Genuine fulfilment in life comes with contributing to other people's well-being and being with them through difficult times, so that we can enjoy the rewards of belonging and support.

## The keys

- → **Relieve yourself of the social obligation to be happy and don't think of it as a right.**
- → **Accept a level of sadness and suffering in life as being necessary or sometimes even worthwhile.**
- → **Stop doing things that make you miserable and put aside thinking about your own happiness for a while.**

Dr. Grant Duncan is a writer, social scientist and university teacher at the Massey University in Auckland (New Zealand). He is the author of many academic publications on social policy ('Society and Politics') and has a special interest in the political issues of happiness ('Should happiness-maximisation be the goal of government?'). He is a poet too. His favourite book? Marcel Proust's 'In Search of Lost Time'.

*'Learn to enjoy*
*a cup of coffee for its own sake.'*

# *Life is our major work of art*

The happy artist's life is all about making art, exchanging art and making himself and others happy with art. Professor **Mariano Rojas** invites us to go further and to become the designer, illustrator, painter, photographer, sculptor and architect of our own life. He has an inspiring masterpiece in mind. Welcome to the gallery happiness and the atelier of well-being.

## Time to create your own work of art

Aesthetic judgments are not solely confined to the realm of objects. It is also possible to appreciate our own life and judge it as something with which we are satisfied or dissatisfied. Of course, we all want a life we can be satisfied with, but this requires us to take good care of ourselves and also to have the wisdom to create a really good work of art.

My happiness research has focused on studying how life satisfaction can be achieved through satisfaction in specific areas in which we all perform as human beings. 'Performing as a human being' usually involves relating with your children, spouse, relatives, friends, colleagues and neighbours, as well as having jobs, purchasing and consuming goods, practicing sports and hobbies, being a member of a community, getting involved in personal activities and interests, and so on. These areas of human activity are called domains of life. I have found that our satisfaction or dissatisfaction in these domains of life do much to explain our general level of satisfaction with life as a whole. I have also found that some domains are more important than others in generating life satisfaction, depending on your own specific situation.

The writer T.S. Eliot (Nobel prizewinner for literature in 1948) invites us to reflect on life as follows: '*Where is the wisdom we have lost in knowledge? Where is the knowledge we have lost in information?*' My academic research, as might be expected, is based on large databases which contain huge amounts of information, which is processed in order to arrive at results which may be considered as 'knowledge'. However, I would also like to point out what I believe to be a few spots of 'wisdom', which have been useful in creating my own work of art.

My research has reminded me that we human beings are much more than mere consumers. This is something that may surprise many economists who, like me, are used to seeing everything in terms of consumption (as their microeconomic textbooks tell them). I have learned that good time management is important. Time is our most valuable resource and we should take special care of managing it in such a way as to increase our satisfaction in those domains that are most relevant to our life satisfaction. Having satisfactory personal relations also requires the allocation of sufficient time to promote them. In addition, we need to allocate time to pursue our own hobbies and interests. For this reason, I have learned that it is important sometimes to say no to extra work and to turn down job offers which would make me more money but allow me to spend less time in other domains of life: for example, to take a midweek break to take my daughters to the playground or to spend more time with my wife. I have learned that my economic satisfaction can be enhanced not only by spending more money but also by devoting more time and attention to the enjoyment of what I already have. I have learned that it is important to enjoy a cup of coffee with a friend just for its own sake, and not as a means to gain some personal advantage or to promote my business network. I have learned to stay in a job where I have good colleagues and a sense of achievement, rather than moving on to a better-paid or more stressful position, which will not gratify me as much.

I see my life as my own work of art and I am trying to allocate my time and my other resources in such a way that my life satisfaction is enhanced. The idea of domains of life has been very helpful in this respect. It is not really a matter of being constantly concerned about how to allocate our personal resources, but more a question of not forgetting to apply some basic wisdom. For example, it is good to bear in mind that we are much more than

mere consumers, and that interpersonal relations matter a great deal. Moreover, we can add some value to our work of art by undertaking actions that contribute to the life satisfaction of others.

I think that I could still use some extra paint brushes here and there, to enhance my work of art still further; there is still space on the canvas where I can increase my life satisfaction. Hopefully, my work of art will one day be as good as my grandma's: she is ninety-eight years old, and hers is a masterpiece.

## The keys

→ **Turn information into knowledge, and knowledge into wisdom.**

→ **Time is our most valuable resource: manage it wisely to increase satisfaction in the domains of life that are most relevant for your life satisfaction.**

→ **Live your life as if it were a major work of art.**

Mariano Rojas is professor at the Facultad Latinoamericana de Ciencias Sociales and at Universidad Popular Autónoma del Estado de Puebla (Mexico). His research during the last decade has revolved around the topic of happiness. His studies deal with the relationship between life satisfaction, income and consumption; the concepts of quality of life and progress; and with well-being deprivation.

*'Bi-cultural individuals are not troubled and anxious outsiders.'*

# *The conflict of living abroad*

Around 175 million people currently live outside the country of their birth, which is about three per cent of world population. The number of migrants has doubled in the last 30 years. Some move because they have to, others because they want to. Most of them are in search of more happiness. But do they find it? Professor **Félix Neto** conducted research among emigrants and immigrants in Portugal and also among groups of victims and offenders in various armed conflicts, from Angola and Guinea-Bissau to Mozambique and East Timor. His results might open our eyes.

# The impact of immigration and serious conflicts

Immigration is changing the cultural and ethnic composition of many countries. In response to rapidly changing demographics, psychologists are focusing their efforts to better understand the impact of culture and acculturation on mental health. One basic question about bi-cultural individuals is whether they are confused outsiders or special individuals with a broader understanding. Until recently, the dominant western view of the multi-ethnic person was of a troubled and anxious outsider, who lacked a clear identity. However, recent research has indicated that multi-ethnic individuals are at no psychological disadvantage in comparison to mono-ethnic individuals. Research conducted among Portuguese emigrants, returned Portuguese emigrants, and immigrants in Portugal revealed that their life satisfaction did not differ from people who had never migrated. These findings appear in line with the view that the majority of migrants adapt well to their new societies, despite difficulties in meeting the demands of cultural changes and of living in two cultures.

What about people involved in serious regional conflicts? Our research focused on one particular aspect – one potential virtue – of these conflicts: forgiveness. Research on forgiveness has led to its inclusion in the list of psychological strengths or virtues that are the domain of the positive psychology movement. Forgiving others who have harmed you is essential for the maintenance of your own physical and psychological well-being. Much of the interest in psychology has focused on interpersonal forgiveness as one way in which individuals, married couples and families try to cope with the hurt and resentment arising from a relational conflict or injury. Much less research has been devoted to intergroup forgiveness. Is intergroup forgiveness a meaningful concept for the victims of violent conflicts? In other words, can a group of victims forgive a group of their violent assailants? We examined the views of people from Angola, Guinea-Bissau, Mozambique and East Timor, who were recently involved in civil wars or wars of occupation, and who, for the most part, had suffered personally as a result. At first, we feared that nobody would be willing to take part in our intergroup forgiveness study, owning to the very painful nature of the experiences, not even if questions were formulated in an impersonal way (i.e., about the meaningfulness of the concept, rather than a personal willingness to forgive). However, and surprisingly enough, we observed the opposite reaction in most cases; the participants were interested in the study and were willing to take time to answer the numerous questions contained in our survey. The simple fact that victims of terrible group violence were not only willing but also interested in taking part in a survey on intergroup forgiveness opens up substantial room for future dialogue between researchers and victimised groups. In fact, a large majority of the participants in our survey agreed that forgiveness as a group process is conceivable. On the one hand, these results may seem surprising, even incredible, in view of the pain and suffering endured by most of the participants. On the other hand, they could be considered as expressing very realistic views, which offer a way forward in the future. Even more remarkable, the participants also appear to have articulated a concept which could be used to define the process of intergroup forgiveness. In this respect, forgiveness certainly deserves its place on the list of positive group attitudes.

## The keys

→ **The majority of migrants adapt well to their new societies.**
→ **Groups of people who have suffered in serious conflicts are nevertheless interested in intergroup forgiveness.**
→ **Forgiveness can certainly be added to the list of positive group attitudes.**

Félix Neto is Professor of Psychology at the University of Porto (Portugal). His research interests include the relationship between culture and well-being. He has published 15 books and more than 200 papers on social psychology and cross-cultural psychology.

# *The meaning of life*

'True happiness is a by-product of finding meaning and purpose in your life,' says Professor Emeritus **Gary T. Reker**. He loves working creatively with words and is fond of claiming this pun: 'You can always take the Me out of Meaning, but you'll never take the Meaning out of Me.' You want to hear more?

## 14 fundamental guidelines

Meaning and purpose are derived from several sources, such as engagement in productive and meaningful activities, doing a good deed, loving a significant other, or producing a creative product. Happiness cannot be pursued for its own sake. It cannot be bought, sold, or traded. Happiness must ensue; it must follow from commitment and engagement in life-affirming actions. The question often arises as to which comes first. Does happiness give meaning to life or does meaning in life lead to happiness? My research consistently shows that finding meaning and purpose in life leads to happiness, not the other way around. This brings us to a critical question: if happiness is a state of mind to which all of us can aspire, how do we get it? What is it about happy people that makes them happy?

Happyologists Professor Michael Fordyce from Florida and Professor Jonathan Freedman of Canada have studied happy people from all walks of life. They found that happy people have many things in common. My research has shown that these same common characteristics are also found in people who have found meaning and purpose in their lives. Dr. Fordyce has summarized these common characteristics in 14 fundamental traits, which most individuals can develop for themselves. The theory behind these fundamentals is simple. If you can be more like happy people, you will be a happier person. Moreover, all of these characteristics of happy people offer guidelines for positive, healthy living.

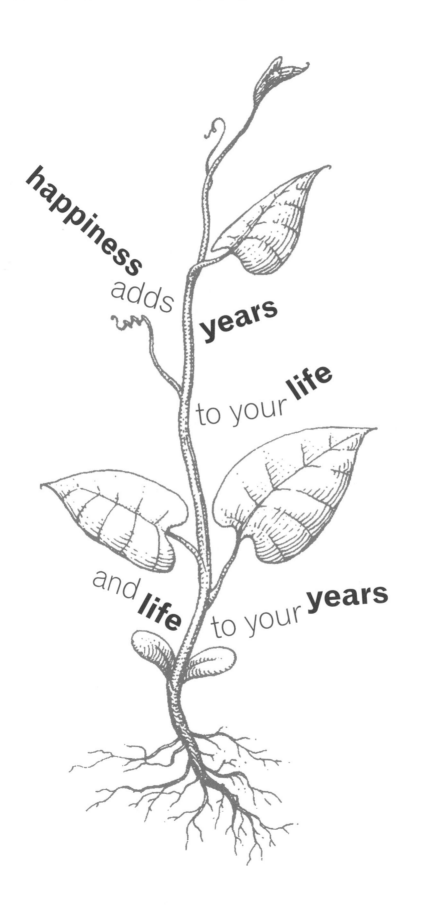

happiness adds **years** to your **life** and **life** to your **years**

→ **Be more active and keep busy.** Happy people, at any age, get more out of life because they put more into it. They get involved. 'Use it or lose it' is their motto.

→ **Spend more time socialising.** Happy people are very social. One of the most important sources of happiness is other people. Research shows that the happiest people are those who work with others. They tend to be members of clubs, groups and organisations.

→ **Be productive at meaningful work.** Happy people place greater priority on 'job significance' than they do on 'job prestige' or 'job income'. They do what they enjoy, and enjoy what they do.

→ **Get better organised.** Happy people plan and organise. They have goals and a purpose. You *get* what you want or desire, if you *know* what you want or desire.

→ **Stop worrying.** Happy people don't worry because worry is a form of unpleasant thinking. They recognise that 90% of worries never come true.

→ **Lower your expectations and aspirations.** Research shows that happy people have modest levels of expectation and aspirations. Happy people know how to avoid disappointments and how to generate pleasant surprises. They strive for realistic goals. Happy people want what they can get. Unhappy people never seem to get what they want.

→ **Develop positive, optimistic thinking.** Happy people think positively. They look forward to desirable goals and are confident that these will be reached. They look at the bright side, no matter how bad the situation.

→ **Get present-oriented.** Happy people live for today. They don't dwell on the past; they don't dream about an idealised future. Happy people have a positive mind set. If you can't be happy now, what makes you think tomorrow will be any different?

→ **Work on a healthy personality.** Happy people are models of mental health. They like themselves, accept themselves, know themselves and help themselves.

→ **Develop an outgoing, social personality.** Happy people are extremely outgoing and friendly. They smile a lot and have a good sense of humour. Older happy people have wrinkles around their eyes.

→ **Be yourself.** Happy people are spontaneous, natural, and real. They say what they think and feel, and are not concerned about what others think of them. Being oneself makes one feel free and authentic.

→ **Eliminate the negative.** Happy people get things off their chest. They don't bottle-up emotions and feelings, since these create psychological distress and physical discomfort. Their motto is: 'Get rid of it, or it will get rid of you'.

→ **Close relationships are number one.** Research shows that nothing has a greater impact on happiness than a close, loving relationship, a close friendship, or close family ties.

→ **Value happiness.** Happy people value happiness. They fully understand that happiness adds years to your life and life to your years.

## The keys

→ **Happiness must ensue. It must follow from commitment
and engagement in life-affirming actions.**

→ **Finding meaning and purpose in life leads to happiness,
not the other way around.**

→ **If you want to be a happier person, try to be more like a happy person.
There are 14 positive guidelines that work.**

Gary T. Reker is a retired life-span developmental psychologist who lives in Canada.
As a university professor emeritus, his teaching and research interests focus on successful
aging processes, such as meaning and purpose in life, optimism, death attitudes, and life
review. He has published numerous articles, book chapters, and a book on these topics.

# The buffer mechanisms

*'People possess a remarkable level of hardiness that helps them mediate the influence of instability.'*

Living and working in Beirut, Dr. **Huda Ayyash-Abdo** has discovered the positive personality mechanisms of people in a tumultuous country like Lebanon: 'Internal traits are more important than external conditions,' she says. And she should know: she is teaching the first course in positive psychology in Lebanon, perhaps in the entire Arab region.

## How to switch negative impact

Subjective well-being (or life satisfaction) has become an area of research to an increasing number of psychologists and social scientists in the last two decades. Our research in this domain in a developing country such as Lebanon has taught us that people do not need ideal conditions to be happy. Liveable and acceptable conditions are sufficient for them to experience satisfaction with life. Socio-economic status also seems to play a salient role in levels of subjective well-being. That said, personality traits seem to correlate significantly with levels of subjective well-being. Among these traits are adaptability, sociability, resilience, self-esteem, optimism, adherence to values, regulation of realistic expectations, and tolerance. Indeed, our research indicates that these internal traits are more important than external conditions.

Lebanon has compromising external conditions, the most significant of which is its chronic political instability that sometimes results in violence. Our research points out that people possess a remarkable level of hardiness that helps them mediate the influence of instability. People use a variety of mechanisms to help them ameliorate the negative impact of political violence and uncertainty. These mechanisms include habituation, denial, sublimation, social connectedness, and engagement in constructive activities that help them to create a different and more positive reality than that of the negative existing one – namely, that of political violence.

The aforementioned personality traits are internal mitigating factors between the individual and the environment. There are also external elements that serve as important buffers between the individual and potentially adverse conditions. One such mediating factor is the presence of family cohesion and stable social support. Another external factor is having a goal and working towards it. This gives a person a sense of purpose and accomplishment.

What do we learn? The presence of negative emotions is not to be avoided or repressed. Indeed, negative affect is natural in certain circumstances. For example, the loss of a loved one merits grief and mourning for a certain period of time. However, the ratio of positive affect to negative affect (i.e., for a person to experience more positive affect than negative affect overall) is a more significant determinant of subjective well-being. In addition, the perception of an event, how it is interpreted, and the importance it is given is equally important in life satisfaction. Not only does a person need to filter through what occurrences trigger negative emotions, but actively engage in activities that elicit positive affect.

## The keys

→ **Internal traits are more important than external conditions: from adaptability and self-esteem to tolerance and adherence to values.**

→ **People use a variety of mechanisms to help them to ameliorate the negative impact of violence and uncertainty: from habituation and denial to social connectedness and engagement in constructive activities.**

→ **The presence of negative emotions is not to be avoided or repressed but we have to engage actively in activities that finally elicit positive affect.**

Huda Ayyash-Abdo is an associate professor of psychology and the chairperson of the Department of Social Sciences in the School of Arts and Sciences at the Lebanese American University in Beirut (Lebanon). Her research interests include developmental counselling, youth development, and the application of appropriate counselling approaches to Lebanon and other Arab countries. She lived and taught in the United States for 16 years before returning to Lebanon.

*'Happiness and schooling do not overlap for many people.'*

# *The happy school*

Are there any inspiring examples of positive education at school? 'Yes,' says Martin Seligman, founder of positive psychology. 'Geelong Grammar School in Australia is the pioneer in the world in taking steps to introduce this type of learning through all aspects of an educational curriculum. In doing so, I believe that the students who go through this programme will be less likely to suffer from depression – which is increasing in epidemic proportions in many western countries, including Australia – and will lead more positive and fulfilling lives.' Dr **Mathew White** is head of this 'happy' school.

## The power of positive education

Happiness and education do not always seem to sit easily in discussion. Education for many people evokes strong emotional reactions about conformity, competition and over-testing. For many of us, it is possible that primary and secondary education are the sources of anxious memories. Happiness and schooling do not overlap for many people.

Education is about the future. It is about equipping children with the capacity to develop a love of learning, but it is also about helping children to develop greater levels of resilience, so that as they encounter life's challenges they will be able to re-engage in its pursuits. Positive education is a proactive, whole school approach to teaching and learning. It deploys both implicit and explicit teaching in curriculum, co-curriculum and pastoral settings to

create an enabling institution. Positive education is an approach that employs the science of positive psychology to encourage students and teachers to experience more positive emotion, develop greater skills for resilience and seek greater meaning.

Geelong Grammar School is Australia's largest co-educational day and boarding school. It is an institution with a significant 150 year history that emphasises service, learning and resilience. Unique to our school is Timbertop Campus, founded in 1953, which takes students outside of their normal daily educational experience to have a year in an outward bound setting, to build deeper levels of resilience and efficacy amongst its students. Since launching the positive programme in 2007 the school has asked the question: should positive psychology be taught in schools? This question raises a number of opportunities that challenge the traditional function of schools. Based on the science of positive psychology the school has developed a theoretical framework and strategy that embraces whole school teaching and learning. It supports good teaching practice, and unifies the language used by faculty to develop a better understanding of what makes life worthwhile. The leading world figures in positive psychology from the University of Pennsylvania have trained over 160 teachers at our school, as well as 270 teachers from other schools.

Central to the positive educational framework is the desire to engage our students in a consideration of the three pillars of positive psychology principals: the good life, the meaningful life and the engaged life. From this structure, our school has been delivering two specifically crafted programmes. These courses have been co-authored and developed by Martin Seligman, Karen Reivich and Jane Gillham from the Positive Psychology Centre at the University of Pennsylvania. They teach students a set of life skills that, combined with seven case topics being explored throughout the school, establish the theoretical structure for discussion about happiness and other emotions in the context of education.

In its implicit teaching approach to positive education the school has focused on the following seven topics taken from the empirical literature on positive psychology: emotion, gratitude, strengths, creativity, self-efficacy, resilience and mindfulness. From these seven topics a set of core-principals and practices are emerging that are starting to be defined as 'Positive Education'. They are helping to stimulate debate and reflection on teaching practice to develop a distinct pro-active approach to mental health issues in youth.

We are now committed to further developing positive education on the sports field, in the orchestra, in the classroom and in our boarding houses. A strengths-based approach, founded on the science of positive psychology, provides the significant rigour that builds on good teaching, learning and pastoral care. It challenges the traditional stereotype that a boarding education is one of cold dormitories, gruel and routine, transforming it to one that seeks to broaden and build our students educational experiences, as we prepare them for life's next step.

## The keys

→ **Education should not focus on anxiety, conformity, competition and testing. It is about the future.**

→ **Students should consider the three pillars of positive psychology: the good life, the meaningful life and the engaged life.**

→ **Focus on these seven topics: emotion, gratitude, strengths, creativity, self-efficacy, resilience and mindfulness.**

Dr Mathew White is Head of Positive Education (HOPE) at Geelong Grammar School, Australia, a pioneer in positive education. He is a fellow in the Melbourne Graduate School of Education at the University of Melbourne. He updates a professional website for leaders in education: 'Why teach positive education in schools?'

# Bhutan's Gross National Happiness

The central importance of happiness in our individual lives stands in strong contrast to the absence of happiness as a consideration in the public sphere. When we talk about the objectives of a nation, we talk about Gross National Product (GNP) and economic growth. There is one country, however, that has chosen to give central stage to happiness: Bhutan. **Johannes Hirata** explores the Gross National Happiness (GNH) of this Himalayan kingdom.

## A government for happiness

Since 2008, Bhutan has been a constitutional monarchy, the size of Switzerland and populated by something less than one million people. It was already in the 1980s that the third King of Bhutan said that 'Gross National Happiness is more important than Gross National Product'. This does not express the view that economic growth is a bad thing. It does, however, make clear that the Bhutanese do not believe in the free market gospel that maximising economic growth will automatically bring comprehensive well-being for all. Instead, while they recognise that economic development is an important building block for a better future, they are keenly aware that economic growth is not an objective in itself, but rather a by-product of good socio-economic development. Pursuing policies that have

# 'It is better to be approximately right than to be precisely wrong.'

intrinsic merit – spreading literacy, developing infrastructure, creating adequate jobs for the increasing numbers of college graduates, and so on – will no doubt also result in steady economic growth. But since this will just be a by-product, this is nothing to write home about.

Of course, the rate of economic growth will certainly be lower than it would have been if economic growth was given top priority, but this is not a 'sacrifice' for the sake of some esoteric objective, rather a conscious choice for comprehensive prosperity – you might as well say 'happiness' – over a misguided obsession with aggregate consumption. For example, Bhutan has resisted the temptation to quickly enrich itself by cutting down and selling its forests, and as a consequence was spared the soil erosion and landslides that neighbouring regions have been suffering on a massive scale.

Some observers are worried about the fact that the government takes an interest in people's happiness. They are afraid of a government that interferes in people's private lives in the name of promoting anything, even happiness. Fortunately, this is not what Gross National Happiness (GNH) is about. Just as governments pursuing Gross National Product (GNP) do not prescribe to their citizens how they may or may not earn their money or how many hours they must work, a GNH policy within a stable democracy of free citizens has nothing to do with state interference. Rather, as in any democratic society (however imperfect in practice), decisions in Bhutan are not imposed by an expert elite but are the result of public debate and a political decision-making process enshrined in the country's constitution. The crucial difference is that policy proposals all over the world can only survive public debate if they can be justified in terms of contributing to economic growth, while in Bhutan they must be justifiable in terms of furthering the well-being of the citizens. Can there be any question that this latter course simply makes more sense?

In defence of GNP, people may say that happiness is an elusive concept and therefore is unsuitable as a policy objective. After all, there are established ways to measure GNP, but you cannot measure happiness – or can you? Well, in fact measuring happiness is possible, and psychologists have long since demonstrated that such measures can be trusted to a very reasonable degree, producing a wealth of eye-opening insights into the relationship between happiness and all kinds of factors. However, it must be granted that even a perfect measure of happiness won't release us from the duty to make contentious judgment calls, especially where questions of justice are concerned. Even so, I definitely prefer an imprecise but relevant concept over a precise but irrelevant one. Otherwise, we would be like the drunk who lost his keys in the dark and looks for them under the streetlight, not because he believes he will find them there but because the light is better. Or, as John Maynard Keynes once put it: 'It is better to be approximately right than to be precisely wrong.'

## The keys

→ **Maximising economic growth will not automatically bring comprehensive well-being for all.**

→ **Economic growth is not an objective in itself, but rather a by-product of good socio-economic development, including happiness.**

→ **A Gross National Happiness policy within a stable democracy of free citizens has nothing to do with state interference.**

Johannes Hirata studied in the Netherlands, France, Switzerland and Brazil. He has been a visiting researcher at the Centre for Bhutan Studies in Bhutan to deepen his understanding of Gross National Happiness and obtained his doctoral degree in economics with a thesis on 'Happiness, ethics and economics'. He is now Professor of Economics at the Fachhochschule in Osnabrück (Germany).

*'It is one thing to achieve happiness;*
*it is another thing to maintain it.'*

# Life begins at 40, 50, 60 and 70

Ask young and old about happiness. The young expect to be less happy when they are old. The old remember being happier when they were young. Both groups expect the average young person to grow less happy with time. But what's the reality? Real life begins at 40, 50, 60 and 70 – says Professor **Margie E. Lachman**.

## Older adults are happier than younger ones

As a lifespan developmental psychologist, I am interested in how happiness changes during the adult years. It is one thing to achieve happiness; it is another thing to maintain it throughout adulthood. One might assume that in the face of aging-related losses of health, memory and loved ones, happiness would decline. In fact, research shows that older adults, on average, are happier than those who are younger. This is sometimes called the paradox of aging. With age and experience comes the wisdom of knowing that, regardless of one's situation, it is possible to be satisfied. This perspective involves the recognition that happiness fluctuates and we are responsible for our own happiness.

At any age period, people differ widely, but the average patterns are telling. On the one hand, older adults are more satisfied with life than younger adults and they are better at predicting their future satisfaction. Yet older adults are less likely to think that things will get better in the future. Older adults expect that things will likely stay the same or possibly deteriorate. Their focus is on maintaining their situation and they recognise that the present may be as good as it gets. Those in midlife and beyond enjoy the fruits of their

labours and try to preserve what they have, with the awareness that things can always get worse. In contrast, young adults expect that things will continue to get better. This view may motivate them to keep working hard, looking for love, trying new things, exploring, discovering, and creating.

People differ in what makes them happy. It may be interactions with friends and family, work, helping others, exercise, food, travel, and so on. These sources may change with age, and there are many pathways to happiness. A key to maintaining happiness involves realising that happiness is transient: there will be some good times and some not so good. It is not realistic to assume that we can be happy all the time, and a likely recipe for continued despair is feeling bad about not being happy. A good strategy for getting back to happiness is to refocus and emphasise the positive. You are in charge of making your own happiness – to a large extent.

In our research in the United States, we have found that a person's sense of control over life's outcomes is closely tied to achieving and maintaining happiness. Many things in life are uncertain and we are never sure how much we can make a difference. Yet those who have a predisposition to believe in their own influence over outcomes in life are significantly happier. Such beliefs are adaptive because they lead to action and efforts to bring about desired results, a 'can do' attitude. At the same time, it is important to recognise that there will be unexpected circumstances that we cannot control. When what is desired is not possible, those who believe in themselves will find alternative solutions and develop other goals as a key to remaining happy. In contrast, those who feel helpless in unfavourable circumstances assume that what they do does not make a difference, and they are less likely to be happy. The reality is that we can only control some of the things some of the time, and happiness depends on recognising both our potential and our limits in creating our life stories.

## The keys

→ **Older adults are happier than younger ones: this is the wisdom of being satisfied.**

→ **People who have a predisposition to believe in their own influence over outcomes in life are happier.**

→ **We can only control some of the things some of the time. Recognise both your potential and your limits.**

Margie E. Lachman is Professor of Psychology at Brandeis University in Waltham, MA, (USA). She has edited two books on development in midlife and is a co-investigator on the national longitudinal study, Midlife in the United States (MIDUS). Her research is on identifying modifiable factors that promote cognitive, psychological and physical health.

*'Spend your time,*
*money and energy on*
*whatever interests you.'*

# The H-market system

There is a market for happiness – and not only by selling books on happiness (an increasing business!). Most publicity for consumption products appeals (consciously or unconsciously) to our quest for happiness. The H-market is booming – as every marketer knows. **Alexandra Ganglmair-Wooliscroft** examines consumer lifestyles. Which pair of gloves will she buy?

## One glove does not fit all

Writing about how to be happy is a daunting task and marketers like myself do not have the best reputation when it comes to studying this idea, often being perceived as trying to 'sell happiness'. Even so, acting and reacting within a market system – spending time, energy and money – is part of most people's lives.

In New Zealand, as in many other countries, the demographic characteristics that describe happier people are clearly visible: having a minimum level of income, (higher) education, a (full-time) job and living in a stable relationship – with New Zealanders considering marriage even more satisfying than simply living together.

Consumer lifestyle studies examine activities, interests and opinions of groups of people in a society and explore how people choose to, or have to, spend their time, money and energy. Lifestyle studies therefore offer further explanation as to what contributes to people's happiness. And what do we see? There are highly educated, well-off people who gain enjoyment from visiting glitzy malls, going to restaurants with friends and spending money on nice things, while another group of equally highly educated, well-off consumers prefers to attend cultural events, give dinner-parties at home and eat organic food. One glove does not fit all and very similar levels of happiness are associated with very different activities.

When it comes to broad consumption choices, activities undertaken with others appear to contribute to increased happiness. Some people prefer to go shopping with friends, others give dinner parties at home, play an active role in their local community, or attend cultural events. Any form of physical activity, matched to the lifestyle of the consumer group, and reasonably healthy consumption choices when it comes to food, also seem to contribute to people's perceived quality of life. The conclusion? To improve the likelihood of being happy it will help to get an education, get married, spend time with other people, exercise well and spend your time, money and energy on whatever interests you.

## The keys

→ **Acting and reacting within a market system (spending time, energy and money) is part of our lives.**

→ **Very similar levels of happiness are associated with very different activities: one glove does not fit all.**

→ **For your broad consumption choices, opt for activities with others, things that improve your health and whatever else interests you.**

Alexandra Ganglmair-Wooliscroft gained her Master at the Wirtschaftuniversität in Vienna and her PhD at the University of Otago, Dunedin, New Zealand where she is now a Senior Lecturer. She researches consumer behaviour, in particular positive consumption emotions and perceived quality of life. Outside university she can be found cycling, running or swimming. She has completed some marathons and Ironman New Zealand.

# *Do migrants win or lose?*

One of the core lessons many people draw from happiness studies is that it is typically a mistake to put great emphasis on the pursuit of money, at least when one has already achieved a reasonably secure standard of living. An intriguing question then arises about international migration: given that migrants' motivations are often related to money, is migration for this reason likely to constitute a similar mistake? Specialist **David Bartram**, a migrant himself, might know the answer.

## Exaggerating the benefits, downplaying the risks

I'm inclined to suspect that economic migration often leads to disappointment: attempting to raise one's standard of living via migration to a wealthy country might not generally lead to greater happiness, and perhaps more is typically lost than gained. Matters would likely be different if we were talking about the world's very poorest people – the idea of a minimum threshold is a significant qualification to the idea that more money normally doesn't bring more happiness. But most people who migrate are not among the very poorest: the poorest don't have the resources for it.

In the eyes of people who don't live in the world's wealthiest countries, those countries no doubt look very attractive. The language sometimes used to describe them is powerful and evocative, and the images on television are even more compelling. And since all wealthy countries restrict possibilities for entry, perhaps they even have a 'forbidden fruit' quality that enhances their attractiveness. But if we generally don't find increased happiness among those who pursue money in their own countries, why would we expect to find increased happiness among those who literally seek their fortunes elsewhere?

After all, wealthier countries are not only wealthier – they are different in other respects as well. Some have a culture of long working hours, an impoverished sense of community, a high incidence of mental illness, etc. In other words, wealth often comes at a price, and migrants are likely to have to pay it, possibly at a premium rate. The benefits of the extra money, though real in some respects, might be dubious in others, especially for migrants: a greater absolute amount often comes with a decline in relative position, as when a migrant who was middle-class in the origin country finds his or her prospects are restricted to the lower reaches of the job market in the country of destination. Sometimes a migrant's only goal is to support the family back home, but even for the sake of their happiness it is seldom the case that remittances are sufficient compensation for their loved one's absence.

Daniel Gilbert's wonderful book *'Stumbling on Happiness'* describes our deeply ingrained tendency to exaggerate benefits and downplay risks when contemplating a course of action. I see no reason to think that decisions on migration are exempt from that tendency.

I do not intend to offer support for those already in wealthy countries who want stricter controls on immigration. For one thing, there is virtually no empirical research on international migration and its resultant consequences for happiness, and my deductive thoughts outlined above might well be wrong. Not all migration is economic in motivation, and even economic migration can bring non-material benefits. Freedom does contribute

*'I suspect I am happy despite migration rather than because of it.'*

to happiness, and so merely having the opportunity to move to a wealthy or safe country might be important for some. In any event, controlling migration effectively requires that a government take some very harsh actions, not just against would-be migrants (arrest, deportation, etc.) but sometimes against its own people as well. But when one's motivation for migration arises mainly from a *desire for more*, then I think there are reasons to worry that migration won't actually satisfy that desire in ways that lead to greater happiness.

As a migrant myself, I risk being charged with hypocrisy in expressing misgivings about migration as a path to happiness. To a limited extent, my thoughts are informed by personal experience: I have lived in four different countries and now find myself much farther from family than I would like, especially now that I have children. Migration has helped to make my life interesting and sometimes exciting. But happy? I suspect I am happy despite migration rather than because of it.

## The keys

→ **Wealth often comes at a price, and migrants are likely to have to pay it, possibly at a premium rate.**

→ **A greater absolute amount of income often comes with a decline in relative social position.**

→ **When the motivation for migration arises mainly from a *desire for more*, migration might not actually satisfy that desire in ways that lead to greater happiness.**

David Bartram is a sociologist at the University of Leicester (United Kingdom). He is originally from the US but is now living in Britain. His research has investigated government policies on labour migration. Publications include the book 'International Labor Migration: Foreign Workers and Public Policy' and articles in journals such as 'International Migration Review'. His main topic is international migration, with recent work focused on understanding the relationship between migration and happiness.

*'Materialism conditions our options and limits our choices.'*

# Always the wrong choice

You are offered two jobs. The first one is interesting. The second one is boring, but pays 20% more. Which one do you choose? You have double-booked an activity. You have to cancel one of them. The first one will give you more pleasure but the second one has cost you double. Which one do you choose? Research shows that in both cases most people opt for the second choice. Many similar decisions affect our future happiness but we insist in making the same old mistakes, time after time. Professor **Leon R. Garduno** offers six hints for the choice that will make you happier.

## Six hints for a better choice

→ Through the media, we are exposed to a constant bombardment encouraging consumption. As a result, our decisions are never truly free from their influence. Materialism conditions our options, limits our choices – and so our happiness becomes dependent on consumption. Research to date on the relationship between income and happiness teaches us that (in addition to the contradictions between competing theories) money does not seem to be the most important factor to explain happiness. There are many other alternative possibilities. In other words, do not place too much importance on money. There are more important things in life. Identify the things that are important to you.

→ To begin with, do not consider what money can buy you for your personal gain, but think of the effect it may have if you use the money for the benefit of others. Several studies have found that people who spend part of their money on pro-social activities are happier than those who use it solely for themselves. If you have money, try to do something for those who have less. This will give you great satisfaction. However, be careful that you are not simply feeding your ego. Do it with all your heart, and really try to help.

→ Look at life as a pie divided into several different slices. Each slice represents one area or domain of importance in your life: family, friends, job, inner life (emotions, desires, adaptation to change, etc.). Consider the relative importance of each slice and try to be consistent with it in terms of the quality and / or amount of time you spend.

→ Assume that nothing is permanent and that everything changes. Do not cling to things unnecessarily. Live for the present and look forward to the future with optimism. You can always make things better. No matter how bad they are now, they will not stay that way: eventually there will be an improvement.

→ Be confident. Work on your self-esteem and on your perception of your ability to achieve the things that are really important to your happiness. Join a group (sports, religious, community support, etc.) where you feel that you can build strong common interests.

→ Consider what the great thinkers, philosophers and mystics have said about happiness: we can find much of value in their ideas. Many seem to agree that happiness is not something that comes from outside of us but from within. True happiness is to be found in the little things of life, like enjoying every moment and in seeing the positive side of everything that happen to us.

## The keys

→ **Do not think solely about what money can buy for you.**
→ **Consider the relative importance of each domain of your life and remember that nothing is permanent.**
→ **Be confident about what you want to do. Happiness does not come from outside of us but from within.**

Professor Leon R. Garduno is director of the Centre for the Study of Quality of Life and Social Development at the Universidad de las Américas, Puebla (Mexico). His main interests are evaluation of social programmes, education and quality of life. His new research deals with the impact of his programme 'Opportunities' on the happiness of a sample of low socio-economic level school students.

*'Happiness is learning to be'*

# Children show the way

Some people say the only time they were happy was before they knew what happiness was: their childhood. But there is no way back. Or is there? What are the main characteristics of children's happiness? The question is not 'what can we teach them', says **Teresa Freire**, but 'what can we learn from them'.

## Building the bridges

Three main contexts of scientific knowledge are crucial if we wish to speak about happiness today: Psychology, Research and Teaching. Although these three domains are related, each one has been relevant for learning, by virtue of their different approaches to what happiness is. What is the most important thing that I have learnt? That to be open to knowledge, novelty, difference, involvement and to others is one of the most important sources of happiness.

I cannot separate this perspective about happiness from my own work with young people. Children, adolescents and youths have been my main laboratory, where I have tried to develop an understanding of happiness and its role during those formative years when life is being built and learnt. Young people make us aware of the naive wisdom necessary to deal with life, when the search for well-being is a main goal. With them we understand how growth and developmental processes are present in the search for happiness, and how happiness is a building process. Young people are always seeking novelty, new challenges and new opportunities to feel, to think or to be motivated to act. And they want to do this in relation to others. With children we understand why others are so important, if we want to make social and affective bridges with the world.

Happiness is being able to choose, to decide and to be with others – and for others. Is to be aware of ourselves because we know others, live with others, and can compare

ourselves to them. We need others to know about ourselves. Happiness is about learning to be, is about learning to relate and being involved. Above all – especially for young people – it is to become more complex and more aware of our own limits, to see just how socially determined we really are. It is to grow. It is to improve, to enhance the self and our relationships. It is to find our place in life. It is to see our own growth through others' growth and development. It is to need others and to share with others. It is to be connected and committed, by bridging with other people and other contexts.

A main question always re-emerges: is happiness a state of being or a process for achieving that state of being? As a state, it is subjective; as a process it can have different directions in terms of how individuals interact with the world and with their internal and external life contexts. If we analyze this through the lens of development and human complexity, we can understand how happiness is built both in terms of individual and social processes. From a developmental point of view, to be socially committed or individually committed are simply two faces of the same coin. Ask a child: why are you happy? Ask an adolescent: why are you happy? And finally ask an adult... Happiness is an unfinished state, if development is a process still in progress. To promote development is to facilitate happiness. So what exactly is this happiness? Happiness is bridging affects, emotions, cognitions, actions, values, strengths, behaviours, people, societies... But bridges don't build themselves – they need to be built.

## The keys

→ **From children we can learn that to be open to knowledge, novelty, difference, involvement and to others is one of the most important sources of happiness.**

→ **To promote development and growth is to facilitate happiness.**

→ **Happiness is bridging affects, emotions, cognitions, actions, values, strengths, behaviours, people, societies... But all bridges need to be built.**

---

Teresa Freire is Professor of Social Psychology at the University of Minho (Portugal). She is the coordinator of the Laboratory of Social Cognition and coordinator of the Research Group for the Study of Optimal Functioning. She often works with children and adolescents. Teresa Freire belongs to the European Network for Positive Psychology (ENPP), being both a member of the Management Board Committee and the national representative for Portugal.

*'The important things
have nothing to do
with success.'*

# *Not who – but how*

'The mainstream literature on happiness is concerned with the "who" question. It asks whether the rich are happier than the poor, if the married, the young, the extraverted or those with clear life goals are happy. Although informative when building scientific theories, knowing that Danes are happier than the French, or that splitting up from a marriage can be tough, has not been directly relevant to my personal search for happiness,' reports **Joar Vitterso** (Norway). 'I therefore welcome a recent development in the field, propelled by a growing number of researchers, who now insist on asking the "how" question of happiness.'

## Become an expert in your own life

As an academic wheeling around in the space of happiness research for a solid quarter of a century, hardly a day passes without at least some contemplation of what it means to lead a happy life. Again and again I grill myself about the ingredients of happiness, repeatedly pondering my options for making the choices which hopefully lead to the best possible life. Sometimes, I must admit, I also ask if the literature on happiness has helped me to get a better life at all. Since I don't believe in short-cuts to this better life, parts of the 'how' literature also appear superficial to me – too 'American', if you will.

However, there are treasures in the 'how' literature and the example I have chosen to present is more than 70 years old. It was written by Joanna Field, the pen name of Marion Milner. Although her life appeared quite successful from the outside, Field realised that it was not as it ought to be. To learn more about who she was and what she wanted from life, Field decided to keep a diary. The writing turned out to be a tedious task. Starting in 1926, Field carefully recorded moments of her daily life to identify barriers to her happiness, and with admirable candour she spent seven challenging years critically analysing her thoughts and feelings. But the efforts paid off, and Field was rather surprised when she finally discovered that the best things in her life had previously been hidden from her. Unexpectedly, the important things in Field's life had nothing to do with success, neither in friendships, work nor play. What made her happy were mostly very small moments of a total change, change in the way she perceived both the outer world and herself. Interestingly, as her insights sank in and her perception of the world and herself changed, the causes of her happiness changed as well. And as Joanna gradually became an expert in her own life, different things began to make her happy.

Joanna Field's most important insight came after she read a book by the Swiss psychologist, Jean Piaget. Piaget described how children seem unable to discriminate between real objects, like tables and chairs. The same is also true of their thoughts and ideas. Consequently – and this is important – **children's feelings tend to go to the extremes.** When a mother leaves her son, he mistakenly believes it is forever, and the misery of loneliness is all that exists for the poor child. Similarly, when Joanna Field was caught by one of her many spontaneous mind-wanderings or feelings of awkwardness, she observed that, like the little child, she was unable to limit its range and imagined consequences. Field referred to these processes as her 'blind thoughts' and their effects were later to become well known in the literature on depression. Unaware of Field's work, Aron Beck identified these processes as 'automatic thoughts'. Learning to know herself – and the work of the psychotherapist Pierre Janet – better, Field discovered that her blind thoughts were a kind of 'chatter'. They were uneasy states of worry, imposing impossible standards to her life. When she realised that her childish chatter came between herself and her surroundings, and when she was eventually able to cope with them, Field was ready for an important step forward: 'When I could break through it, and only then, was I able to see clearly enough to choose those circumstances under which happiness could grow; to learn for instance, to limit my activities, not to run after every new thing, not to expend all my energies on the effort to keep up with what other people did, just because they did it, so that I had no vitality left for those needs that were personal to me.'

The improvements in Field's life came as a result of comprehension. With her new understanding, Joanna Field was able to develop her own rules for living and to fully realise that happiness came when she was most widely aware of her surroundings. Her story confirms not only that it takes a lot of effort to change, it also testifies to the wisdom of the famous inscription on the ancient temple of Apollo at Delphi: 'Know Thyself'.

## The keys

→ **It is hard to become an expert in your own life but when you succeed, different things make you happy.**

→ **Break through the chatter of your blind thoughts, so that you can see clearly enough to choose those circumstances under which your happiness can grow.**

→ **Happiness comes when you are most widely aware of your surroundings.**

Joar Vittersø holds a Ph.D. in social psychology from the University of Oslo and is a professor of psychology at the University of Tromsø (Norway). His research interests focus on life satisfaction, positive emotions and the measurement of happiness. He is a board member of the International Positive Psychology Association and has written extensively about happiness and subjective well-being. His most recent publication: 'Was Hercules Happy?'

# *Shades of green*

Ireland is in the world top 20 of happy countries. People with Irish ancestors around the world wear green on St. Patrick's Day. In fact, the country is said to have forty different shades of green. No wonder Dr. **Finbarr Brereton** reports on the influence of green – which in his case means the environment.

For me, as an environmental economist by training, the most interesting finding in recent happiness research is the critical importance of the environment to human well-being. This not only means the essential ecological functions that the environment provides to maintain human life as we know it on our planet, but also the local environment where people live and work on a day-to-day basis. **What struck me most about the results was the lack of emphasis individuals placed on the environment, largely due to it being a 'free' commodity.** Because environmental goods, such as clean air and beautiful landscapes, which are critical to sustainable development and quality of life, are not traded on open markets like common consumer goods (cars and televisions being the most obvious examples), they tend to be undervalued by individuals and not given the importance that reflects their true value. There was a recent example of this in Ireland, when the country was in the grip of the coldest winter for the last 30 years. In an attempt to prevent pipes from freezing, individuals left their taps running constantly, which resulted in water shortages across the country. Whether or not this course of action prevented pipes from freezing is immaterial: the key point is that because this essential resource was 'free', people saw no reason to preserve it. My message to people would be to go out and take note of the environment around you, conserve it, engage with it – not only because we need it, but also because it really will make you happy.

> Dr. Finbarr Brereton is a research fellow at the UCD Urban Institute
> in Dublin (Ireland) with a special interest in environmental economics
> and the influence of the environment on subjective well-being.

# *Intro or Extra?*

Are you extra or intro? 'Research shows that extraverted people
tend to be happier than introverted persons,' states **Marek Blatny**.
'Nevertheless, I myself am introverted – but I am not unhappy.'
Marek is searching for a deeper answer to this seeming paradox
in his research on life-span development.

## The influence of my temperament

Since the 1980s we have discovered that well-being or happiness depends on external factors
and circumstances to a much smaller extent than had been expected. What is much more
important for subjective well-being are fulfilled expectations, good interpersonal relations,
purpose in life, and a sense of one's value. Well-being is influenced mainly by temperament
characteristics, personal traits connected with our experiencing of the world around us.
Current psychology identifies two personality traits with this kind of biological, tempera-
mental basis: extraversion/introversion and emotional stability/lability. Research has
repeatedly shown that people who are extraverted and emotionally stable tend to be
happier in their lives than introverted and emotionally unstable persons.

During the 1990s, I was involved in research into relationships between personality traits
and well-being, and their detailed analysis. I kept being confronted with the fact that some
people tended to be sad, while others tended to experience things joyfully. However, other
research at this time also yielded the positive finding that people differ in the *degree* of their
happiness rather than by being either happy or unhappy. Few people reported that they
were really unhappy. I think of myself as an introverted person who is inclined towards
melancholy (despite the fact that company can cheer me up). I cannot, however, say that
I am unhappy or dissatisfied. It is only that I do not experience such ecstasy of happiness
as my friends of a 'happier' nature.

I have thus satisfied my desire for knowledge in research and perhaps even done my share
for the science of personality and well-being. But since psychology is not only a science but
also a helping profession, I started to ask myself what I, as a psychologist, could offer people –
how I could help others to experience happiness and to reach a state of satisfaction.

I found the answer in humanistic psychology, which helped me not only in my professional but also personal life. Humanistic psychology was among the first fields within psychology to deal with positive aspects of human life in a systematic way. The works of Carl Rogers or Abraham Maslow have influenced a number of current researchers concerned with well-being and happiness. Humanistic psychology is also among the principal inspirations for positive psychology, a recent trend in psychology which emerged at the turn of the millennium. Humanistic psychologists believe that people are born good and only unfavourable external conditions can lead to situations where one's development is not optimal and fails to match one's potential. The tendency to grow, develop and adapt actively is believed to be the key motivational force in humans – a concept known as self-actualisation. Humanistic psychologists believe that each person has a certain potential – talent, ability, skill – which they can develop and fulfil. The key conditions for healthy personal development are a sense of security and loving nurture – an awareness of being accepted for what I am, with all my good and bad qualities. Rogers uses the term 'unconditional positive acceptance'. This regard and respect of others towards us is gradually adopted and internalised, thereby helping us to develop a self-concept and self-esteem.

This is what I learned in my practice as a psychologist and in my personal life. The first step towards happiness is self-acceptance – the fact that we must love ourselves for what we are, whatever our strengths and weaknesses are. Only by letting go of worries about who we are, will we be able to develop our potential. Only then can we grow, commit to a goal, work for others – and be happy.

## The keys

- → **External factors are less important than internal ones (fulfilled expectations, good interpersonal relations, purpose in life, and a sense of ones value).**
- → **Extraverted and stable persons are often happier than introverted and unstable ones. But people differ in their degree of happiness.**
- → **Our key force is self-actualisation – and the first step is self-acceptance.**

Marek Blatny is director of the Institute of Psychology of the Academy of Sciences of the Czech Republic and a Professor of Social Psychology at Masaryk University in Brno (Czech Republic). His project on life-span development is based on research with people who have been monitored since 1961. Another long-running project is a prospective longitudinal study of the quality of life of children surviving cancer.

*'Create your own currency
that no one else can buy.'*

# The Takayoshi Currency

'Using Japanese data, I have examined whether economic growth is positively associated with people's life satisfaction. The answer is no,' reports Professor **Takayoshi Kusago**. 'After I started these studies, I have noticed clear differences in my personal behaviour and value system.' Now he presents his own Takayoshi Currency. It can only be bought by himself.

## Your personal value system

I was once a rationalist who cared mostly about the effectiveness of my work and paid great attention to productivity as a key measure for my life. I evaluated my well-being in a similar manner to the Gross Domestic Product-driven assessments of well-being enhancement. Economic prosperity was the most important base for me and my family, and non-economic aspects were secondary. My subsequent cross-disciplinary study of psychology, sociology, philosophy and economics has since convinced me of the shallowness of these 'old' thoughts. Economic prosperity does not promise to increase social trust, social ties and dialogue for the expansion of these values, which are essential to strengthen people's life satisfaction and happiness.

I am now fully convinced of the importance of building and developing good social relationships with my own family, friends and neighbours, partly because of my interaction with Bhutanese colleagues and their Gross National Happiness project. Now I am happy to join meetings with local communities and four years ago I started monthly family meetings, where everyone has an equal voice to discuss issues through dialogue.

In addition, I have also created a special currency called Takayoshi Currency (TC). This currency cannot be bought by anyone expect myself. It is accumulated if I am able to use time to increase my own happiness. For instance, when I meet a good friend and enjoy the conversation, TC increases, say, by 1,000. When I spend a day helping the elderly as a volunteer, the currency goes up by 20,000. You get the idea. I do not have to remember the exact amount or the degree of increase. However, this way of measuring certainly helps me to set priorities and to think about how I can better use my time for my own life satisfaction and that of others. My ultimate goal is to increase my own currency 'reserves' through the life I live, a life based on a holistic approach of well-being, a decent economic base, health, knowledge, hope, dreams, community, culture, politics and the environment.

In addition, I have learnt to pay closer attention to the 'process' as well as to the outcome of public policies. The 'process' requires public commitment to a particular issue – usually people in need. However, this, process must be reflected by the people in question. I now look into people's well-being, by pushing myself to learn how people relate to their livelihoods in their own social and economic contexts. Subjective questions are now the core inquiries of my field work on people's well-being. And changes of well-being and empowerment processes have become my key research work. Better late than never.

## The keys

→ **Economic prosperity does not promise to increase social trust, social ties and dialogue for the expansion of these important values.**

→ **Respect your own value system and create your own measures to promote it, like the Takayoshi Currency.**

→ **In public policy, pay more attention to the 'processes' of those who are most closely involved and affected.**

Takayoshi Kusago, Ph.D. is Professor of Social System Design, Faculty of Sociology at the Kansai University in Japan. He has been working as a researcher and practitioner for the past two decades. For the last several years he has devoted himself to subjective well-being studies. He is currently working on alternative development indicators suitable for developed country contexts by modifying human development indicators with subjective data.

# Beyond good and bad

'When we meet people and are asked *"how are you?"*
or *"how are you doing?"* we would seldom dare to give a negative
answer. Numerous surveys worldwide show that the vast majority
of respondents report above-medium levels of happiness, including
people in disadvantageous conditions, such as those who are old,
poor, disabled or have endured misfortunes in their past.'
Where do we find the strength to be happy?
Professor **Dov Shmotkin** develops an integrated theory
on the pursuit of happiness in the face of adversity.

## Our secret agent in a hostile world

The inclination to be (basically) happy can often appear contradictory, not only to a
variety of pessimistic philosophical traditions, but also to an empirical body of evidence
which shows that 'bad is stronger than good'. This evidence indicates that undesirable,
harmful or unpleasant outcomes have a greater psychological impact than desirable,
beneficial or pleasant ones. Thus, while people can usually adjust to most adverse
conditions, certain negative events (e.g., disability, unemployment) may lower happiness
permanently. Psychological trauma, which often represents ineradicable loss or suffering,

may perpetuate its harsh impact by depleting resources and instigating further cycles of loss. The predominant power of 'the bad' over 'the good' is reasonably explained by the critical implications that negative experiences may bear for a person's protection and survival.

But how can most people be happy if the bad in their life is stronger than the good? Indeed, this discrepancy between the two bodies of evidence cannot easily be dismissed. It genuinely reflects two conflicting principles of positivity and negativity in human life. The conceptual model that I propose may introduce a more integrative formulation about the role of happiness. In my model, subjective well-being (the more academic term for happiness) is not treated merely as a desired outcome, but rather as a dynamic system whose role is to constitute a *favourable psychological environment*, which allows us to function normally and competently with minimal disruptions. Complementary to subjective well-being in this model is a system termed the *hostile-world scenario*, referring to an image of actual or potential threats to a person's life or, more broadly, to a person's physical and mental integrity. The hostile-world scenario is nourished by beliefs about catastrophes and afflictions, such as accidents, violence, natural disasters, wars, illness, aging, and death. This image of adversity scans for any potentially negative conditions or for an even worse condition, when a negative one already prevails. When activated adaptively, the hostile-world scenario helps people to stay vigilant to threats in their struggle to remain safe and well. However, an extreme hostile-world scenario generates a sense of living precariously in a disastrous world.

Subjective well-being and the hostile-world scenario regulate each other by various mechanisms, in order to fulfil their respective tasks of promoting pleasure and accomplishment, while ensuring safety and protection. A detailed description of these mechanisms is beyond the present scope of this text. Generally, a state of subjective well-being can counteract, or dismantle, the negative repercussions of a highly activated hostile-world scenario. But this is not an adaptive move in all conditions: if we face a real danger, we need to cope with it, rather than staying in elusive well-being. In fact, in certain conditions it is even warranted to co-activate both subjective well-being and the hostile-world scenario: for example, when novel situations may stimulate our subjective well-being, while the hostile-world scenario simultaneously ensures our alertness to potential dangers. These and other mechanisms illustrate how subjective well-being constantly negotiates with the hostile world, so that life is not overridden by the nightmarish imminence of catastrophe, nor is it driven to the naivety of a fool's paradise.

The quest for happiness is still a source of considerable perplexity. Happiness has many different faces (what we really experience, what we tell to others, what we remember), which may be contradictory at times. Is happiness a realistic outcome within tangible reach of most people, or is it an elusive and treacherous experience which ultimately leads those who seek it into greater unhappiness? Protagonists for both ideas can readily be found.. My approach is that happiness is essentially more dialectical than commonly assumed – because it functions as our secret agent in a hostile world.

## The keys

- → **Happiness is a dynamic system whose role is to constitute a *favourable psychological environment*, which allows us to function normally and competently with minimal disruptions.**
- → **The hostile-world scenario helps people to stay vigilant to threats in their struggle to remain safe and well.**
- → **A state of subjective well-being can counteract, or dismantle, the negative repercussions of a highly activated hostile-world scenario.**

The work of Professor Dov Shmotkin expands studies on subjective well-being across the life span, as well as on long-term traumatic effects amongst Holocaust survivors. Shmotkin is affiliated to the Department of Psychology and the Herczeg Institute on Aging at Tel Aviv University (Israel). He is a member of research teams that have conducted national surveys of Israel's older population.

*'No man is an island.'*

# *The culture of happy relationships*

'No man is an island. Across the world, relationships are important for people's well-being. Emotional sharing, intimacy and communication, with friends, family and colleagues promote social support, regulate stress, and increase happiness, well-being, and health. But such relational practices differ from culture to culture and the influence of relationships on people's well-being is not the same across all cultural contexts.'
Dr. **Konstantinos Kafetsios** discovers the differences.

## Two different cultures

In order to keep social order, culture regulates the norms of people's behaviour. This applies as much to relationships as to anything else. For this reason, it is important to realise how the cultural 'rules' of relationships can impact on people's happiness. In cultures that promote collectivist cultural values and an interdependent sense of self (typically South European and Eastern cultures), a person's beliefs, emotions and behaviour are influenced by the opinions of others around them, usually their family and close friends. This happens less in societies that promote more individualist social values (typically North European and North American cultures), where the average person develops a sense of self independently from others, and is more accountable to his or her own needs and values.

This would lead us to expect that relationships are more influential on well-being and happiness in collectivist cultures than in individualist cultures. Research is still ongoing, but findings from our own and other studies on this topic do not necessarily agree with this assumption. Paradoxically, we find that in collectivist cultural contexts people develop smaller social networks of close friends and relatives, and that related practices – such as emotional sharing, communication and social support – are not necessarily connected to personal needs and emotions, but are more concerned about defining these roles and the rules of relationships. Recent studies in Greece, Korea and China show that in comparison to relationships in countries like the US, the Netherlands and the UK, supportive relationships do not have the same beneficial effects on personal well-being and positive emotions.

In collectivist countries and communities, individuals interact with a smaller number of people, and this can have an impact on well-being. Moreover, having stronger ties to fewer people (typically members of the family) means that personal needs and emotions are more strongly regulated at day-to-day level, which can be detrimental for the expression and sharing of positive emotions. In countries where independence is promoted, the expression of emotion and its sharing with others are used more freely on a day-to-day basis and this may increase happiness and well-being.

However, it must be remembered that within any given culture an independent or interdependent sense of the self is not uniform, but can vary from person to person as a result of parenting practices and personalities. In this respect, it is also interesting to think about the person-to-culture fit for happiness. Recent studies on day-to-day social relations in Greece and the UK show that people whose 'cultural self' is closer to the culture's dominant values (interdependence in Greece and independence in the UK) experience more positive emotions in their day-to-day relationships than those who are not. If you utilise culture-inappropriate rules of relating, or if you relate daily with people who do not share the same cultural rules of relating, you may encounter difficulties and distress.

Consequently, it is important not only to realise whether an individual adopts independent or interdependent relational practices, but also to understand the culturally dependent sense of self of those with whom this individual relates and the communities in which he/she participates.

## The keys

→ **Identify the dominant relational norms in the country where you live. Are people influenced by the opinions of family and close friends (interdependent) or not (independent)?**

→ **Identify the relational norms – independent or interdependent norms – which you apply yourself.**

→ **Interact with persons who share cultural rules of relationships similar to your own and, if possible, choose communities which reflect these values and practices.**

Dr. Konstantinos Kafetsios teaches social psychology at the University of Crete (Greece). He is author of the book 'Attachment, emotion and close relationships' and of several research papers in the social psychology of emotion and personal relationships.

# *The secrets of future public policy*

Colombia is a surprising country in the world happiness-index. Despite bad 'objective' indicators, people give themselves scores that bring them in the Top 20 list. In the international well-being group (IWG) **Eduardo Wills-Herrera** has created a network of researchers from all over the world who are interested in validating new 'subjective' scales. He reveals the secrets of future public policy.

## Emphasis on subjective measures

As an organisational and development studies scholar, I have learnt that the progress of nations or societies cannot and should not be measured only from 'objective' measures such as gross domestic product per capita or income per capita, but also from 'subjective' measures directly assessed with the populations concerned, by asking such simple questions as 'how do you feel?' or 'how satisfied are you with your in life in general?' Research has shown that these are valid measures and that they can be used to make interpersonal or inter-cultural comparisons. With these new 'subjective' scales, we can understand how different dimensions such as personal security, community, health, standard of living, etc. all add to a person's sense of well-being. We have also tested new criteria such as satisfaction with spirituality, and are learning that this dimension is not equally important to all people, depending on the cultural context in which they live.

*'Encouragement of social networks*
*for affective and material support of the most vulnerable*
*must become an important public policy objective.'*

From answers to these questions I have learnt that people give more importance and weight to non-material values when assessing satisfaction with their lives, such as the importance and quality of social relationships, family life and the search for meaning. That is why we can often find more satisfied people in societies that have been defined as 'underdeveloped' on economic or objective grounds. For my own country, Colombia, this is a particularly interesting finding, which requires more research and understanding. Despite bad 'objective' indicators, unstable environments and social conflicts, people turn to social networks and to spirituality in order to find satisfaction in life. They search for meaning and support, which in turns gives them a sense of higher well-being, compared to people who live in more wealthy societies.

In order to use measures of subjective well-being as indicators for public policy, it is important to distinguish different concepts and meanings associated with these indicators. We are not only looking to identify 'happiness' – a hedonistic short-term feeling – but also 'well-being', which from an eudaimonic point of view (from Aristotle) means the ability to flourish as a person, to possess what is most valuable for a person, to be true to your own spirit. In this sense, well-being becomes the ultimate goal for both public policy and personal realisation.

Quality of work and job satisfaction are important dimensions for well-being. These factors depend on internal (locus of control, optimism, extraversion, intrinsic motivation) as well as external attributes (payment, career development, task autonomy, feedback). Unemployment, on the contrary, is linked with higher levels of mental illness, stress and unhappier lives. It is not only the case that companies whose employees feel healthier and happier are more productive, but it is also important to know and assess the impact of business and private enterprise on the population in general, and how the commercial sector can contribute to higher levels of well-being and reduced levels of environmental and social damage. Additionally, social networks in organisations may contribute to the generation of positive energy for work, which may in turn influence higher performance.

I also wish to emphasise the importance for public policies of subjective well-being measures within the context of the social indicators movement. Global problems such as climate change, the depletion of natural resources, an increased level of inequality and societal insecurity all point to the increased importance of the social indicator movement, which looks for alternative measures for understanding the development and progress of societies. Emphasis on subjective measures of well-being will lead to a change in the short term, with regard to methods for the formulation, design and implementation of new objectives for public policy. Creating higher levels of self-efficacy, self-esteem and perceived control for the population, particularly for low-income or vulnerable groups, is crucial. So, too, is an assessment of the realisation of these goals, using subjective indicators which point to the importance of social and human development. Encouragement of social networks for affective and material support of the most vulnerable must become an important public policy objective.

## The keys

→ **People attach more importance and weight to non-material values when assessing satisfaction with their lives: social relationships, family life and the search for meaning.**

→ **Quality of work and job satisfaction are important dimensions for well-being.**

→ **Emphasis on subjective measures of well-being will lead to a change in how we formulate, design and implement new objectives for public policy.**

Eduardo Wills-Herrera is an organisational and well-being scholar at the Management School of Universidad de los Andes in Bogotá (Colombia). He is engaged in research on subjective well-being in Colombian society and organisations. He holds a Master in Development Studies from the Institute of Social Studies in The Hague, Netherlands and received his PhD in Organisational Behaviour from Tulane University, New Orleans. He believes in each human being's right to search for his own path to self-growth and happiness.

*'Economics is a discipline that best serves those with higher material stakes.'*

# The loss of happiness

For more than half a century **Robert E. Lane** has been one of the most respected, thoughtful and creative political scientists in the United States. He finally poses the 'big' question: 'why are so many in the rich world unhappy and depressed these days?'

## The tragic erosion

Market economies increase subjective well-being in less-developed countries, because they provide prosperity and thus pull people out of the mires of poverty and oppression. But market economies begin to lose their marginal utility in industrialised nations, because they do not necessarily provide the goods that increase well-being – or if they do, only as incidentals. The main sources of well-being in advanced economies are friendship and a good family life. Once one is beyond the poverty level, a larger income contributes almost nothing to happiness. In fact, as prosperity increases, there is a tragic erosion of family solidarity and community integration, and individuals become more and more distrustful of each other and their political institutions. It is urgent to alter our priorities, so that we increase our levels of companionship, even at the risk of reducing our income.

Let us start with two observations: (1) the neurons in the emotional centres of the brain fire before the neurons in the cognitive centres; (2) most 'thinking' is unconscious. Research and theory following these observations strongly suggest that reasons are not causes but rationalisations of what is 'decided' by prior emotional responses. Because only the rational processes are accessible to what we experience as 'consciousness', we attribute causal force to them and create a mental world of reason based on what we 'know'. The Enlightenment provided the philosophical underpinnings of this illusionary rational structure. Economics, the discipline that best serves those with higher material stakes, gave this illusionary world view a kind of moral legitimacy, by justifying rational choice in terms of utility interpreted as material well-being. Only when the studies of well-being showed that it is, in fact, much more a function of social relations than of material possessions, was the elaborate structure of economics and rational choice seen to be part of the larger illusionary world produced by our cognitive limitations.

The combined research of neurology and emotional life are finally beginning to penetrate the basic epistemological errors of economics, law, political science and philosophy. Whether the necessary research will deliver its products in time to prevent rational man from destroying the human habitat is uncertain. A return to scarcity is likely to reinforce interpretations of well-being based on material goods and to increase the anxiety and depression that now characterizes the West. If, along with the human habitat, the human genome perishes, the long evolutionary struggle to produce consciousness may never happen again.

## The keys

→ **Once people are beyond the poverty level, a larger income contributes almost nothing to their happiness.**

→ **The main sources of well-being in advanced economies are friendship and a good family life.**

→ **It is urgent to alter our priorities, so that we increase our levels of companionship, even at the risk of reducing our income.**

Robert E. Lane is Eugene Meyer Professor Emeritus of Political Science at Yale University (United States). He is a fellow of the British Academy, a past president of the American Political Science Association and a past president of the International Society of Political Psychology. His latest book is called 'The Loss of Happiness in Market Democracies'.

*'The core is being able to fulfil our targets and aspirations at the broader levels of society.'*

# The predictor 'trust'

Dr. **Luisa Corrado** from Cambridge University leads international research on analysing the social geography of well-being, using data from the European Social Survey on 15 European countries, for which 20,000 people in 180 regions are regularly asked to rate both their overall happiness and their longer-term sense of fulfilment ('life satisfaction'). She finds a strong predictor of happiness: trust.

## Beyond the stereotypes

The map of European well-being puts paid to some long-standing national stereotypes. In particular, the idea that people are happiest along the sunny banks of the Mediterranean does not appear to be true. Most southern European countries are consistently among the lowest-scoring countries in the survey, while the highest scores are registered in the chillier surrounds of Sweden, Finland and the Netherlands, as well as among the table-topping Danes. Women generally class themselves as happier than men, while the old and young tend to be happier than people in their middle years.

We are now analysing what makes people in some countries happier than others. One of the most consistent trends is that those with the highest levels of happiness also report the highest levels of trust in their governments, the police and the justice system. Happier people also tend to have plenty of friends and acquaintances, as well as at least one very close friend, or a partner. The report appears to confirm the old adage that money can't buy you happiness. In countries where the population generally says that they trust the government and other institutions, a high income makes people happier still. But in those countries where such trust is lacking, even the richest tend to be less happy. The degree to which people have been educated has a similarly limited impact on their overall well-being. But the degree to which peoples' jobs give them a sense of self-respect does appear to influence their happiness levels.

Fostering and promoting individual well-being is becoming a central focus in policy. The bulk for establishing national 'well-being accounts' to supplement existing economic data is, in fact, the recognition that public contentment is the outcome of both individual, social and institutional factors. And what I have learnt so far from the research in this area is that the well-being of a country and the well-being of its fellow citizens are not independent from each other.

Starting from the personal level of a person's relations, friends, family and loved ones is certainly important. But the core is being able to fulfil our targets and aspirations at the broader levels of society. As such, institutional support and policy intervention are strongly needed. National policies that recognise the importance of measuring and fostering individual well-being can also have positive economic and social effects, such as more productive workers and greater social cohesion. Consequently, the fostering of well-being could also lead to the fostering of growth, which is the ultimate policy target.

People throughout the European Union appear to be relatively happy. The main reason is not financial. The most important factors influencing happiness appear to be the quality of our social interaction with others and the confidence we have in our country's institutions.

## The keys

→ **The degree to which peoples' jobs give them a sense of self-respect does play an important role.**

→ **The most important factors appear to be the quality of our social interaction with others and the confidence we have in our country's institutions.**

→ **Institutional support and policy intervention are strongly needed.**

Dr. Luisa Corrado received the European Science Award for her outstanding international research on the social geography of income and well-being. She currently is the Marie-Curie Fellow at the Faculty of Economics, University of Cambridge (United Kingdom) and an associate professor at the Tor Vergata University of Rome (Italy).

# *Conflict of needs*

Human beings are a social species. The evolution of our brains has been primarily driven by needs associated with the desire for communication with our fellow human beings. Not surprisingly, world religions, as well as theories about happiness and well-being, deal with the role of social relationships. Commonly, they reflect on three basic needs. How do we reach them? And how do we reconcile potentially conflicting needs? **Martin Guhn** and **Anne Gadermann** share their insights.

## Higher levels of collective happiness

Self-Determination Theory states that there are three universal human needs that must be met if we wish to be happy (assuming that basic needs for food, shelter, physical health, and safety have already been taken care of). These needs are:

→   the need to have others who we care about and who care about us (relatedness);

→   the need to feel competent in activities that are valued by others (competence);

→   the need to have a sense of being in control of our own behaviour (autonomy).

These three needs have been subject to considerable research. Research on relatedness (or variants thereof, such as attachment or social support) has shown that social support (e.g. from friends, family, neighbours and colleagues) is associated with happiness, subjective well-being, life-satisfaction and health. Likewise, perceptions of ones competence (or similar constructs, such as self-efficacy or need for achievement) have been linked to well-being, and so too have high levels of perceived autonomy (or related concepts, such as control beliefs).

The question of why or how some people, but not others, have high levels of relatedness, competence and autonomy has spurred other lines of research. Developmentally, it seems to be critical that children should grow up with a secure sense of attachment to their care-givers, which is fostered by the care-givers' predictable and consistent provision of care, support, high (and accomplishable) expectations, and a clear set of (moral) rules. In other words: children need the enduring and loving involvement of one or more adults, in care and joint activity with the child.

Are relatedness and autonomy conflicting needs? Not necessarily. Self-Determination Theory states that relatedness and autonomy can co-exist and, from a developmental perspective, it is considered ideal when a person develops a state of 'autonomous-relatedness'. However, at times, the needs for relatedness and autonomy are perceived as conflicting or even incompatible, and it has been found that social contexts which engender conflicts between basic needs help to set up the conditions for alienation and psychopathology.

In societies that are becoming increasingly multicultural, the coexistence of different subcultures with their respective value systems can lead to conflicts between relatedness needs and autonomy needs amongst members within a subculture, and between members of different subcultures. For example, an intergenerational conflict within an immigrant family may arise when a child wishes to pursue activities that are valued among its peers from the 'new' culture (e.g. going out to a party), but which are not acceptable in the culture of their family and/or home country. Likewise, members of different subcultures might feel either restricted in their autonomy or in their desire to establish a relatedness in situations where customs or role expectations clash (e.g. dress codes; gender roles; human rights).

How can individuals or entire societies reconcile conflicts between their needs for related-ness and autonomy that arise from different values and role expectations? The key to this challenge, we suggest, lies in understanding how social competences (such as empathy, helping behaviour and listening skills) can facilitate ways in which individuals and groups from different subcultures renegotiate their respective role expectations and values to the point where they are not conflicting but complementing each other. Also, we propose that societies increasingly need to provide structural support and resources to facilitate interactions between people from different subcultures in a way that promotes common sources of joy and pride; for example, by staging school or community events, to which children and parents contribute by drawing from their cultural resources, such as music, art or food recipes. In short, we need to understand how people use social skills to mediate in situations of conflict between autonomy and relatedness which occur due to a clash of values, and we also need to create opportunities for activities that motivate pro-social behaviour in schools, communities, and other public places.

A blueprint for the principles which can inform the design of such common activities can be found in the group experiments of Muzafer and Carolyn Sherif. In these experiments, children in a summer camp, who were continuously being engaged in grouped competitive activities (e.g. sports games), developed anti-social and aggressive behaviour towards children of the opposite teams even outside of the competitive activity (e.g. during breakfast). However, when children were faced (through an experimental manipulation) with a challenge that was of concern to everyone (i.e. the water pipe to the camp had been shut off), not only did the children collaborate to solve the problem, but their behaviour became consistently friendly and supportive towards the children they had treated with disrespect just days before.

Many societies provide substantial resources to meet universal human needs; for example, via the education system, healthcare, social welfare, childcare, parental leave policies, and democratic structures. The one area which, in our view, is underrepresented and undervalued in our modern post-industrial societies is the extent to which structures and resources in communities are used to regularly engage citizens in collaborative, pro-social and multicultural activities, and to provide children with frequent opportunities to develop their social competences.

## The keys

→ **There are three universal human needs that must be met, in order to be happy: relatedness, competence and autonomy.**

→ **To obtain high levels of these needs, careful education to promote social competences and pro-social interactions in children is crucial.**

→ **Conflicting needs can be reconciled into complementing needs, when societies provide structural support and resources to engage people in collaborative, social, and inter-cultural activities.**

Martin Guhn, PhD is a postdoctoral fellow at the Michael Smith Foundation for Health Research & Human Early Learning Partnership, University of British Columbia (Canada), with a special interest for cultural and contextual factors and children's social and emotional competence. Anne Gadermann, PhD is a postdoctoral fellow in the Department of Health Care Policy at Harvard University (USA), with a special interest for children's and youth well-being.

# *The European cake*

European countries have quite different levels of happiness. Divide the European cake into four parts and mark the contrasts between east and west, north and south. **Ingrida Geciene** compared the happiness of people in 31 countries. She unveils the link with the political and religious background of each part of the cake.

## In four parts

Some recent approaches on subjective well-being argue that in advanced Western societies, high economic security leads to an 'increasing emphasis on subjective well-being and quality of life concerns; for many people, these become higher priorities than economic growth'. In order to examine such assumptions we compared people's opinions in 31 Western and Central-East European countries on subjective indicators of quality of life, life satisfaction and happiness.

The results of this analysis revealed two different patterns of subjective evaluation of the quality of life: a highly positive evaluation of well-being in Western Europe (8-7 points out of 10) and a more negative evaluation prevailing in Central and East European countries (6-4 points out of 10). These results generally reflect the main division between the economically advanced countries of the West and the less economically developed post-communist countries. Consequently, these data seem to reveal the great impact of economic factors on the subjective evaluation of the quality of life: in other words, people in poorer countries are less satisfied with their existence. However, some post-communist countries such as Slovenia and the Czech Republic are at the same level of subjective well-being as Latin European countries such as Italy, Spain, Portugal and France, which do not fit precisely into this grouping. It therefore seems that it is not enough simply to study the impact of economic factors in matters relating to subjective well-being.

Within the economic factor, the strongest impact on life satisfaction in both blocs of Western and Central-East Europe is made by the level of income (the higher the income, the greater life satisfaction). Links between subjective indicators (life satisfaction and happiness) and other factors are not so direct. Factors such as stable interpersonal relation-ships and a sense of belonging are more important in Western European countries than in post-communist countries. Thus, it can be supposed that people in poorer post-communist countries suffer more from a lack of financial security than in advanced Western countries. Consequently, needs such as a sense of belonging and stable relation-ships count less for them than income, in terms of being satisfied with life.

Some other important factors influencing subjective well-being were found whilst examining different, long-lasting cultural traditions in both parts of Europe. This distinction primarily deals with the self-determination of individuals in respect of their relations with other individuals, the state and the world. In this case, it is possible to speak of two main groups of countries characterised by different cultural patterns: *state-oriented countries*, where the population think that the state should take more responsibility to ensure that everyone is provided for (predominantly typical for post-communist countries); and *self-oriented countries*, where the population feel that they have completely free choice and full control over their lives (prevailing in Western and, above all, Northern countries). Data indicates that a stronger orientation towards the state has a negative impact on the level of happiness, while a stronger orientation towards the self has a strong positive impact on higher life satisfaction.

*'It would be unwise to underestimate the effect of underlying and often quite different cultural factors.'*

We found significant differences in levels of happiness among the post-communist countries. These can be partly explained by the differing duration of communist ideological influence on the country's population. The least happy people were in Ukraine, Russia and Belarus and it is precisely these countries which experienced the longest (almost 70 years) impact of this ideology. Several generations of people were forced to be passive about their own life development and unreservedly to accept the regulations of state. Over several decades this world-view became traditional. After the collapse of communism, this made it very difficult for large numbers of people to adapt to the new socio-economic and political situation. Consequently, these people, who still expect that the state will provide their basic needs, experience a discrepancy between their expectations and reality, particularly where post-communist states are impoverished by the process of transformation and cannot maintain their previous social policies. As a result, this discrepancy helps to determine the dissatisfaction of people from the post-communist countries with changes, state policy and their own lives.

The importance of world-view for life satisfaction is also partly revealed by differences between the Western European countries. Latin European countries, with a long-lasting Catholic tradition, show lower levels of life satisfaction than Northern European countries, with a Protestant or mixed tradition. Despite the fact that there is no direct relationship between religious denomination and life satisfaction in the data used for analysis, it can be supposed that these different traditions have an indirect influence. The influence of the dominant tradition can be partly demonstrated, for example, in the way that Latin European countries are characterised by a higher percentage of fatalists (people who consider that few things in life depend on personal intervention), while Northern European countries contain a higher percentage of voluntarists (people who feel that they have free choice and complete control over their life). Nevertheless, such assumptions are too imprecise to enable more significant conclusions to be drawn.

After analysing the impact of the new post-materialist cultural tradition on the subjective evaluation of the quality of life, we found that there is no significant relation between subjective indicators of well-being and some of the most important post-materialist values, such as the value of friends and leisure in personal life. In all cases, this relation is clearly a much weaker factor (nearly 10 times) than income. Moreover, there is no meaningful difference between Western and Central-East Europe in this respect. This finding questions the eligibility of the assumption that in wealthier countries happiness is more closely related to a post-materialist orientation than in economically poorer countries.

To sum up, despite the complexity of the explanations of the subjective evaluation of quality of life in different European countries, it can be argued that the level of life satisfaction and happiness is most closely related to economic factors (especially income) and less with the presence of stable relationships and cultural worldview components, such as the level of state dependency or self-dependence. Therefore, it is reasonable to assume that with the stabilisation of the political situation and the improvement of economic and social conditions in the post-communist countries, it will be possible in future to observe an increase in the subjective level of well-being amongst the populations of these lands. Nonetheless, it would be unwise to underestimate the effect of underlying and often quite different cultural factors which relate to greater life satisfaction and happiness. The reduction of the obsolete orientation towards complete state dependency and the growth of a more voluntaristic orientation towards self-development and self-actualisation in the post-communist transformational societies are importance, not least because of their implications for the cultural integration of Western and Central-Eastern Europe.

## The keys

→ **In general, people of poorer countries are less satisfied with life, but it is not enough to exclusively study the impact of economic factors.**

→ **Stronger orientation towards the state has a negative impact on the level of happiness, while a stronger orientation towards the self has strong positive impact on higher levels of life satisfaction.**

→ **Voluntarists seem to be happier than fatalists.**

Ingrida Geciene is director of the Institute for Social Innovations in Vilnius (Lithuania) and a lecturer in the Communication Faculty of Vilnius University. She leads research on youth, migration and changing identities in post-communist countries.

*'Bad things happen
but focusing on them
only makes them worse.'*

# High Five

The high five is a celebratory hand gesture that occurs when two people simultaneously raise one hand and push, slide or slap the flat of their palms against each other. It is a symbol of understanding, success, satisfaction and elation. **David Watson** has spent a lifetime in his search to find the high five of happiness.

## Highlight principles

Much of our work on happiness has focused on the issue of individual differences. That is, we have been very interested by the fact that happiness comes relatively easily for some people, whereas others have to work much harder at attaining it. Nevertheless, it is possible for anyone to improve his or her level of happiness by following a few basic principles. I will highlight five principles here that have emerged as particularly important considerations in our research. Everyone can benefit from these 'high five' principles, even those for whom happiness does not come easily.

→ The first principle is to recognise that happiness is a subjective state of mind – rather than an objective condition – that largely reflects a person's inner outlook on life. It is best to focus as much as possible on the good and positive aspects of one's life, rather than dwelling on the negative. It is very difficult to be happy if one spends a lot of time brooding about past mistakes, stewing over insults and frustrations, or worrying about bad things that might happen in the future. Bad things do happen – but focusing on them only makes them worse.

→ The second principle is that envy is a particularly powerful enemy of happiness. Bertrand Russell once wrote, 'If I can cure myself of envy, I can acquire happiness and become enviable.' If you start comparing your situation to that of others, it is almost inevitable that you will eventually be able to think of people who are better off in some ways (greater wealth or success, better possessions, superior skills, and so on) than you are. People who spend a lot of time comparing themselves to others therefore find it a real challenge to be happy. Focus on what you have, rather than on what others have (or on what you don't have).

→ The third principle is that human beings are social animals, and we are happier when we are connecting with other people. Almost any activity – no matter how mundane – is more enjoyable when others are involved. It is therefore extremely important to get together with others to maintain old relationships or build new ones, even when you don't particularly feel like doing so. One of the most terrible aspects of disorders such as depression is that they can cause people to turn away from others, and become socially aloof and isolated. This, in turn, can create an enduring cycle of misery. It is particularly important to develop stable, long-term social relationships (such as friendships and committed romantic relationships) that will provide key sources of advice and support during difficult times. People with good support networks are much better able to withstand the effects of stress. Finding ways to help others is another good way to feel better about yourself and your life.

→ The fourth principle is that it is important to have goals, interests or values that give your life meaning. Some people find meaning through their faith and religion. Other people may find meaning in their work or career, or through their hobbies or close relationships with others. The specific source of this meaning is not important. Indeed, what seems very meaningful to one person may appear largely meaningless to another. The key thing is to find something that gives purpose to your life and allows you to approach each day with renewed energy. One interesting paradox that has been noted by many happiness researchers is that people devote much of their lives to striving after things – money, education, success – that ultimately have little actual effect on their happiness. This does not mean that this striving is a waste of time, however. Pursuing goals of this kind can also help to give life meaning.

→ Our work also highlights a fifth principle, namely, the importance of physical activity in improving a person's sense of inner well-being. People feel better when they are physically engaged, and individuals who are physically active have higher overall levels of happiness and life satisfaction. Exercise regimens have been shown to be very effective in increasing well-being and reducing depression. It is important to add, moreover, that exercise does not have to be long or intense to be effective. In fact, our work and that of others demonstrates that brief, moderate exercise is extremely effective in improving your mood – and thereby your outlook on life. I often find that a 15 to 20 minute walk is all I need to feel refreshed and energised.

## The keys

→ **Recognise that happiness is a subjective state of mind: focus on the good and rid yourself of envy.**

→ **Humans are social animals. We are happier when we are connecting with other people.**

→ **It is important to be physically active and to have goals, interests or values that give your life meaning.**

Dr. David Watson is Professor of Psychology and head of the Personality and Social Psychology Training Programme at the University of Iowa (USA). He received his doctorate in Personality Research and Assessment from the University of Minnesota in 1982. David Watson has broad interests in personality, health and clinical psychology, and has published widely in the top journals in these fields. He has served on the editorial boards of numerous journals and is the associate editor of the 'Journal of Abnormal Psychology'.

*'The Gross National Product per capita of Kenya is 1% of that of the USA, but Kenyans feel as healthy as Americans.'*

# Around the world

In recent years, **Carol Graham** has been studying happiness in countries around the world. These include very poor and very rich countries, and countries of all different cultures, ranging from Chile to Uzbekistan and from America to Afghanistan. 'What is most remarkable about my findings is how similar the basic determinants of happiness are in countries that are so different, ranging from bastions of prosperity to failing states mired in poverty and adversity.'

## It's a story of adaptation to good and bad fortune

Ultimately, there seem to be strong similarities in what determines happiness across humankind, regardless of the contextual environment. There is a consistent relationship between happiness and age. It is U shaped, with the lowest point on that U being around the mid forties in most countries. Another strong and consistent relationship is that between happiness and health. Healthy people are happier and it is also likely that happy people are healthier. Employment status also matters: virtually everywhere I and others have studied happiness, the unemployed are less happy than the employed. There are a very few exceptions, such as Afghanistan, where the definitional lines between employment and unemployment are murky. Married people are typically happier than the average in most places, including the United States, Europe, Latin America and Central Asia. This result does not hold for Russia or for Afghanistan, however, perhaps because of an imbalance in gender rights in those places.

Not surprisingly, the relationship that has dominated economists' discussions about happiness is that between happiness and income. My studies across the world support the conclusion that many other scholars have already reached: money matters to individual happiness, but it only matters so much. Wealthy people are happier than poor people virtually everywhere, but after a certain point other things, including relative income differences, start to matter as much (if not more) than absolute levels of income. My work shows that these concerns for relative income differences – or more colloquially 'keeping up with the Joneses' – exist at remarkably low levels of income, including in very poor countries in Latin America and even among poor migrants in China.

One reason that the basic correlates of happiness are so consistent across countries is that happiness questions are open-ended: the definition is left up to the respondent. Thus people in Kabul define happiness as *they* see it, and those in New York define it as *they* see it. This allows for the comparison of happiness across countries and cultures, and makes happiness surveys a powerful research tool for exploring the effects of other things on well-being. These include the welfare effects of institutional arrangements and/or those of phenomena such as crime, corruption and pollution.

However, the lack of an absolute definition of happiness means that the results are, to some extent, relative. Human beings are remarkable at adapting to both good and bad circumstances. Thus individuals who have become accustomed to poor health and much crime and corruption are less likely to report unhappiness when posed with these challenges than are individuals that have better norms of health and higher levels of security. Kenyans, for example, are as satisfied with their health as are respondents in the United States, where health conditions are better by an order of magnitude. And freedom is more important to the happiness of those who live in contexts with more of it than it is to those in contexts where functioning democracies are a scarcer commodity. Individuals adapt upwards as well as downwards: those that are accustomed to more freedom and income, for example, require more freedom and income to attain the same levels of happiness as those with less of these public and private goods.

This human capacity to adapt is, no doubt, a positive force for preserving individual psychological welfare in the face of extreme adversity, such as in contexts like Afghanistan. Average happiness levels in Afghanistan are above the world average and on par with Latin American levels, even though objective conditions in most quality of life domains are materially much worse. And, unlike most other places in the world, respondents in Afghanistan are not made unhappy when they experience crime and corruption, as they have become so accustomed to these phenomena. This suggests that the same individual capacity to adapt to adversity can result in collective tolerance for very poor norms of health, security, and governance. This may help to explain why some societies remain trapped in a very bad equilibrium, even though they co-exist – in a world of global information – with others that have standards of living that are an order of magnitude better.

This world-wide story of adaptation is an example of how understanding happiness provides insights into the puzzles of human development. At the same time, it poses clear challenges to applying the results directly to public policy, unless one is willing to accept that individuals in Afghanistan merit norms of health, security, and freedom that are far inferior to those in Canada or Chile.

## Why are Afghans smiling?

'Afghanistan has been at war more or less continuously for more than 30 years. The country has been invaded and effectively destroyed many times. But our recent research reveals that, relative to international norms, Afghans remain surprisingly happy. In our survey, 81% of Afghans said that they had been smiling the day before. Smiling yesterday is a commonly used measure of innate happiness, and Afghans who were smiling yesterday are likely to have been smiling the day before, too. We conducted the surveys across eight regions of Afghanistan, in collaboration with researchers in Kabul. We found an overall high level of happiness. The reasons why so many Afghans smiled were intriguing. Adaptation to crime and corruption appears to be key. Of 2,000 respondents – only 11 percent of whom were women: fear of violence leads many women to avoid talking to unfamiliar men – 25 percent reported having been a victim of corruption in the past 12 months, and 11 percent were victims of crime. Yet victims were no less happy than the average, as were those who reported being unable to walk safely in their neighbourhoods. This is a marked departure from most other places in the world, where being victimised or afraid in one's own neighbourhood causes unhappiness. As crime and corruption have become the norm, these phenomena do not appear to be having the usual effects on well-being. The ability to adapt to adversity is good from an individual perspective, but from a societal perspective, it can lead to complacency in the face of rampant crime and corruption.'

Carol Graham in The Washington Post

## The keys

→ **There seem to be strong similarities in what determines happiness across humankind, regardless of the contextual environment: age, health, employment and income.**

→ **Human beings are remarkable at adapting to both good and bad circumstances.**

→ **The same individual capacity to adapt to adversity can result in collective tolerance for very poor norms of health, security and governance.**

Carol Graham is Senior Fellow at The Brookings Institution, University of Maryland (USA). Her research focuses on poverty, inequality, public health and novel measures of well-being. Her most recent book is called 'Happiness Around the World: The Paradox of Happy Peasants and Miserable Millionaires'. The Brookings Institution is a non-profit, public policy organisation, conducting high-quality, independent research to provide innovative, practical recommendations that advance a secure, more open, safe, prosperous and cooperative international system. It is consistently ranked as one of the most influential, most quoted and most trusted think tanks.

# *Training the Happy-Muscles*

Successful athletes know that they have to focus on winning, not on losing. Why do people who want to increase their happiness, then, focus on their unhappiness? **Miriam Akhtar** is one of the first positive psychologists in the UK and has developed a 12-step training plan for the happiness muscles.

## Mind, body and spirit

From my work as a positive psychologist, the main thing I've learnt is that with happiness it really is a case of 'what you focus on is what you get'. Happiness is like a muscle that can be developed and when you put your focus on it, it grows. We know that about 40% of our happiness is under voluntary control, so that's a lot to play for. It means that there are things that we can do that will increase our happiness. Activities such as savouring good experiences, expressing gratitude and appreciating the good things in your life (the key, in my opinion, to switching from a glass half empty to a glass half full), prioritising time with loved ones (good personal relationships and an active social life are characteristics of the happiest people), finding new ways to use your strengths and practising optimism (the natural self-defence for the mind against depression).

Happiness is an holistic pursuit not just for the mind but for the body and spirit, too. Food affects mood and so does physical activity. If you're depressed and don't feel motivated to use the cognitive techniques that will grow your happiness muscle, try doing

WHAT
YOU
FOCUS
ON, IS
WHAT
YOU
GET

something physical instead, like walking or dancing. This will release endorphins and you will experience a natural lift in your mood without any hard mental work. Spirituality is also important – having a sense of meaning or purpose, a connection to something bigger that focuses you outside of yourself. There is some amazing research on meditation. For example, we now know that the regular practice of mindfulness meditation can develop the left pre-frontal cortex, the seat of positive emotions in the brain. So the more you meditate, the more you grow your capacity for positive emotions.

I find with my coaching clients that although they want greater happiness, they are often focused on their unhappiness –which is exactly what they don't want. So when they're telling me about the things that are compromising their well-being, I ask them to focus instead on what it is that they really want. So if they're very focused on a source of stress, we focus instead on what they want, such as relaxation, and then investigate ways to achieve that goal authentically. What you focus on is what you get.

The result of my research is a 12-step training plan to develop greater happiness: express gratitude, use your strengths, live with purpose, find your power, get physical, the happiness diet, learning optimism, bounceback-ability, improving relationships, spiritual happiness, rest & renewal, the fun factor. Anyone can practise these strategies to develop greater well-being. Our goal? To grow your personal happiness and join with others to increase the tonnage of happiness on the planet.

## The keys

→ **Happiness is like a muscle that can be developed, and when you put your focus on it, it grows.**

→ **Happiness is an holistic pursuit, not just for the mind but for the body and spirit, too.**

→ **A twelve-step training plan of practical strategies can make your happiness muscles grow.**

Miriam Akhtar MSc is a positive psychologist, coach, trainer and author in Bristol (United Kingdom) and a specialist in practical strategies for a happier life. She holds the coveted Masters in Applied Positive Psychology, one of the first generation in Europe to qualify as a positive psychologist. She is a member of the International Positive Psychology Association.

*'Pleasure and pain both vanish over time.'*

# After the shock

Crucial events in our lives – marriage, the birth of a child, divorce, the death of spouse, disability, an increase in our standard of living, etc. – strongly affect our happiness levels, but is the effect of these shocks on our psychological well-being temporary or permanent? **Katja Uglanova** discovers a substitute for happiness: habit.

*But there was none to care, her opinion was not sought,*
*And so to the altar the girl was brought.*
*To make her sorrow fade, ere it was too late,*
*The clever husband took her to his estate,*
*Far from city, deep in the countryside,*
*Where she amongst strangers must evermore reside.*

*At first she cried, smashed china, was enraged,*
*And even tried to seek divorce,*
*But the things went smoothly, not really worse.*
*In household routine she became engaged,*
*Got used to it. Habit is God's gift, it is His tribute*
*To happiness, its equal substitute.*

A.S. Pushkin, 'Eugeny Onegin'

# Habit: a substitute for happiness?

For the heroine of '*Eugeny Onegin*', the challenging task of getting used to a loveless marriage was only made possible thanks to an important psychological mechanism, '*hedonic adaptation*', which makes favourable and unfavourable circumstances produce weaker emotional reactions over time. Adaptation is a blessing when we have to deal with potentially damaging experiences, such as romantic break-up or losing a job, but it has a reverse side – the pleasure initially derived from positive events, such as an increase in salary, getting a bigger house, or even marriage – gradually disappears as the weeks, months and years pass. Hedonic adaptation serves several important functions. Firstly, persistently strong emotional states (especially negative ones) may have detrimental physiological consequences. Secondly, it is important that new experiences 'overwrite' previous ones, because they provide new information, which helps us in guiding our behaviour and finally leads to more efficient functioning.

Do people adapt to anything? Yes, they do – our adaptive potential is great. It used to be assumed within the so-called '*hedonic treadmill model*' that individuals have stable levels of happiness, determined by genes and early life experiences, and that life events do not change these levels in the long run. Someone might become happier after being promoted at work, but after a while the effect fades. Research studies have provided evidence that, on average, people adapt to marriage, divorce, childbirth, rises in income and widowhood surprisingly quickly. These findings challenge our deeply-rooted convictions about sources of happiness, since they suggest that we constantly overestimate the expected pleasure potential of various events, activities and achievements.

Does this mean that our efforts to move to a better home, find the right partner or get a better job are all in vain? No – adaptation is not a cast-iron law. The speed of this process and its trajectory varies across several dimensions: events, personality and context. Firstly, patterns of adaptation vary across events; adaptation to marital dissolution, for example, seems to be more rapid and complete than to unemployment. Of course, there are some experiences to which people never adapt. We almost never get used to becoming disabled. Some circumstances, such as noise, even produce a stronger reaction over time. However, **the good news is that there are also things which never cease to bring us joy** – meeting friends, our hobbies, our favourite songs. I have a personal example here. I am allergic to cats, and yet I always have them around me – because I adore them. Fortunately, you can get used to living with an allergy, whereas the positive emotions derived from having a pet will never fade. Finding and perpetuating activities that continue to be rewarding is certainly an important path to happiness.

Secondly, personality is a very important predictor of how quickly a person adapts. After a partner's death, some people remain resilient, some suffer for a period of time and then gradually revert to their normal mood, while others plunge into chronic depression from which they never recover. Personality 'works' in different ways. It influences our choice of coping strategies. Neurotic individuals (emotionally unstable people with predominantly negative emotional states) are likely to engage in ineffective coping strategies, such as denial, whereas extraverts chose more effective ones, such as the search for social support. Personality also dictates whether we see the glass as half empty or half full: neurotics focus on negative events, whereas extraverts assign more importance to positive experiences. As a result, high levels of neuroticism might lead to a decrease in happiness, whereas high extraversion is likely to increase it. Moreover, personality affects the probability of certain events. For example, **happy, optimistic people are more sought after on the 'marriage market'** than depressive, pessimistic individuals, and people who experience divorce were likely to have been unhappy, even before they got married.

Finally, the characteristics of the socio-economic and cultural context play a role, although little comparison of different contexts has so far been carried out. Nevertheless, comparative analysis of adaptation to major life events in Germany and Russia has revealed an interesting finding: in Germany, men return to their 'usual' level of happiness after just two years of marriage, whereas Russian men seem to adapt at a slower pace, and can therefore profit more from marriage in terms of happiness, at least at the beginning of their marital career. This is a good example of how different contexts produce different responses to similar life experiences.

To sum up, hedonic adaptation is not an immutable law of human psychological functioning, and people are not bound to remain at their 'personal' set-points of happiness, as was once assumed. The more insights we get into adaptation, the more flexibility we discover. It seems that people's reactions to life's experiences are, at least to some extent, constructed by the societies in which they live and by the personal resources at their disposal. However, we still do not fully understand why people display such different patterns of reaction to similar experiences. The challenge for the (near) future is to find out what personal resources and contextual features can help people to cope with tragedies or to prolong the effect of more positive life events.

## The keys

→ **On average, people adapt to marriage, divorce, childbirth, rises in income and widowhood surprisingly quickly.**

→ **Adaptation is not an iron law. The speed of this process and its trajectory varies across several dimensions: events, personality and context.**

→ **Finding and perpetuating activities that continue to be rewarding is an important path to happiness – even after shock events.**

Katja Uglanova used to work as a lecturer at the Higher School of Economics in St. Petersburg (Russia). Her research area is adaptation to major life events. She is now working to get her Ph.D at the Bremen International Graduate School of Social Sciences (BIGSSS) in Germany.

*'There are no goals*
*beyond your own desires'*

# The mix of ex and in

Does the sun shine on you or do you shine yourself? Does the place you are born play a bigger role than the body you are born in? Does happiness come from the outside or from the inside? Prof. **Joaquina Palomar** is looking for the balance.

## From the inside or the outside?

External factors refer to the environment in which an individual is born, grows up and develops. They include a nation's poverty or wealth, the security provided by a country to its citizens, the freedom experienced in order to express and choose what one desires, the opportunities for development offered, the prevailing conditions of social equality, and many others. Studies focused on external factors have revealed enough evidence to make it very clear that the objective conditions in the lives of individuals have a decisive impact on their happiness. And this is especially true when the population lacks the most indispensable material conditions to live with dignity or when the nation in which one lives has problems with governability or severe social conflicts. National surveys conducted in various countries have demonstrated that happiness is greater in developed countries than in developing countries, and the correlation indexes between income and subjective well-being indicate a curved line relation, with a greater impact on subjective well-being when income levels are lower. Included among other external factors having a strong impact are those we can refer to as *'life events'*, which generate an important flow of personal experiences. Events such as accidents have a strong random component. Nevertheless, an individual's reaction to these events – what they are able or not able to do in the aftermath – depends to a significant degree on their personal resources.

Individuals' internal factors or resources have a decisive impact on subjective well-being and happiness, even when environmental conditions and life events are, in many cases, highly adverse. Variables such as intelligence, health and temperament are especially noteworthy. The internal resources of individuals may be classified as innate or learned. They can be referred to as life abilities, resilience or personal resources, and are developed in the processes of socialisation experienced by individuals. Enough studies have shown that individuals with greater life abilities or personal resources are happier.

My experiences as a psychologist and researcher have also shown me that there are resources which give individuals increased possibilities to function better in their work, family and social worlds: locus of internal control, the identification of feelings, emotional regulation, motivation to achieve, and coping directly with problems. More specifically, when individuals are capable of identifying their emotions, they can attribute the results of their actions to their own behaviour and not to random events or luck. When they have the motivation and persistence to enthusiastically attempt to achieve what they have set as their goals; when they resolve the problems that present themselves along the way in a direct manner; when they speak truthfully, expressing clearly what they need and seeking support for what they need from persons in their complex network of relations established in the worlds of work, love and friendship – in these circumstances, it is much more likely that they will be happy or have greater subjective well-being. In the same way, when individuals value their work, their efforts and their achievements, they are less likely to compare themselves to others, so that their well-being is less dependent on social comparison.

On the obverse side of the coin, it has been demonstrated that when individuals do not know what they want or what they feel; when they are unaware of or hide the problems which present themselves; when they fail to clearly express their goals; when they fail to understand or are not willing to pay the price necessary to achieve these goals; when they become frustrated because these goals are not within their reach; when they blame other people for the origin of their misfortune – in these circumstances, they will very likely be unhappy and will have very few opportunities to change their present and immediate future.

The state of being happy or unhappy does not remain fixed during a person's entire life. Happiness levels are sensitive to changes in life conditions and the various stages in the life cycle through which human beings must pass. Throughout their entire lifetime, whether consciously or unconsciously, individuals evaluate what they are doing and what they have achieved, with the aim of adjusting their behaviour to seek ever greater happiness.

Of course, the difficulty in improving subjective well-being can be explained by the large number of factors with which it is associated, including some of a socio-cultural nature, the modification of which is not within the reach of individuals. Certain factors within the individual context can sometimes be modified, but not without considerable time and effort. There are no goals beyond your own desires. Ask yourself which are your deepest wishes – and try to achieve them.

## The keys

→ **The external, objective conditions in the lives of individuals have a decisive impact on their happiness (e.g. money, security, freedom, opportunities and equality).**

→ **The internal, subjective abilities and resources of individuals have a decisive impact on their happiness (e.g. locus of internal control, emotional regulation, motivation and coping).**

→ **Changes in external and internal conditions may change our well-being. Some of these changes are within our reach. Others are not.**

---

Joaquina Palomar-Lever is a full-time professor at the Iberoamerican University in Mexico City (Mexico). She obtained her Master Degree and Ph. D. in Psychology from the National Autonomous University of Mexico. She is member of the Researchers National System and has published in (inter)national journals in the areas of values, family, poverty and quality of life.

*'The older we get, the better we handle our emotions.'*

# The four questions

The audience has been listening in silent enthusiasm throughout the lecture on 'The Psychology of Happiness'. Now it is time for the questions. Professor **Reynaldo Alarcón** knows that the same four questions always come back, time after time. Here are the answers.

## Age, marriage and personality

**What things make people happy?** In Lima, in groups of diverse ages, I found the following answers in the following order: to be in good health, to be on good terms with God, and to have a good family. I observed, however, that these three 'things' changed according to gender, age and marital status. For example, for young university students in their twenties, the most prized objective was professional success, while the 60-year-old group expressed the desire (previously mentioned) to have a good family and be on good terms with their Maker. It is certainly true that the 'things' which make one person happy will not necessarily make other people happy. Happiness is very personal.

**What is the impact of age?** Frequently, it is assumed that old people are less happy than young ones. There are several facts which support this hypothesis: declining health in old age, being left alone through the loss of a partner, the progressive loss of friends and relatives, plus all the other problems that come with age. However, research relating age and happiness shows that people in their sixties and seventies are often happier. Part of the reason why the elderly feel happier is connected with their ability to handle their emotions better. They have learnt to control both positive and negative events. They do not get overly excited when told that they have won the lottery, nor if they receive bad news. They process this emotional stimulus primarily through cognitive thinking. It should be noted, however,

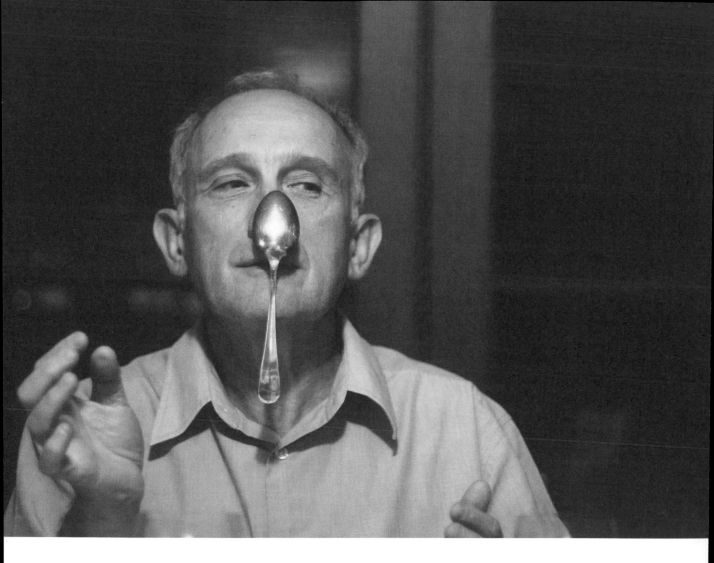

that this information corresponds to elderly people living in their own homes or in a family context. In contrast, older people living in care homes often display depressive symptoms, loneliness, an irritable character and other problems which make them unhappy.

**Does marital status influence the happiness of people?** In our research we have found that married people are happier than single people. Among married men and women there are no significant differences between the levels of happiness. It may be presumed that married people, both men and women, have satisfactory and gratifying affective experiences throughout their married lives. It has been found that an affective balance between the couple and mutual gratification contribute to marital stability. On the other side of the coin, negative experiences and egocentric behaviour in a marriage act as factors which can lead to crisis. Some researchers have observed that men and women who are unhappy in their marriages suffer common mental alterations: neuroticism, authoritarianism, aggressive behaviour, etc.

**What are the personal characteristics that make you happy?** We have found that there are some psychological factors that clearly promote happiness, such as extroversion. It is certainly true that extrovert people obtain higher levels of happiness than introverts. Feeling satisfied with life, being comfortable with who we are and what we have achieved, is a key factor for life satisfaction. This judgment is a result of self-evaluation, and it is on the basis of this positive self-evaluation that people consider themselves as 'valuable': they are confident that they have the capacities and qualities to face life and to determine their future actions. There is a very close relationship between happiness and self-esteem, but this should not be allowed to lead to narcissism or exaggerated self-admiration for your own personal qualities. Finally, it has also been found that the 'frequency of positive affect' contributes to the state of personal happiness. This means that any act or comment which rewards or recognises the value of a person in their daily relationships will make them happy. All of us long for recognition. While positive affects – which are moderate emotions – increase our well-being, more intense emotional experiences do not favour happiness. The Greek philosophers already knew that the sensorial pleasures do not create happiness. On the contrary, they are inclined to upset the balance on which a happy life depends. And this is a great truth – whether you are young or old, man or woman, married or single.

## The keys

→ **Getting older doesn't make you unhappy. You learn to handle your emotions better.**

→ **In general, married men and women report a higher degree of happiness.**

→ **Important personal characteristics are extroversion, self-esteem, and giving and receiving positive affects.**

---

Reynaldo Alarcón is Emeritus Professor and Doctor of Psychology and Philosophy at the Universidad Nacional de Mayor de San Marcos in Lima (Peru). He has published eight books and 173 psychological articles, including empirical research and theoretical reports. He is Doctor Honoris Causa for the Ricardo Palma University and a member of the Inter-American Society of Psychology and of the American Psychological Association. Since 2000 he has worked in the area of positive psychology, having published various research papers and lectured at conferences. His latest book is called 'Psychology of Happiness'.

*'Happiness can be found
by constructing a good story
and then living your way into it.'*

# Your story

**All the world's a stage.**
**And all the men and women merely players.**
**And one man in his time plays many parts...**
**William Shakespeare**

Shakespeare did not invent this metaphor. It was already
in common use in the 16<sup>th</sup> century and he would have expected
his audience to recognize it. So does **Jonathan Adler** talking
to people after the September 11<sup>th</sup> attacks in New York.
We are all protagonists in our own life story – and also the narrator.
Crafting this most important fiction holds the key to real happiness.
Especially in the wake of adversity.

## The most important fiction

Bad things happen to all of us. Every life is peppered with the unexpected and
the uncomfortable. These events challenge us with the task of meaning-making;
they force us to question how our lives can continue to make sense in light of what has
happened. In essence, unanticipated adversity dares us to revise our lives.

A growing body of interdisciplinary research broadly labelled '*the narrative study of lives*' suggests that each of us carries with us a story about our lives that is continually evolving. This story helps smooth our sense of self over time; it connects the person we have been to the person we currently are and to the person that we will become. It unifies, while so much of modern life splinters and compartmentalizes. The story also imbues our life with a sense of purpose – it answers that most challenging question: '*why?*' Bad things that happen to us challenge the story we've been telling. They can shake us from our story-line and can even cause us to doubt the meaning of every chapter that has already been crafted. One of the major reasons life's struggles feel so bad is that they usher in this sense of narrative uncertainty, that robs us of the unity and purpose we find so reassuring. But for this very reason, the challenges we face also provide us with the opportunity to step out of our stories, exchanging the role of the protagonist for the role of the narrator.

In my own research, I have studied the ways in which people grapple more and less successfully with narrating life's turning points. I am especially interested in stories of those periods when people work towards happiness in the face of adversity. What I have found is that all stories are not created equal, when it comes to psychological well-being. It turns out that different ways of telling our story have profoundly different impacts on how happy we are.

One of the most compelling examples of how our stories relate to our happiness concerns the way the main character is portrayed. You are the protagonist in your life story and it turns out that the type of character you are matters a lot. Specifically, it matters whether this main character is portrayed as being in control of his or her circumstances, as opposed to being completely powerless to the whims of fate. In stories about wrestling with difficulties, this theme – called 'agency' – predicts how happy a person is, above and beyond the impact of other qualities that might predict happiness, like personality traits. In one of my studies, people who sought the help of a psychotherapist in order to manage some difficulty told their stories before beginning treatment and then again after each session of therapy. I found that the portrayal of the main character in these stories shifted towards including more and more of the theme of agency over the course of treatment. And even more interesting, the changes in their stories happened before they reported feeling happier. This suggests that in the wake of life's challenges, happiness can be found by constructing a good story and then living your way into it.

The stories we craft about our lives are just that – stories. We know that memories, especially memories of highly emotional events, cannot be assumed to be completely accurate recordings of what really happened. But the stories' imperfections do not render them powerless when it comes to our well-being. Indeed, the stories we tell about our lives imbue our day-to-day existence with a sense of meaning and purpose. This is why I think about each person's life story as '*the most important fiction*'. Conceiving of your story as one of the keys to a meaningful and happy life is a wonderfully empowering insight; for regardless of your life circumstances, the story that you tell about your life is malleable and in your control.

## The keys

→ **Remember that when bad things happen they present you with an opportunity to step back and revise the story of your life.**

→ **Realising that you are both the main character and the narrator in the story of your life empowers you to shape the plot of the story – and the way you live it.**

→ **Sometimes changing the story can precede changes in your happiness, so find a way to revise your story and then live your way into it.**

Jonathan M. Adler is an assistant professor of psychology at the F.W. Olin College of Engineering in Needham, Massachusetts (USA). His research is focused on the ways in which the process of responding to challenges fuels identity development and well-being. He has published scholarly articles on the relationship between well-being and people's life stories, their stories of psychotherapy, and their stories of the September 11th attacks in the United States. His work has been covered by The New York Times, as well as by Elle Magazine.

*'People primarily get feelings of happiness from other people's affection and opinions.'*

# Married or single?

*Cleverly puts a question in the Answerbag on the Internet: 'Is it better to be single or married?' This is the first answer she gets: 'Neither, actually (Ironhead)'.* Professor **Leonard Cargan** has followed marrieds and singles over a 22-year period. Does he have a better answer?

## Being single on Noah's ark

Since they are believed to have fewer responsibilities, a stereotype applied to people that are single is that they are happier than those who are married. To determine whether this belief is a myth or a reality, it is first necessary to know what factors are important to happiness. For the marrieds, the most important items for their happiness are their marriage, love, and their children, whereas for the singles the most important items for their happiness are their friends and personal growth. As can be seen, the widest difference between marrieds and singles on factors important to happiness is in regard to the role played by marriage and children. This finding seems strange, since the low ranking of marriage by singles for their happiness contradicts their almost unanimous belief that they would marry in the future. Similarly, our study also revealed an increase in importance of children for the happiness of singles. This may explain the vast increase in single-parent adoptions and births.

Turning to the stereotype on happiness, it is now possible to answer the question as to who has the bragging rights about being happiest with their status. The above findings indicate that people primarily get feelings of happiness from other people. It is their affection and their opinion of us that most influence our feeling of happiness.

This being the case, it is not surprising that the stereotype regarding singles and happiness is a myth, despite the fact that most of both statuses claim to be happy. National studies, as well as our own studies, consistently show that married people are happier than unmarried ones.

A final question with regard to the matter of happiness is whether happiness is affected by your status and gender within each of the two statuses, since marrieds are made up of those who married once and those who are remarried, while those who are single are made up of those who have never married and those who are divorced. Similarly, all four of the groups can be divided on a gender basis. Although the differences are limited, among the marrieds, the order of happiness is the married-once females, the married-once males, the remarried males and the remarried females. First marriages therefore appear to bring more happiness feelings than remarriage. Also with slight differences, the order in claims of happiness among the singles is divorced males, the never-married females, the never-married males and the divorced females. It appears that being a divorced female is not a happy situation, when compared to the life of a divorced male. This breakdown on happiness feelings allows for a final breakdown, utilising all of the statuses involved. Again with limited differences, the happiest in order are the married female, the married male, with the single male and the single female almost tied at the bottom of the list. It may be prudent for us to leave the whys and wherefores of these findings to the imagination of the reader, since you own beliefs – and marital status – will no doubt affect your opinions…

## The keys

→ **The most important sources of happiness for the marrieds are their marriage, love and their children; for the singles the most important things are friends and personal growth.**

→ **Married people are happier than unmarried ones.**
  **First marriages appear to bring more happiness than remarriage.**

→ **Divorced males fare better than divorced females.**

Leonard Cargan is Professor Emeritus at Wright State University, Dayton, Ohio (USA). He has published numerous articles and books on sociology, singles, marriage and the family. He also founded a programme for singles. His most recent book is called 'Being Single on Noah's Ark'.

*'Happy people need room to breathe.'*

# The final three

'I have studied happiness scientifically for nearly twenty years. Through the course of my career, I must have read, thought about, and conducted studies on happiness from almost every angle I can imagine,' writes Professor **Eunkook M. Suh**. 'Given my profession, I am often asked the question: "So, at the end of the day, what is your pick for the most crucial determinants of happiness?" Embarrassingly, I usually try to dodge this question (it's a tough one!), but for this book, I have finally come up with my answer.'

## Crucial conditions

Research offers an endless list of factors which relate to happiness in some way (e.g., having a dog). However, most of these relations are relatively insignificant or are in fact caused by other hidden reasons. This is not the case with the three conditions which I intend to propose. They each seem to have a considerable impact on happiness, regardless of your job, religion, income, skin colour or age.

→   Firstly, an optimistic, cheerful temperament is possibly the strongest single factor in determining a person's happiness level. Whether you think this is fair or not, it is the truth. Trying to deny it is like the ostrich burying his head in the sand. Hundreds of studies support this conclusion, including those which have compared twins' happiness. Research finds surprisingly little difference in the objective life conditions

of happy versus unhappy people. The key difference, however, appears to be in the ways happy and unhappy persons react to and interpret life. These factors are strongly shaped by the person's personality. If you think you are born with the 'less-happy' gene, try to break out from the vicious cycle of feeling bitter about yourself and feeling even more unhappy. Instead, acknowledge this part of you (like the fact that you have brown eyes instead of blue), and try to emulate the positive and energetic life styles of happy people. Sometimes it works.

→ Another very reliable finding about happy people is that they have a much richer social life than others. The default behaviour of a happy person is to seek other people; depression states, on the other hand, strengthen the desire to be alone. Imagine the fate of a person who is not capable of experiencing joy through in social interaction. Such individuals, given the crucial role of others in our long-term survival, will be slowly weeded out of the evolutionary process. For this very reason, happiness and social interaction were glued together by the most primitive, evolutionary forces. Even introverted people, contrary to what you might think, are happier when they are in social situations. In other words, your relational life needs to be fairly high on your checklist for key conditions for about happiness. But be careful: make sure your are being social foe the right reasons. Is it intrinsically rewarding, fun and meaningful, or is it primarily coloured by tension and obligations?

→ A sense of personal freedom is my final candidate for the crucial conditions of happiness. Among the three factors in my list, this one is perhaps the most controllable. I am not necessarily talking about freedom from physical constraints (e.g. imprisonment), but more about the kind of subjective freedom which is harboured in the mind. As social and cultural creatures, we often become excessively concerned about how we are evaluated by others. A life whose sole purpose is to be popular and well-received by others will be both exhausting and barren. It is very difficult for me to imagine any kind of personal happiness in such a life. In fact, members of overly collectivistic and hierarchical societies (e.g. Japan) report surprisingly low levels of happiness. People are socially conditioned to pay too much attention to others in these societies, at the expense of their own sense of personal freedom. To be happy, people need room to breathe and opportunities (at times) to transcend the expectations, rules, and standards set by others.

I do not mean to suggest that these three conditions are sufficient by themselves, nor that they will guarantee happiness. However, if you aspire to restore or increase your happiness, I would suggest that this is where you should begin. They are crucial – all the rest is detail.

## The keys

→ **The strongest factor is a positive, optimistic and cheerful temperament. If you don't have it yourself, try copying it from others.**

→ **Build a rich social life – not as an obligation, but because it is rewarding, meaningful and fun.**

→ **Look for personal freedom and room to breathe, so that you can transcend the expectations, rules and standards set by others.**

Eunkook M. Suh is a psychology professor at Yonsei University in Seoul, Korea. He obtained his Ph. D. at the University of Illinois, where he was a student of the world specialist on happiness, Dr. Ed Diener. Suh has published influential scientific articles on happiness, culture and the self, which have been referenced over 2,500 times by other researchers. With Ed Diener, Suh has co-edited the book 'Culture and Subjective Well-Being'

*'A large number of the people who are already happy do not lead lives of decadent self-content and stagnation.'*

# The engine of progress

'Time and again, modern-western society is portrayed as the road to unhappiness and depression,' says **Jan Delhey**. 'Yet, this is not what we find in social surveys.'

## Modernity is better than its reputation

Being a sociologist, my main interest is in how living conditions influence human happiness. True, research has time and again revealed that subjective well-being is not simply a reflection of our life circumstances, how rich we are or how prestigious our job is. These things are filtered by our personalities, by values and life goals, by aspirations and comparisons with neighbours. This means, amongst other things, that plenty of adaptation is going on. To a large extent, humans become attuned to good circumstances (more easily) and ease into bad ones (less easily). Yet despite such filters and adaptation processes, living conditions *do* influence how we feel about our lives.

**Within nations,** research constantly finds that people who are objectively well-off are more satisfied with their lives than the poor and deprived. There is a satisfaction gap between those at the top and those at the bottom of the social ladder. Popular lore claims that you can't buy happiness. Even so – and contrary to the received wisdom – happiness does, at least, tend to be closely related to income and affluence. Yet the satisfaction gap between the 'haves' and the 'have-nots' is not equally large everywhere. Indeed, it is much smaller in rich societies than in poor ones.

**Across nations,** there is a clear pattern that happiness is to be found in places which are characterised by good living conditions. People are, on average, happier in wealthy, free, well-governed, egalitarian, tolerant and capital-rich countries. No wonder that we find the highest happiness scores in nations such as Denmark and Switzerland, and lowest in Iraq and Zimbabwe. And the same conditions which drive average happiness up also drive happiness inequality down. What can we learn from these key findings?

Firstly, good or bad 'objective' living conditions *do* influence our subjective appreciation of life, so that commonly used indicators such as life satisfaction do indeed tell us something about the state of nations. This makes them important for policy-makers. Secondly, cross-national comparisons give us a pretty clear picture of the conditions which are conducive to happiness. By progressing towards these conditions, national happiness levels can be raised. Increasing GDP, no matter what the cost, does not necessarily do the trick, but growing welfare in a broader sense, which trickles down to all strata of society, is quite effective. Thirdly, it is the primarily the modern condition which is most conducive to general well-being, notwithstanding the current fashion for modernity-bashing in current sociological diagnosis. The new 'iron cage' of McDonaldisation; moral decline and growing anomie; the corrosion of character in an ever flexible and fast-changing economy: time and again modern western society is portrayed as the road to unhappiness and depression. Yet this is not what we find in social surveys. **The large majority of people in advanced-modern societies assert that they are quite happy and satisfied with their life.** This does not necessarily prove that the sociological diagnoses are completely bogus. However, they underestimate the benefits of modernity, which include (amongst others) increasing autonomy and freedom to live our lives the way we want. These benefits correlate with the sea change in human values which is taking place in affluent societies, i.e. the switch from materialism to post-materialism.

Does this inevitably mean that we are all going to live happily ever after? Not necessarily. **Progress does not create itself**, it has to be created by human action. It is certainly true that 'happy' people can play an important role in this process, precisely because they are often the people who are most critical about the society in which they live. They have a higher standard of what progress actually means, and they support (much more than unhappy people) the principles that are known to be conducive to human happiness. Hence, a large number of the people who are already happy do not lead lives of decadent self-content and stagnation. On the contrary, it may turn out that the 'happy many' are in fact the true engine of further progress.

## The keys

→ **Good or bad 'objective' living conditions *do* influence our subjective appreciation of life. Cross-national comparisons give us a clear picture of the conditions which are conducive to happiness.**

→ **The large majority of people in advanced modern societies assert that they are quite happy and satisfied with their lives.**

→ **It may turn out that the 'happy many' are the true engine of further progress.**

---

Jan Delhey is Professor of Sociology at Jacobs University in Bremen (Germany). He studied sociology in Bamberg, Groningen and Berlin. His PhD supervisor was Wolfgang Zapf, one of the leading figures in the social indicators movement. His research interests include cross-national comparisons of human happiness, interpersonal trust and social change. The key drivers of his personal happiness are his wife Andrea and his son Niklas.

*'More than 90% of people consider their sense of humour to be average or above average.'*

# The double edge of humour

'Humour is a double-edged sword: it may benefit people but it can also hurt them,' says **Willibald Ruch**. He has been studying humour and laughter for more than 30 years. A recent research project involving some 15,000 people scientifically discovered for the very first time the specific role of humour in relation to general satisfaction with life.

## Improving our sense of humour

Ridicule and sarcasm may have lasting, destructive effects on people. Recently, we conducted a study involving more than 70 nations and we found that a substantial proportion of people throughout the world has pronounced fear of being laughed at; i.e., they suffer from gelotophobia, a fear that has presumably been brought about or intensified by repeated and stressful experiences of having been mocked or not taken seriously during their childhood and adolescence. While cultures have reserved particular words – such as sarcasm, irony or ridicule – to denote the phenomena which often make us feel uncomfortable, we assume that seeing the funny side of things, not taking oneself too seriously, joking, hilarity, amusement, merriment, glee, mirth, nonsense, humour, etc. are intrinsically 'good' for humans. Amongst these terms 'a sense of humour' seems to be the most esteemed. Researchers who have studied the social desirability of human traits

often find humour to be among the top traits – even in lists containing as many as 500 alternative options. To say that someone lacks a sense of humour is an insult, and studies show that displaying a sense of humour is one of the most effective ways of attracting a desirable partner or for looking like a desirable mate. Studies reliably show that more than 90% of those questioned consider their sense of humour to be average or above average. Clearly, everyone wants to have a sense of humour. But what is it good for?

I studied various facets of humour for a number of years: humour as an aesthetic perception, as the ability to create funny situations, as a coping strategy, a world-view, a virtue, a temperament, a predominant mood, and so on. We found that **people reveal their true character by what they think is funny.** Humour can help you to cope with adversity and people who are able to make witty comments are often also creative in other fields. Frequently, we found that humour can have an immediate but short-lived effect on a person's mood and general frame of mind; it makes people playful and lifts their level of cheerfulness. Humour may result in an outburst of laughter, which is often accompanied by short-lived happiness in the form of hilarity or joy. In other words, humour protects us from negative affects (coping with adversity, reducing fear) and encourages positive affects (being amused and elated). Less well documented is the manner in which humour can lower negative (e.g. reduce levels of stress hormones) and enhance positive biological factors (e.g. increase pain tolerance).

But can humour contribute to long-term happiness? Does it do more than offer us short-lived highs and help to reduce the effects of our lows? During a recent study involving 15,000 people, we were able to make a first-ever assessment of the correlation between humour and general satisfaction with life. Interestingly, we found that people with a more developed sense of humour tended to be more content with their life. The greater the humour, the greater the contentment. However, correlation does not prove causality. For this reason, we developed a series of tests to see if we could improve a person's sense of humour – and then measure its effects. It is commonly assumed that a sense of humour is immutable and there is indeed some empirical evidence for a heritability of humour. Nevertheless, with a structured 8-step programme we were able to achieve significant sense of humour increases in a sample of more than 100 participants. The programme consisted of a series of ordered of steps, ranging from easy (e.g. finding humour in everyday life, rediscovering the child in the adult, verbal humour, etc.) to difficult (e.g. laughing at yourself, humour under stress). Strikingly, it was clear that the participant's general satisfaction with life increased in line with the increase in their sense of humour. Moreover, this effect was still present during later follow-up testing. In a different study, we found that keeping a humour diary – taking time each evening to write down the funny things that happened during the day – had a similar effect. These results imply that **humour can be trained and has a causal effect on life satisfaction**; i.e. the cognitive appraisal that we are living our lives well.

In other words, developing humour skills and building up humour memories do have a beneficial effect on our well-being. Humour is associated with pleasure in life. It helps us to maximise positive and minimise negative affects. Adopting a more composed view of life and seeing things in their proper perspective is helpful. 'Always look on the bright side of life,' as the Monty Python team says. If we develop a philosophical sense of humour, we won't take everything too seriously and we will be better able to deal with the life's adversities. However, humour is also for sharing, and others will occasionally need your help to lighten up when they are too serious and or to cheer them up when they are too gloomy. Furthermore, helping others is a source of contentment, and humour often helps us to achieve this. In short, humour needs to be cultivated for the benefit of the individual, his or her immediate peers and society at large. Humour has the potential both to be destructive and to contribute to a better life. It affects short-term and long-term forms of happiness. Not surprisingly, humour was considered to be a cardinal virtue in the 19th century. However, it is only now that we are beginning to understand the value of humour as a factor for enhancing people's lives beyond the level of mere entertainment.

## The keys

→ **Most of us want to have a sense of humour but are afraid of being laughed at.**
→ **Humour protects us from negative affects and encourages positive affects.**
→ **Humour can be trained and has a causal effect on life satisfaction.**

Willibald Ruch was born in Austria and is currently a professor of psychology in the Department of Psychology at the University of Zurich (Switzerland). He first started studying humour and laughter 30 years ago and more recently became interested in the perspective which positive psychology provides to research and application.

# *Different people...*

Even twins follow different paths to find their happiness. So why should the same route to happiness work for you, your friend, your partner, your neighbour or your colleague? 'I've seen friends taking the same advice for happiness with differing degrees of success and I realised that the starting point in my research of happiness should be our individual differences,' says **Andreja Avsec**. 'I know that what works for me probably won't work for you.'

## ... different recipes

I cannot imagine that all the different recipes for happiness will be suitable for every single person. For example, suggestions about the best way to organise your life – such as making lists, not procrastinating, planning and fulfilling goals – is not help much to someone who is already a perfectionist. For a woman who devotes herself each day to her family, her children and to many others, it is clear that positive interpersonal relationships are crucial for her experience of happiness, but she will probably needs something 'extra' before experiencing true happiness: perhaps a little a bit of hedonistic pleasure. Similarly, a self-confident individual, with high self-esteem and narcissistic tendencies, will not be helped towards greater happiness by exercises in front of the mirror, repeating affirmations about what a worthy person he really is!

Based on these assumptions, I started to study personality predispositions and what they can tell us about happy and unhappy people. I came to the conclusion that they have a great deal to say. I was disappointed in the first instance to discover the degree to which personality defines happiness, cheerfulness, contentment, satisfaction, etc. If you are extravert, you probably experience many positive emotions. On the other hand, if you are neurotic, dissatisfaction is likely to be your daily companion. Of course, I was not satisfied with this somewhat simplistic finding. To be honest, I am a bit of a neurotic myself, and am often dissatisfied with things – and so I could hardly accept the idea that I am predisposed to have a 50% chance of being unhappy most of the time! With a percentage like this, it is clearly worth while making some effort to get to know ourselves. For example, if I know that I tend to perceive stimuli as threats or that I worry too much, I can be aware of these tendencies and I can try to judge them differently in particular situations.

Individuals sometimes (consciously or unconsciously) follow advice for happiness which intensifies their natural predispositions. But studies of gender stereotypic personality traits indicate that extreme traits seldom contribute to happiness. Personality traits stereotypically attributed to males (agentic traits) include: principled, independent, competitive, courageous and dominant; while personality traits stereotypically attributed to females (communal traits) include: sensitive to the needs of others, affectionate, warm, attentive and compassionate. Agentic and communal traits are beneficial for the individual's well-being but only when they are not expressed in an extreme form. Being self-confident and dominant is beneficial to your well-being, but being arrogant or aggressive (both extreme expressions of agentic traits) is not, because this extreme orientation toward the self contradicts your orientation toward others. Likewise, being warm-hearted and understanding is beneficial to your own well-being and the well-being of others, but being servile and gullible (extreme expressions of communal traits) is not, because these traits prevent the necessary expression of agentic traits.

*'Being self-confident is beneficial to your well-being, but being arrogant is not.'*

It is interesting to note that many studies have confirmed that agentic traits contribute to an individual's well-being, whereas communal traits do not. This sounds egocentric and is probably not what most of us expect. However, the problem with these studies is that well-being was in most cases assessed on the basis of self-esteem questionnaires. Fortunately, positive psychology also directs psychologists to analyze the real meaning of well-being in more precise terms. More specific assessments of well-being indicate that both orientations are important to happiness. An individual must be independent, courageous, even dominant, but at the same time should balance this orientation towards the self and others with traits such us warmth, tenderness and compassion.

## The keys

→ **Become aware of your personality traits and predispositions, and take them into account when deciding your path to happiness.**

→ **Be aware that the intensification of your natural predispositions to extremes is usually not beneficial for your well-being.**

→ **Try to balance two basic orientations in your life: towards yourself and towards others.**

Andreja Avsec is a senior lecturer in the Department of Psychology at the University of Ljubljana (Slovenia). Her research programme focuses on personality, gender differences and positive psychology.

# The focus of our energy

'In India people are always seeking to achieve the continuous state of happiness (Annanda) known by different names such as Kevalya, Nirvana, Samdhi, etc., as found in different scriptures.' Dr. **Hardik Shah** connects the focus of our energy to our search for happiness.

The *Bhagavad Gita* is a sacred Hindu scripture, considered to be among the most important texts in the history of literature and philosophy. It is part of the *Mahabharata* and, amongst other things, it states: 'Of all gifts, good health is the greatest. Of all wealth, contentment is the greatest. Among kinsmen, trust is the greatest. Freedom (Nibb-ana) is the ultimate happiness'. The ancient *Taittiriya Upanishad* describes the various degrees of happiness enjoyed by the different beings in creation. It states that: 'Life is art, and the whole life of man is a story of self-expression. We suffer if we do not express ourselves.' This implies that if we are able to express ourselves fully, this will bring us happiness.

One recent research study at the University of Wisconsin-Madison has shown that **people can train themselves to be compassionate**, and that there are actual physical changes in their brains when they think compassionate thoughts and do compassionate deeds. If it has been observed that we can learn compassion – just as it has been observed that we can learn to be helpless or sad – then why can't we learn to be happy, and train ourselves to be happy in different situations? Some of our actions are half hearted, with little or no emotion, with no real conscious purpose and with no real integration between self and goals. Actions of this kind lead to unhappiness. In contrast, our actions with total integration, conscious effort and genuine emotion often make us happy. In particular, conscious effort makes us aware of our senses during our actions. Conscious effort, sensible emotional commitment and training can therefore contribute towards the learning of happiness and may help us to discover the final art of being happy.

Many dark forces cast shadows in our life and act as passive forces or hindrances for happiness. They make our actions more mechanical and less sensitive. We need to explore the origins of these forces in the field of positive psychology, which can help us to replace the mechanical and unconscious parts of our life with more conscious efforts, which will allow us to explore and realise our own potential to create happiness. **Sensitivity and emotions play a very critical role in these actions.**

# Hardik Shah

We need to be sensitive to the needs and expectations of 'significant others', in order to make the conscious efforts that will help us to reach our goal. To train ourselves in the learning of happiness, we need to focus on the conscious parts of our being: instinct, moving, thinking, emotion and sex. And we shouldn't focus our energy exclusively on the factors which make individuals happy, but also on exploring the deeper roots which, if cultivated and nurtured, make mankind as a whole both happy and joyous.

Dr. Hardik Shah has a doctorate in management from Nirma University in Ahmedabad and is currently working as an assistant professor at the Academy of Human Resource Development, one of the leading HRD institutions in India. His major interests include learned helplessness, appreciative inquiry and competency building.

# *Changing the focus*

In international rankings for the national degree
of happiness, Thailand scores better than France or Italy.
Economist Dr. **Sauwalak Kittiprapas** looks for the reasons
behind this result and has been involved in public policy focusing
on improving happiness in her native country: 'While searching
for happiness from outside, we finally find that real happiness comes
from inside our own selves'. An international change of focus.

## The new weight

When happiness is talked about, people in different cultures may understand the term
in different ways. They can each use different concepts, words, and values. Moreover,
happiness itself also has many different levels, starting from the lowest level of material
gain to the highest level of a clear conscience. However, it seems that the factors affecting
the higher levels of happiness are intangible, involving concepts such as freedom, wisdom,
'positive' values, quality of mind, etc. This implies that policies which simply focus on
promoting material wealth (reflected by Gross Domestic Product, GDP) have ignored
many of the more important aspects which contribute towards the higher levels of human
happiness. Policy-makers have spent a lot of money to boost economic growth, which they
believe can raise the happiness of their populations; whereas promoting real happiness
through the inner-self can be achieved at low cost.

We *SEARCH* **for HAPPI**

**OUTSIDE.** *But real happiness comes from* **INSIDE.**

**NESS** *from*

On the basis of the various messages that I have picked up from the national and international exchanges for which I have worked, I would suggest that we need a paradigm change in development policy and a rethinking of conventional economic assumptions relating to human behaviour. Buddhist economic theory appears to offer an alternative paradigm towards happiness. Traditional objective measurements are no longer sufficient to indicate the well-being and happiness of people. Consequently, subjective well-being measurement is also needed to assist in better policy-making. This means that useful policy implications can be drawn from subjective well-being research; for example, reducing poverty as well as social and economic inequality; meeting the basic needs of the poor; enhancing people's standard of living; keeping people healthy and educating them well; utilising technology to improve general well-being; improving employment opportunities and working conditions; promoting social capital based on trust, unity, family relationships and social networks; promoting freedom and a clean environment; supporting self-contentment and positive values, spiritual well-being and intellectual development.

This being said, there is no 'one-size, fits-all' policy. The combination of public policies appropriate for each particular country will be variable, depending on that country's specific circumstances (levels of socio-economic development, culture, religion, political system, degree of openness, etc.). That is why micro-research on happiness is important: it provides useful insights which allow the development of detailed policies better suited to groups, societies and nations with different cultures.

Although research has concluded that wealth is not unimportant, its dominance in relation to happiness tends to decline at the higher levels of income and may have no real effect on happiness in the long-run. If happiness is to be the goal of public policy, policy-makers will need to shift their traditional policy focus – attempts to encourage increased GDP – and instead give more weight to others levers, such as poverty reduction, especially in poorer countries and societies where income levels are too low to cover basic needs. The meeting of such basic needs not only increases the happiness of the poor directly, but a certain degree of income gain would also produce more happiness indirectly (as a result of the diminishing marginal return of happiness in relation to income). In addition, given the negative effect of social comparison and income inequality on individual and societal happiness, it is rational for public policies to aim at a reduction of poverty and income disparity as a means of increasing the country's overall happiness. Moreover, in order to reduce the negative impact of social comparison, the concepts of self-contentedness, acceptance of ones lot and intellectual and spiritual development should all be promoted.

According to Buddhist economics and philosophy, the origin of happiness is linked to a particular state of mind and wisdom; in other words, a well-trained mind can bring happiness. Each individual can apply this philosophy to his or her own life and can observe changes inside his or her mind. While searching for happiness from outside, we finally find that true happiness is to be found inside ourselves.

## The keys

→ **The traditional focus on material wealth does not always improve happiness.**

→ **Promoting real happiness through the inner-self can be achieved at low cost.**

→ **Public policies should aim at reducing poverty and income disparity, rather than boosting high economic growth.**

Dr. Sauwalak Kittiprapas is founder and Director of the International Research Associates for Happy Societies (IRAH) and former Director of the Public Policy Development Office (PPDO) in Bangkok (Thailand). She is an economist, who has published many articles on happiness and is also author of the book 'Happiness: New Paradigm, Measurement, and Policy Implications'. She says she has found greater personal happiness by being involved in happiness issues.

# The new framework

**A vital problem in research regarding happiness is the lack of a commonly accepted framework.** In Western academia, psychology and neuroscience provide an explanation of human feelings and behaviour in scientific terms, whereas in Eastern studies spirituality and religion are considered essential, due to their role in understanding the subtle and subjective dimension of human behaviour and the environment, both materially and socially.
I tried to build a framework which identifies happiness patterns by making use of both Western and Eastern concepts of happiness. The two main applied theories are Experienced Utility and Buddhist Economics. Although these two theories differ substantially, they share their emphasis on happiness as cognition.

→

The conclusion is that **if an individual can live with balance in terms of his body, his mind and the environment, this balance can lead to happiness.** This implies that it is not only the variables of self-dimension which matter; within the individual's environment, society and nature also provide significant influences. This happiness framework is constructed in order to explain human happiness in a holistic perspective, and to show how it relates to eastern culture. Under the Buddhist Economics concept, happiness at the 'self' level, or the level of the body and mind relationship, can be obtained from practice in perception, concentration and wisdom, which are the core elements of the teachings of Buddha. However, environments such as family, community, society and nature also encourage human happiness, because human beings are social animals. For this reason, the happiness analysis should consider and incorporate both internal and external factors.

Further studies regarding happiness should create a framework that considers both objective and subjective issues, as well as cultural constraints, in order to lay the foundations for the study of human happiness, which may become a new paradigm in developing the traditional economic model.

Kanokporn Nitnitiphrut (Thailand) graduated in economics with a thesis on happiness and has designed a common framework of happiness for the East and the West. She is member of the International Research Associates for Happy Societies (IRAH).

## 'Who will survive on an isolated island?'

# Sense of coherence

The opposite of 'bad' is 'not bad', but that is not 'good'. The opposite of 'ill' is 'not ill' but that is not 'healthy'. In our search for health and happiness, we shouldn't focus on illness and unhappiness, but on their opposites. Dr. **Sakari Suominen** unravels the origin of health: salutogenesis and the sense of coherence. Problems, he says, are inevitable in life. The trick is how you deal with them.

## The origin of health

It is inevitable that we will encounter various problems in everyday life. In fact, a total avoidance of such problems will ultimately lead to a loss of the things which make life worth living. The decisive factor in determining whether or not these 'encounters' cause a long-term breakdown of well-being is the level of generalised resistance resources which are at the individual's disposal. These resources are the means by which we are able to solve the problems of everyday life. They can be directly linked to ourselves (e.g. 'personal skills and education'), or they can be provided by the environment in which we live in (e.g. 'help from friends'). If these resources are sufficient, problems can usually be solved. Successfully coping with problems can even promote well-being. We all know the good feeling that occurs when we manage a difficult task. However, in the opposite circumstances, we can experience an unpleasant feeling of overwhelming strain and stress. In the long run, it is this stress which is believed to be responsible for the breakdown of both our health and our well-being.

I have built my research on the work of Aaron Antonovsky. He unravelled the mystery of health and introduced the term 'salutogenesis', which could be translated as 'the origin of health'. He focuses on causes of health – or, in broader terms, the causes of well-being – rather than the opposite (i.e. the causes of illness and unhappiness). A central concept in his theory is sense of coherence (SOC). This is a global orientation that expresses the extent to which an individual perceives her or his life as comprehensible, manageable and meaningful. This encompasses three universal dimensions of human life.

→ **Comprehensibility** refers to the individual's intellectual capacity, i.e. the ability to memorise, to appraise and to draw ones own conclusions.

→ **Manageability** refers to a person's readiness to be in interaction with the community in which he or she lives, i.e. the willingness to co-operate with others, in order to get things done.

→ **Meaningfulness** refers to an individual's perception that life has some deeper meaning beyond the 'trivia' of everyday existence. For instance, this feeling can be acquired by taking care of one's children or other loved ones.

What then does a strong SOC mean? It refers to a person's readiness to make the most of the resources provided to him or her. To give a simple example, if two persons are stranded on an isolated island, one with a strong SOC and one with a weak SOC, the person with the strong SOC will be better able to utilise the resources provided by the environment and will have a greater chance of survival than the person with a weak SOC. In survey research, strong SOC has been found to associate independently with good health (determined in various ways). This means that this association cannot simply be explained by common underlying third factors which explain both SOC *and* good health (for example, a high level of education). The implication is that a strong SOC can protect health. To date, however, there is no clear evidence to show how SOC could be strengthened, and more research is needed in this field.

Happiness can be divided into two different types of feeling: a more intense, sometimes even instantaneous, emotional experience or a more thought-based sensation, best characterised by concepts such as contentment or life satisfaction. These latter concepts refer to the extent to which the individual feels that he/she has achieved the various personal goals in their life.

But how are the concepts of SOC and happiness interrelated? According to survey results, in many ways they are alike, or at least have features in common. For instance, people who claim to be happy and people with a strong SOC are both less likely to suffer from depression.

Having said this, in theoretical terms the concepts differ in an interesting way. It is easy to imagine that a person with a strong SOC is likely to be happy most of the time. But this is not necessarily the case. On the contrary, one of the features of people with a strong SOC is their ability to maintain their spirits and their belief in their ability to overcome their difficulties in the long run, even in the presence of considerable strain or when confronted with unpleasant life events, such as a divorce. On the other hand, a person who is happy cannot perceive their life situation as being difficult or dissatisfying. In other words, the concept of SOC relates to the resources which can be utilised for the creation of happiness, whereas happiness itself is more about the outcome, i.e. how a person feels. This means that the reverse is also true: the experience of happiness and strong SOC do not necessarily coincide. A person can be happy, but if their SOC is weak, their happiness can be impaired by even minor setbacks. This is not the case if their SOC is strong.

The concepts of happiness and salutogenesis do not contradict each other. In fact, they more or less complement each other. The former deals with the outcome, whereas the latter deals with a potential mechanism which may eventually lead to that outcome. The concept and theory of salutogenesis therefore provides an interesting approach towards the conditions necessary for happiness.

## The keys

→ **Problems in life are inevitable. Successfully coping with these problems promotes well-being.**

→ **One of the causes of health and well-being is sense of coherence (SOC): a global orientation that expresses the extent to which an individual perceives his life as comprehensible, manageable and meaningful.**

→ **Happiness itself is an outcome. Salutogenesis and sense of coherence deal with the resources that can be utilised for the creation of this outcome.**

Sakari Suominen is an associate professor in the Department of Public Health at the University of Turku (Finland). He is a medical doctor, a public health researcher and an academic teacher of medical students. His studies have focused on sense of coherence and health, the health of children and adolescents and health care research. He has also worked within the field of authority supervision and guidance for health care and social services. Sakari has a passion for wooden boats.

# *Living a lie*

Do the test. Watch a sitcom, movie or drama on television and notice how many of the problems are caused by someone being dishonest. Dramas wouldn't be possible if there were no lies. We seem to tell at least between two and five lies a day. Sometimes they make life run a little bit easier. Dr. **Claire Beazley** puts the finger on a lie that might seriously block happiness: the lie about failure.

## Honesty and failure

One essential of inner well-being is to be consistently honest about yourself, and with yourself and others, in what you say and what you do. Behaving honestly is something you should do all the time; it should be a way of life. All possible outcomes should be accepted, explored and shared. This involves listening to and acting on feelings as well as thoughts. **Feelings are friends**; they are a minute by minute status report, telling you how you are getting on with the world around you. Feelings alert you to successes and problems very early on, allowing you to fine-tune your actions. My research on taking sick leave for minor illness, which many employers believe is wimpy, selfish or lazy, shows that people who listen to their feelings and make choices that accord with their own internal needs actually take less sickness leave. Honesty also involves understanding that if something is really experienced by you, it is really true for you in your current state of being and awareness. It also involves accepting that the same thing may not be true for another person.
Does being honest mean selfishly blurting out anything and everything regardless? No. A mentor of mine suggested that everything you say should fulfil any two of these three criteria: it should be honest, necessary or kind.

# 'Honest failure is a misunderstood friend.'

**If acting honestly all the time is such a good idea, why don't we do it?** The main reason is that it requires honesty about failure as well as success. In many societies, people who claim to be wiser and right more often than other people enjoy massive prestige and material reward. This cannot be justified if they fail just like other people. The problem is that some failure is inevitable; no one knows enough to always accurately predict what will be true for themselves, let alone everyone else. So the wealthier we become and the wiser we believe ourselves to be, the more we fear to lose, the more we demonise failure and the more we shy away from honesty. My experience is that honest failure is a misunderstood friend whom you should welcome as an inspirational companion and teacher. Research on organisations and businesses which treat success and failure even-handedly and seek to learn from failure rather than punish it, shows that they are more successful and have higher levels of worker well-being than failure-intolerant workplaces. Shared failures can be an opportunity for everyone to learn. Did you know that the post-it-note and bakelite, the first plastic, are the outcomes of failed experiments? If you were someone who knew everything, got everything right and never failed, you would have nowhere new to go, nothing to learn and you would not be reading this book.

What is the outcome of suppressing truth? My experience with the epidemic of stressed patients who can no longer cope with work is that they know what is wrong and what needs to be done. However, they have suppressed this knowledge because **they believe that the consequences of being honest will be more painful than the daily burden of living a lie.** Instead of conforming to modern medical practice and labelling them as depressed and anxious, I tell them that their distress is a healthy, truthful alarm system begging them to be honest, because the burden of untruth has become impossibly heavy. Suggesting this alternative viewpoint almost always brings a sense of release and freedom – and the ring of truth. Released into acting honestly, they can stop trying to live the lies and allow themselves to be an open, honest failure (being off work with stress is the big failure of our time) or have the courage to expose the failures of others.

# Praise and flattery

People know themselves surprisingly well and flattery is often recognised as dishonest, thereby leading to future mistrust. When it comes to praise, Carol Dweck found that praising the qualities of the action or event, rather than the person who did it, lessens anxiety about maintaining the same high standard every time. People are more likely to persevere in the face of difficulty in future and try new things. For example, it is better to say 'that was an excellent cake' rather than 'your cakes are always delicious'. When dealing with something which has gone badly, start by giving a factual, concrete description of how it affected you, or by asking the other person to give a concrete description of their own actions and feelings. This is usually less threatening and produces better results than simply offering opinions.

## The keys

→ **Be consistently honest about yourself, and with yourself and others, in what you say and what you do.**

→ **Be honest about your failures, too. Shared failures can be an opportunity for everyone to learn.**

→ **People who are released from suppressing the truth can stop trying to live the lies and allow themselves to be an open, honest failure.**

Dr. Claire Beazley has been working as a doctor for more than 20 years. Latterly, she graduated as a Master of Science in Applied Positive Psychology. She has a particular interest in fitness for work and the relationship between emotional intelligence, self-determination and sickness behaviour. She is doing further research in this area at Lancaster University (United Kingdom).

*'We all have an interest and a role to play in shaping a happier future.'*

# A new view on progress

Thirty high-income countries are part of the international Organisation for Economic Co-operation and Development (OECD). **Jon Hall** leads the global project on measuring their progress. After ten years of research, he knows for certain that they need to widen the lens through which policy-makers view and measure progress. 'By progress I mean an improvement in the equitable and sustainable well-being of a society. Happiness is an important part of that well-being.'

## The direction of our travel

For a good part of the 20th century, there was an implicit assumption that economic growth was synonymous with progress; an assumption that a growing Gross Domestic Product (GDP) meant that life must be getting better. The world now recognises that it isn't quite as simple as that. Despite high levels of economic growth in many countries, many experts believe we are no more satisfied (or happier) with our life than we were 50 years ago; that people trust one another – and their governments – less than they used to; and that increased income has come at the expense of increased insecurity, longer working hours and greater complexity in our lives. Much of the world is healthier and people live longer than they did just a few years ago, but environmental problems, such as climate change, cast a shadow over an uncertain future.

As societies, we manage what we measure and we get what we measure. So it is vital that we measure the right things if we want to travel in the right direction. There continues to be a preoccupation among policy-makers and the media with measuring the performance of the economy. This is, of course, important. But it is also important to remember that a healthy economy is not an end in itself: our economies matter because they provide citizens with access to goods and services, and provide the money to improve other aspects of their well-being (money can be spent on tackling environmental problems, improving our hospitals, and so on). However, if it is well-being that ultimately matters to people, then it is well-being that we should ultimately be paying attention to. Direct aspects of well-being need to be measured – alongside indicators like GDP – if we are to get a balanced view of the genuine progress of a society.

But what things do we need to measure to get this balanced view? It is important to consider both the human system and the ecosystem. Each system contains a range of factors that determine our well-being. Each factor needs to be considered. Direct measures of human well-being should be at the centre of the assessment. Our physical and mental health, our knowledge and understanding, the quality and extent of our work and free time, our material well-being, our levels of freedom and self-determination and the quality of our interpersonal relationships are all very important factors in determining our happiness. Human well-being is supported by three areas of human activity: the economy (our income and wealth), our cultural heritage, and the way we govern ourselves (where aspects like human rights, civic and political engagement, security and violence, trust and access to services all come into play). Our economies, governance and culture are important insofar as they are key supporting pillars to human well-being, rather than being important for their own sake. **Having a strong economy, effective governance and vibrant culture is not well-being in itself,** but these factors do – typically – provide an enabling environment in which human well-being will improve. Ecosystem well-being is also crucially important for people's general well-being, because of the services it provides (clean air, fresh water, food, and so on), as well as the pleasure it brings. To understand the state of our ecosystems we need to look at the health of our land, fresh and sea water, biodiversity, air quality and atmosphere.

So what have I learned about happiness? I know that happiness is not equivalent to GDP. I know that different things make different people happy in different ways. I know that to fully understand our quality of life and well-being we need to look at the sorts of factors I have outlined above. And I know that we don't yet give sufficient attention to these things. I also know that before a society can measure progress and well-being, it needs to know what these things look like. And because we all view things in different ways, defining these concepts more precisely is a conversation that each society should have with itself. There can be few – if any – more important conversations. Everyone should be involved, because we all have an interest and a role to play in shaping a happier future.

## The keys

→   **A healthy economy is not an end in itself. Direct measures of human well-being should be at the centre of the happiness assessment.**

→   **Human well-being is supported by three areas of human activity: the economy, our cultural heritage and the way we govern ourselves.**

→   **Ecosystem well-being is also crucially important for people's well-being.**

Jon Hall has led the Global Project on 'Measuring the Progress of Societies' at the Organisation for Economic Co-operation and Development (OECD). He came to the OECD from the Australian Bureau of Statistics, where he spent seven years, mainly leading a ground-breaking project to publish the first set of measures of Australia's progress. He has a master's degree in statistics from the UK and an executive masters in public service administration from the Australian and New Zealand School of Government. An Australian and British citizen, Jon has also worked for the British public service, for the World Food Programme in Zambia and as a spectacularly unsuccessful house painter, security guard and waiter in the USA.

'*This book is certainly one of the milestones towards the construction of a universal model of happiness.*'

# *Universal happiness*

'When I ask my Chinese patients if they are happy or not, many of them look at me with empty eyes, not knowing how to respond,' says Dr. **Samuel Ho**, who set up the first Positive Psychology Laboratory in China. He says that it is now time to bring the Eastern and Western views together in a universal model of happiness.

## Yin & Yang

If it is odd for people in academia to talk about happiness in America, it is even more so in Chinese societies. The Chinese conceptualisation of happiness is a view of dialectical balance. Ultimately tracing back to the ancient *Yin-Yang* philosophy, everything from the cosmos to human life is a never-ending, cyclic process of change between good and bad, happiness and misery, and so on. In other words, happiness is dependent on unhappiness, and unhappiness is hidden in happiness. Placing too much importance on happiness may disrupt the balance of life. The ancient Chinese thinking of Taoism believes that good things are inevitably followed by bad things. Accordingly, one should not focus too much on happiness, in order not to attract unhappiness into one's life. In fact, when I set up the Positive Psychology Laboratory in my department about ten years ago, some people suggested (sarcastically) that I should set up another 'negative psychology laboratory' on the other side of the building, in order to keep the department's *feng-shui* in balance.

Since then, ten years have passed and positive psychology and happiness are now thriving concepts in academia, in the community, in Hong Kong and in other cities of China.

In my early work in the area of positive psychology, I was fascinated by a study by Ed Diener on subjective well-being, which showed that the Chinese considered happiness to be less important and thought less frequently about it than the peoples of other nations. However, the overall happiness level of Chinese people was not particularly low, in spite of the fact that their purchasing power parity was amongst the lowest of all the nations included in the study. These findings are consistent with my practices as a clinical psychologist. When I ask my Chinese patients if they are happy or not, many of them look at me with empty eyes, not knowing how to respond. My question at that time was this: if Chinese people are less inclined to think about their own happiness, might there not be some other indigenous dimensions of happiness which would better indicate their true levels of well-being? Like many of my predecessors, I began to search for answers along the interdependent construal dimension of the Chinese.

As mentioned above, cultivating a balance in life and maintaining good human relationships are the essence of the Chinese philosophy. For this reason, it is understandable that the Chinese understanding of happiness is more interpersonal, in contrast to the more intra-individual western model of happiness. The Chinese often believe that personal happiness may damage social relationships. For instance, individual success may lead to jealousy or envy by others. **Chinese collective culture emphasises the well-being of significant others or groups more than that of individuals.** Mere self-appraisal of one's own well-being may not be enough to unfold the total experience of happiness among the people of such a culture. The patients who have difficulty in answering the question of whether or not they are happy would find it much easier if I simply changed the question, and asked them instead whether or not their wife and children are happy. Their answers are usually a valid indicator of their own happiness levels. I first thought that this interpersonal dimension of happiness was unique to the Chinese people, or, at most, applied only to the peoples of Asia. But when I shared this view in international meetings and conferences, many colleagues from other countries told me that this interpersonal dimension of happiness also reflects to their own experiences at home. This suggested to me that our globalised world may have already moved beyond the era of 'cross-cultural psychology', so that we can now work together to build a universal model of happiness. This *World Book of Happiness* is certainly one of the milestones towards the construction of such a universal model.

Finally, I would like to offer the following ways to happiness, taken from *I Ching* (the Book of Changes), an ancient Chinese book on philosophy. According to *I Ching*, you can nurture your own happiness by sharing your happiness with other people, by making others happier, by forming harmonious relationships and by freeing others from constraints. I trust that these ways of happiness are not only applicable to the Chinese, but to people in other cultures as well.

## The keys

→ **Yin and Yang: happiness is dependent on unhappiness, and unhappiness is hidden in happiness.**

→ **The interpersonal dimension of happiness seems to be universal.**

→ **We may have already moved beyond the era of cross-cultural psychology, so that we can now work together to build a universal model of happiness.**

Dr. Samuel Ho is an associate professor in the Department of Psychology at the University of Hong Kong (China). In 2000, he established the first Positive Psychology Laboratory in China, since when he has been actively engaged in research and clinical work in the positive psychology field. According to Ho, his involvement in the positive psychology movement was one of the most risky yet most satisfying things he has ever done in his life.

*'For the majority of teenagers school is a dull and uninspiring place.'*

# The best teenage drug

MTV asked teenagers what makes them happy. The answer was not what most worried, weary parents might think ('sex, drugs and rock 'n roll?'). Spending time with the family was the top answer. Their heroes? For half of them: their parents. **Katie Henson** is not surprised: 'Adolescence doesn't have to be a problem.' She has found the best drug for teenagers: flow.

## The school for success

The teenage years tend to be seen as problematic, with traditional psychological research and media portrayals focusing on topics such as teen pregnancy, substance abuse, violence, suicide, eating disorders and academic difficulties. Positive psychology holds an alternative view of adolescents, believing that most teenagers will be well behaved and will not become delinquents, addicts or dropouts. Indeed, less than 10% of families with adolescents experience serious relationship difficulties. Even so, the view that adolescence is a period of high trauma, stress and delinquency has prevailed for many years. A great deal of research into adolescence has focused on educational attainment and has tried to unpick the reasons why particular groups tend to perform poorly in their schooling. Positive psychology offers many theories that may help understand poor academic performance amongst adolescents. One of the keys is 'flow'.

Many research studies have found that the occurrence of flow is associated with beneficial outcomes in adolescents, such as increased concentration, enjoyment, happiness, strength, motivation, self esteem, optimism and future mindedness. These findings remain valid even when other factors such as socio-economic status, academic grades and ethnic background are taken into account. Researchers have also found that **adolescents who spend more time in flow are happier, more cheerful, friendlier and more sociable.** In addition, flow has also been found to be positively associated with intrinsic motivation and enjoyment in adolescents, and negatively associated with pessimism. Adolescents who experience few periods of flow tend to be more bored, less involved, less enthusiastic and less excited.

Adolescents spend the majority of their time in compulsory education. Consequently, the occurrence of flow within the school setting is perhaps the most important area on which future research should focus. Researchers have already confirmed that for the majority of teenagers school is a dull and uninspiring place. In fact, the boredom is so commonplace that most teens consider tedium to be a normal part of their development. However, for those students who do attempt to engage positively with the education system, the benefits are great. For example, students who experience high levels of flow have higher levels of commitment to their education and higher achievement rates than their low flow peers, with the amount of flow experienced during an academic course being a better predictor of success than measures of scholastic aptitude. However, it is not clear from these studies whether these beneficial outcomes are due to the flow experienced whilst engaged in academic activities or the tendency for flow activities to become preferentially replicated, meaning that the adolescents who experience higher levels of flow tend to engage in more schoolwork because they find it intrinsically rewarding. On average, high-flow students spend seven hours more per week engaged in productive activities than low flow students. Furthermore, high flow students also spend more time engaged in schoolwork and homework and less time watching television.

School-related activities were found to create the most flow in teenagers, but if we want to actively create a learning environment that is conducive to flow experiences, then it is beneficial to examine the types of learning that are most likely to lead to flow. Exams, individual work and group work all produced above average levels of flow, whereas listening to the teachers give presentations and watching educational videos provided few flow opportunities. The scholastic subjects that tend to lead to the highest levels of flow experience are vocational courses, computer sciences and the arts. Of the academic subjects studied in schools, mathematics produces the highest levels of flow, while subjects such as English and science have much lower levels and history is consistently found to be the least flow-inducing subject.

Flow is highly beneficial for teenagers who are able to experience it. Not only do they perform better academically (which will positively impact their future lives), but they are also happier, more motivated and optimistic. Since flow is so beneficial in academic settings, educators may wish to keep the theory of flow in mind when designing future curriculums. If we can engage teenagers and teach them how to find flow in their tasks and activities, they are more likely to lead focused, engaged and happier lives.

## What is flow?

Flow is a concept coined by psychologist Mihaly Csikszentmihalyi. It refers to an experience which is totally absorbing, so that time seems to pass in an instant and we become unaware of everything going on around us, even hunger, temperature and self-consciousness. Flow is thought to be highly beneficial for our happiness. The experience occurs when we become engaged in a challenging but controllable activity that requires a high level of skill. Activities which produce flow experiences are intrinsically motivating and as a result they are valuable, in that they produce a state of being that is an end in itself. Furthermore, such activities are also believed to allow an individual to flourish and function at their best levels of performance.

## The keys

→ **Adolescence doesn't have to be a problem.**
→ **Flow is highly beneficial for teenagers: they are happier, perform better and are more motivated.**
→ **Educators must create stimulating learning environments, with tasks and activities which are conducive to flow experiences.**

Katie Hanson is a graduate of the MAPP program (MSc Applied Positive Psychology) at the University of East London. She has a keen and varied interest in all areas of positive psychology, well-being and happiness. She is currently working at Sheffield Hallam University in England, researching student well-being and success, with a particular focus on how we can predict and foster academic success amongst students who are underrepresented in higher education and who traditionally underperform academically.

# The Child and Youth Well-Being Index

Happiness is the product of our experience of life in all its social,
psychological and physical dimensions.

For the past years, I have been involved in a project which is seeking to assess trends
in the well-being of America's children and young people since 1975. In other
words, we seek to provide information which indicates whether the well-being
of young people on average, and for various subgroups of this age range,
is improving, deteriorating, or staying the same. If changes are occurring, we then
seek to identify the areas in the lives of our children in which these changes are
taking place. The project reports to the American public on these issues every year.
The Child and Youth Well-Being Index (CWI) is a composite index, similar
to a Consumer Price Index, based on dozens of social indicators relating to
the well-being of children and young people. Our findings indicate that in terms of
their happiness young people respond to the same aspects of their lives as adults
in similar studies. More specifically, these are the most important indicators of
what makes children and young people happy:

→   1.  Stable, supportive social relationships with family and friends.
→   2.  Having a fulfilling life and being emotionally stable.
→   3.  Living in a safe environment, free from the fear of crime.
→   4.  Being in good health.
→   5.  Participating in community institutions, such as schools.
→   6.  Doing well and gaining status in those institutions, realising their potential.
→   7.  Having a good level of access to material goods and services.

Kenneth C. Land is Professor of Sociology and Demography
at Duke University (USA). He is the author or co-author of over 200 books,
book chapters, journal articles and reports on mathematical and statistical
models for the social sciences, demography, criminology and social indicator/
quality-of-life studies.

*'It is not about the glossy magazine style happiness that links sex and smiles through the retelling of orgasmic tales.'*

# And what about sex?

'Sexual energy can be used to heighten your overall vitality and passion for life. It can act as a motor for the creation of art, writing, music, or even for social or political ambitions. When sexual energy flows naturally, we experience the greatest possible harmony in our human relationships,' says **Cassie Robinson** in London.

## The rich tapestry of sex

In 1994, a gathering of sexuality scientists declared: 'Sexual pleasure, including autoeroticism, is a source of physical, psychological, intellectual and spiritual well-being.' Nevertheless, today's public debate about sexuality is still primarily focused on risks and dangers: abuse, addiction, dysfunction, infection, paedophilia, teen pregnancy and the struggle of sexual minorities for their human rights. Public discourse about the physiological and psychosocial health benefits of sexual expression, including its positive physical, intellectual, emotional, and social dimensions, has been almost entirely absent.

In my research, I have sought to bring to life the rich tapestry and multidimensionality inherent in the different ways in which people experience and embody their sexuality, and to link these factors to well-being and happiness. By moving my research away from the performance definitions of sexual response – in other words, by not viewing it through a medical, consumerist or political lens – I have instead supported the possibilities of

an erotic consciousness that is complex, transformative and evolving. In referring to happiness, **I do not mean the glossy magazine style happiness that links sex and smiles through the retelling of orgasmic tales**, which is still so focused on performance and aesthetics. Instead, I have used the hedonic/eudaimonic paradigm to consider well-being; hedonism being the desire for stability and familiarity, with resistance to change, whilst eudaimonia aligns itself with a striving for change, meaning, possibility, curiosity and interest. By talking about sexual expression as part of the eudaimonic well-being domain, we move away from the tendency to see it only as something that has to be managed or controlled.

My research established a number of factors linking sexual expression with well-being. These included the emotional aspects of sexual expression that impact on connectivity with oneself and with others, the process of self-awareness, self-acceptance, taking owner- ship, taking action, becoming alive, integrating into a whole and finding balance in relation to one's sexual self, as well as the enabling energies that it generates and the developmental and transformative impact which results. The findings suggest that by aligning the positive affects of sexual expression with eudaimonic well-being, the province of sexuality develops a wider and more important meaning. **Sexuality offers a way to discover the potentialities of each person**, the realisation of which leads to their greatest fulfilment.

People seeking to deepen or improve their happiness can do so by embracing sexuality as a central aspect of their life and by declaring their intention to expand their experience, understanding and application of this magnificent energy. By learning and discovering their authentic sexual self, participants in my research described how the expression of this energy opened them up to the world, giving a sense of wholeness, flow and aliveness. By looking beyond the physical performance of the sexual act to include the emotional, relational, and spiritual dimensions of sexual experience, it is possible to connect with a broader view of sexual expression which can expand your sense of self, love, creativity and well-being. Whereas hedonism can motivate people to perceive their internal and external environment in more stable ways, eudaimonism motivates people to understand themselves and the universe by expanding their knowledge structures. I would categorise sexual expression as a vehicle through which to achieve this, and therefore as a way for a person to cultivate their life in the direction of greater complexity and meaning.

A belief system which communicates sexual expression as an enhancing, life-affirming, natural energy, thereby allowing individuals to respect, value and own their own selves, will also allow them to accept others better on a deeper level. Perhaps most importantly, once people have the permission and information necessary to become their best sexual selves, they are more likely to demand (and create) a social system that works better for everyone, not only in matters relating to their health, their sexual and relational choices, and their pleasure, but also their consideration for one another and how they engage with the world to exploit their full potential for a greater purpose.

Your experience of sexuality is ultimately your own creation and I would encourage you to give your sexuality a vital, positive place in your life, as is your right, allowing you to develop the conditions that integrate your sexuality with your health, your well-being and your life purpose.

## The keys

→ **Reposition sexual expression, so that it is no longer seen as something that has to be managed or controlled.**

→ **Embrace sexuality as a central aspect of life, with the intention of expanding your experience, understanding and application of this magnificent energy.**

→ **When we learn to respect, value and own ourselves on a sexual level, we will also be better able to accept others on a deeper level.**

Cassie Robinson is a positive psychologist and creative pioneer (Master of Science in Positive Psychology at the University of East London, United Kingdom). Her main interests lie in social potential and social emergence. She is a researcher in Social Innovation, Design and Psychology in London.

*'For something to make you happy,*
*you must learn to really love it.'*

# *The power of love*

'We're heading for something. Somewhere I've never been.
Sometimes I'm frightened. But I'm ready to learn. Of the power
of love.' Millions of people know these lyrics from Céline Dion,
one of the best selling artists in the world.
Prof. **José L. Zaccagnini** tends to agree with her.
He explores the real power of love – which takes us
far beyond the pleasures you might expect.

## Three lessons I have learned

**The first thing** I discovered some ten years ago, when I left Cognitive Psychology and took
up 'happiness' as a research topic, was amazing. Although both philosophic and popular
psychology had been asserting for years that happiness is 'obviously' what everybody looks
for in life, I quickly learnt that is not true at all. Most people – during most of history –
have been too busy trying to survive. Human beings, as species, are biologically designed
to survive and to raise children. That is our function. Only in well-developed societies,
where more than the basic needs of life are fulfilled, human rights are guaranteed,
education and health are provided and a degree of free time is available, can a person pay
attention to his/her own happiness, and take this as a personal goal. But even so, most
people in the developed countries of the West do not stop to think about their own

happiness. Instead, they spend their lives **assuming and pursuing what our culture tells us are 'desirable social goals',** such as getting a good job, a good mate and family, amassing money and/or power, enjoying material pleasures (good food, sex, sport, drugs, media entertainment), and so on. And they normally do not check to what extent these goals are really worth the life they (and others) are forced to live to achieve them. That is how our western way-of-life works, but the daily life conflicts which it entails may make us think that perhaps it is far from perfect.

**The second thing** I discovered is something which explains why our cultural models are not perfect. Most of those 'cultural goals' do not guarantee long-lasting psychological well-being. In fact, scientific research shows that none of them make you happy, unless you do deal with them properly. For something to make you happy, you must learn to really love it. Not just need it, or be hooked on it, or can't live without it, or 'I must to have it'. No, you really have to love it. Because it is one thing is to get rid of negative emotions (which happens when you finally get something you think you need) but it is a very different thing to develop positive emotions (something you can only do by loving something/someone). **So it is not only what you have, but how you approach what you have**, that can make all the difference. This is why subjective well-being is more closely related to personality (the way you face life) than to any other matter. There are people who get what they want and are still not happy, just as there are people who do not get what they expect and are happy all the time. For this reason, when people ask me as a psychologist what they must do to be happy, I always say: 'The most important thing is not to embitter your own life by focusing on bad things and disregarding the good things'. All this, of course, helps to explains why research has shown that very rich people are not necessarily happier than the not so rich, and why very powerful or handsome or gifted people are not happier than the rest of us. Even rich countries are not necessarily happier than their less rich neighbours, providing these neighbours have sufficient means to live and human rights are respected. In short, our western way of life does not guarantee happiness.

**The third thing** I learned from my work is that a happy life can be pursued in very different ways. Ways that we can divide under three main headings.
→   The first is trying to get a 'pleasant life'. This means that people search for positive emotions by seeking to acquire things and experiences, such as good food, sex, cars, houses, yachts, travels, music, dance, entertainment, etc. Some people are addicted to pleasure. But the pleasure you get from these kinds of things is not lasting. You get fed up with it very quickly And then it is necessary either to increase the doses or to change to a new type of pleasure. In other words, the happiness and well-being you can get from the 'pleasant life' approach is clearly limited. As a well-known Spanish

philosopher once said, the pleasures of life are sold by the media as a way to freedom and happiness, but *'to follow the desire for pleasure in life is not to be free, but to be a slave of your own desire'*. In the long run, this always moves us away from rather than towards psychological well-being.

→ The second way to seek happiness is by means of an 'engaged life', in which people obtain satisfaction from through interesting work or activities. This usually means devoting your life to art, business, romantic love, literature, your family, your company, etc.. If you really 'love' these activities, you can keep doing them for a long time. As a result, this kind of life can give much more psychological well-being than the 'pleasant life'. Very often, however, this 'engaged' life style means that you will be very self-centred,, so that you do not to pay enough attention to the things outside your scope, including most of the people around you. As I once heard in a film, to be 'honest to yourself' does not justify your being 'dishonest' to everyone else. In other words, an 'engaged' often means that you can become enclosed within yourself. In the end, this leads to an impoverished life, which once gain moves us away rather than towards balanced psychological well-being.

→ Finally, the third option for happiness is the 'meaningful' or 'ethical' life, in which you devote yourself to 'values which are always related to the improvement of other people's lives'. This is the option chosen by the Gandhi's, Mandela's and Luther King's of the world: full commitment to the rights and needs of humanity. But it can also be found in a parents' loving commitment towards the life and happiness of their children. In fact, it includes any way of caring about other people lives. Again, **you must really feel 'love' for the people you care for,** in order to get happiness from your care. For example, if you do it because it is your duty (i.e. Gods 'commands' you to do care), it will not work. This is why religious people are not always happier than lay people. But when you really learn to love other people, you always get a maximum of psychological well-being (as empirical research has shown). In fact, this has been the message of all the great spiritual leaders – Buddah, Jesus Christ, Mohammed – throughout human history. Today, psychologically speaking, we can say (paradoxically) that it is necessary to love people, not only because they need it, but because we need it to be happy.

So if I am asked how to obtain true happiness in life, my advice may seem contradictory. On the one hand, I always begin with the ancient advice of the oracle of Delphi: 'Man, know thyself'. As we now know, to be happy you must 'love' the goals to which you devote your life. So when choosing these goals, make sure that you take a real good look inside yourself; do not just follow what is being said and done around you. Try to imagine what it would be like to achieve these goals. Do you really think that you can reach them?

And most important, try to imagine how much it will cost you and how will you feel once you get there? Do you think that they will give you the fulfilment you seek? **To be happy, you must begin by loving the 'real yourself'** (i.e. your life), and not a false and biased image created by the media or by any other external influence. But on the other hand, I will also tell you to look outside yourself, because we also now know that the best way to be happy is by devoting yourself to other people around you. Be aware of the well-being which can result when you share a peaceful and loving life with other people. Be aware that this type of psychological well-being is better and sounder and more durable than any other kind of well-being which you can reach by other means. And so my final advice, my recipe for happiness, is this: try to build a life in which you do the things that you are good at, in order to improve the quality of other people's lives. And try to do it every single day of your life. You can do it in many different ways, as long as you learn to love what you are doing as a means of expressing your love for other people. Perhaps it will not be easy to find your own way, and it is often easier to follow any external advice. But it is only by persevering with your own way, by making your own choices, that you can finally reach your own happiness. Of course, there is nothing wrong in getting pleasure from life, and it is also a good thing to have work which engages you. But if you do not find a way to relate these things to the positive well-being of others, it will not work. Not for you and not for the rest of world.

## The keys

→ **Only by following your own way can you finally attain your own happiness.**
→ **We can only increase positive emotions by means of loving something or someone.**
→ **Know yourself and use this knowledge for the benefit of others: try to build a life in which you do what you are good at, in order to improve other people's quality of life.**

José L. Zaccagnini studied and worked at the University of Madrid and is currently Professor of Psychology at the University of Malaga (Spain). He worked on artificial intelligence, developed expert systems in the field of psychological diagnosis and published papers on cognitive psychology. Since 1995 he has been working at the University of Málaga with the Cognition and Emotion Research Group, researching within the framework of positive psychology. His main topics of interest are 'friendship' and 'emotional conflicts'.

*'Your time reflects your choices.'*

# Time is the enemy

'Time is the enemy' and 'Time is your friend'. Both sayings are popular in lyrics. In business, time management is one of the most popular courses. But we cannot manage time. The only thing we can manage is our own activity. 'Time is a mustang that you cannot tame.' In her research on happiness, Dr. **Ilona Boniwell** has discovered the crucial importance of the time factor. In the background the lyrics continue: 'Time is a wish, you can throw coins at a fish but you're still gonna have to feed it.'

## Time is a friend

I am really interested in studying people's relationship with their time and the impact that time has on our happiness and well-being. Time is such a central problem nowadays. Learning to balance it is a skill which very few of us possess. Research shows that **satisfaction with our time is one of the most important predictors of our overall well-being.** However, this is not achieved by squeezing every last second, in order to become even more effective. Rather, it is about learning how to be happy with your time, and sometimes this can also mean working less.

The main lessons learnt from my studies include the importance of having some time for yourself on a daily basis. People who claim this 'me time' are much happier with their time as whole. They are more able to find the balance between time for themselves and time for others, time for the things that have to be done and time for the things that they want to do. Another finding is the importance of completing 'something' every day. We are satisfied with our time when we achieve something. It doesn't need to be something big; it can be just finishing a small chunk of a larger project. Finally, only those people who take responsibility for their time are really happy with it. It is all very easy to blame something or someone – your employers, e-mails, workload – but unless and until you assume responsibility for your time, nothing will change.

Do you feel that you are spending your time on what really matters to you or do you feel that time is running through your fingers, leaving no trace? Your time reflects your choices about the way you live your life, and as such offers a key to happiness.

## The keys

- → **Make sure you create some time for yourself on a daily basis.**
- → **Complete at least 'something' every day.**
- → **Only those people who take responsibility for their time are really happy with it.**

Dr. Ilona Boniwell (University of East London, United Kingdom) is the programme leader for the first postgraduate Masters Degree in Applied Positive Psychology (MAPP) in Europe. She is an active researcher and one of the first positive psychologists in the UK. She was the founder and first chair of the European Network of Positive Psychology, organised the first European Positive Psychology Conference, consulted BBC2 on the Happiness Formula series and is the author of the bestselling book 'Positive Psychology in a Nutshell'. She is a prolific speaker and often addresses international psychology and professional audiences.

# A politics of happiness

'It is often claimed that happiness is a very personal thing;
that every person has to find his or her own specific way of being
happy. Even so, I have never researched a topic which turned out
to be so predictable,' says **Mark Elchardus**. He challenges
politicians to create the conditions for 'the greatest happiness
of the greatest number'. These conditions seem to be more
or less the same for everybody.

## A shift from cure to care

The happiness of a sample of about 4,500 Belgians turned out to be extremely predictable,
on the basis of a limited number of variables measuring the conditions under which these
people live, their relationships with others and a number of attitudes. The measure of
happiness used in this study was fine grained. Happiness was measured on the basis
of 36 questions, comprising standard questions about satisfaction with life, an extensive
series of questions concerning satisfaction with different aspects of life (work, family,
neighbourhood, body, etc.), supplemented by questions relating to the moods they had
experienced over the last two weeks. The very high predictability of happiness indicates
that even though the specific way in which we experience happiness might vary from
person to person, the conditions that have to be fulfilled in order to have a reasonable
chance of attaining that happiness are to a large extent the same for everybody.

Such an observation opens the possibility of a politics of happiness. Not, of course, in
the sense that governments could or should be called upon to prescribe happiness or (even
more nightmarishly) prescribe the way in which we ought to be happy. Such horror is
the subject of dystopias, like Aldous Huxley's '*Brave New World*'. Even so, the predictability
of happiness makes a new and fruitful relationship between happiness and public policy

possible. Modern governments can now be expected to create the conditions under which the 'greatest happiness of the greatest number' can be attained. This, to me, seems to be the most important conclusion of the renewed attention now being paid to happiness and the scientific investigations which have ensued. In this short note I want to look at the policy areas which are crucial for such a politics of happiness.

The factors which explain our degree of happiness are quite limited in number. They can be grouped into three categories: conditions, other people and wisdom.

Other people turn out to be crucial for happiness. Not in the sense of Sartre's existentialist *'l'enfer, c'est les autres'*. On the contrary, **hell is the absence of others** and loneliness is the single most important destroyer of happiness. Loneliness often comes as an accident, through the loss of a partner to sickness or divorce. Yet the risk of loneliness, even under averse conditions, is strongly reduced when people have extensive social networks, participate in voluntary associations (do not bowl alone), and spend their leisure time outside the home. This is where governments can play a role, by actively promoting and stimulating voluntary associations, neighbourhood life, leisure time pursuits and cultural life which brings people together and strengthens the social fabric. An additional argument in favour of such a policy is the fact that participation in voluntary organizations and active leisure outside the home are per se associated with higher degrees of happiness, independent of their contribution to the reduction of the risk at loneliness. No evidence was found that watching television makes people unhappy, but it certainly takes up time that could be used for pursuits which contribute more to happiness.

An important condition of happiness is health. It is (one is tempted to add, obviously) more difficult to be happy when seriously or chronically ill. Nevertheless, it is striking that people who are chronically ill, but are assured of sufficient care, either by their family or professional providers, are much more happy (or less unhappy) than other patients who are chronically ill. A politics of happiness has therefore a double responsibility: promoting health and providing care. Health can be promoted through life styles and preventive medicine. A politics of happiness would promote such policies, particularly ones geared towards people with less schooling. **A health-gap is indeed growing between the highly educated and the less well educated**, and it is related less to access to cure than to life style. Happiness therefore requires a shift from cure to care. This is a daunting challenge in European societies with a quickly aging population, a demographic development which is moreover coupled with the threat of an insufficient supply of people willing (and motivated, and able) to provide care. This is a crucial area for a farsighted, daring and innovative politics of happiness.

Another important condition for happiness is financial security. The contribution to happiness of a shift from an average to a high income is (very) modest. For a shift from a high to very high income it is non-existent. In other words, it is largely true that money doesn't make you happy. However, the lack of money can certainly make you unhappy. There is a sharp drop in happiness when one goes from situations where there is sufficient income, and people can 'make ends meet', to situations where there is insufficient income and people cannot make ends meet. Economic insecurity – uncertainty about one's job and future income – is also detrimental to happiness. A politics of happiness should combat both poverty and economic uncertainty. Richard Layard has already pointed out the inherently egalitarian character which a true politics of happiness possesses, simply because it is much easier to make the unhappy happier than to make the happy happier still. Because poverty and economic uncertainty are so detrimental to happiness, a politics of happiness is not only egalitarian, but also shows great similarities with the welfare states, as they have emerged over the last half century in North-Western Europe.

A third important condition is time. The experience of time pressure decreases happiness. Time pressure is endemic during the 'busy' years: between the ages of 25 and 50, when a career has to be made, a family founded, children raised. Time pressure in this phase of life creates a mid-life dip, as a result of which the middle aged tend to be less happy than young people under 25 and older people over 60. **The remarkable thing about time pressure is that its negative effect on happiness is much stronger when people want to 'slow down' or 'take it easy'.** That ambition is often thwarted, and the ensuing frustration causes unhappiness. Contemporary societies should invest in developing innovative time policies, distributing work time, family time and leisure time more evenly and intelligently over the life cycle, taking into account the fact that in the rich societies this cycle has, over the last half century, been significantly prolonged.

With the possible exception of time policies, the policy areas relating to the politics of happiness are familiar. However, if we view them from the vantage point of the greatest happiness for the greatest number, we are invited to look at these policy areas in a new way, which raises a set of new challenges both for the immediate and more distant future.

A politics of happiness does not, of course, eliminate personal responsibility. Even when conditions are favourable, people have to be willing or aware enough to make use of them. Under similar conditions some people are more happy than others, and these differences are to a large extent explained by attitudes such as the willingness and determination to remain the master of one's life, an optimistic outlook or a capacity to be content with what one has (although not too quickly or too easily). These are the attitudes which the Ancients called wisdom, and they are still relevant today – and they are still equally difficult to attain, always demanding a delicate balance. They are also frequently the subject of the many available books, techniques, therapies which offer to assist us in our personal quest for happiness.

A simple way to help in this quest is to compare the experiences of happy and unhappy people, living under comparable material conditions, enjoying similar health, coping with equivalent amounts of time pressure, and enjoying similar wisdom. What counsel can one derive from the way the happy people live? The answer turns out to be disconcertingly straightforward and down to earth: try to become a home owner; ask yourself whether your desire to 'slow down' is not in fact a desire to invest more time in various other pursuits (sports, travel, companionship, reading, gardening, etc.); don't overburden your already well-filled agenda. Every now and then, pause and make a list of your activities. Note if they are necessary and enjoyable. Eliminate activities that are neither necessary, nor enjoyable. Join voluntary associations, meet friends, spent leisure time actively, and don't watch too much television. Treasure friends and cherish friendship; it is a mistake to limit your life to your partner or your family. This seldom brings happiness – even with the very best relationships and families.

## The keys

- → **Governments should actively promote voluntary associations, public health and care provisions, whilst at the same time combating poverty and economic uncertainty.**
- → **Contemporary societies should invest in developing innovative time policies, distributing work time, family time and leisure time more evenly and intelligently over the life cycle.**
- → **Ask yourself whether your desire to 'slow down' is not in fact a desire to invest more time in various other pursuits.**

Mark Elchardus is Professor of Sociology at the Vrije Universiteit Brussel in Brussels (Belgium). He has written numerous articles and books on cultural sociology and happiness. He keeps an eye on recent developments in attitudes and thinking, education and media, with special attention to social and political responsibility.

## '*We are not victims but survivors.*'

# *Two doctors in Mumbai*

'My parents moved to Mumbai when I was just one year old, and I have lived here ever since. I love this city, with all its energy, life, filth, noise and impossible traffic. I have often experienced a feeling of unfairness at the difficulty faced by the poor in gaining access to quality care at affordable costs. Sometimes it seems like the poor have no right to live.' Dr. **Joshi Wasundhara** is looking for happiness in the most difficult circumstances. He starts with two of his colleagues.

## Whatever happens…

My passion is to work on urban health issues for the poor. My vision is of an empowered society with affordable access to quality healthcare for all. To do this, I want to create a strong organisation which can work with government and the private sector, whilst at the same time having its own impact on the health of women and children in urban India. It is all a question of happiness. I have not done any research on this subject, but much of my work is concerned with making people happy in their workplace.

Let me begin with the story of two doctors. Both are paediatricians, both are women and both are survivors. What first struck me was the marked difference in their levels of happiness and energy. Both began their lives in what would be termed as 'normal' families and had 'arranged marriages', which is traditional in India. They were both in abusive relationships, in which they continued for many years, before finally ending them. At the same time, they both continued to pursue their careers. Today, when you meet them, one is a highly successful person, who is involved in many different activities and is full of energy. The other is also reasonably successful, but has an air of melancholy about her, and tends to not achieve all that she could. I was curious about this and decided to listen to them more closely.

The only difference that I could discern is in the story which they tell to themselves and the world about who they are. The first woman almost revels in her achievements and celebrates having overcome the difficulties in her life. **She sees herself as a survivor, who would not be beaten by circumstances. In short, she believed in making her own destiny.** The other woman sees herself as a victim of unfortunate circumstances, believing that fate has dealt her a cruel hand and that her destiny is to suffer. In other words, she sees herself in the image that people around her have casting for her, without ever being truly aware of whom she really is.

What makes some people accept their lot, while others complain and the remarkable few thrive and make the most of it, whatever happens? I raise these questions because I believe they help to define who is happy and who is not. 'Happiness is not the absence of pain.' Happiness is what we do and what we seek to achieve, often in spite of the things which are happening around us. Happiness is being able to celebrate who we are and what we do. It is being able to celebrate, even in adverse circumstances. It is seeing the opportunities presented by these circumstances, and then further celebrating our ability to overcome them. It is the story we tell ourselves.

I live in Mumbai, a crazy, congested and (some might say) dirty metropolis, which is throbbing with life and energy. I work in government hospital, where I come into contact with healthcare workers, doctors, nurses, housekeepers and administrative staff. The hospitals are a bit like the city, crowded and crazy, with much too much work, made worse by inefficient systems and inadequate resources. In every hospital I hear the same refrain: 'our staff is not motivated: how can we change that?'

To answer this, we decided to interview those few members of staff who *were* identified as being well motivated. We hoped that this would help us to understand what keeps people going in this kind of environment. These were people who had made a difference and were successful. They had faced exactly the same circumstances as everyone else, but they had persevered, whereas the others said that these circumstances prevented them from performing even their regular duties properly. Here again, I found the same differentiating factor as with my two doctor friends. The key distinction lies in **the story which people tell themselves about who they are**, the circumstances they face, and whether they see themselves as having the power to make a difference.

Those who were successful did indeed see themselves as being powerful, in the sense that they believed that they could make things work. They refused to be 'victims' and continuously sought ways to cut through (or work around) the complicated red tape and bureaucracy. One doctor said to me: 'When I go into an office to ask for something, I go in believing that it is my right to get it.' Another said: 'I don't give up. I keep on pursuing different lines of approach until I get what I want'. And when they hit an immoveable obstacle or a failure, they simply walk around it and move on.

I am amazed by this ability to focus on the things that work, on the things that can be celebrated in life. It is a remarkable tool for happiness in this world. It allows you to deal with all of life's painful moments, whilst still retaining that happy feeling. This is what our work in the hospitals of Mumbai is all about.

Hospital staff work in a service profession. Except for doctors (and not even all of them), most do not see themselves as contributing to the well-being of society. They are simply doing their job as the hierarchy prescribes. As a result, their stories about their work are not about saving lives or making people better. Instead, they are about having to work hard without recognition. And this makes them unhappy. When we started working with these staff, we wanted to uncover their stories of heroism and healing. And we discovered that there are, indeed, plenty of these stories to tell. Telling them, however, was often an emotional process, but if this process was carried out within a large group, the change in perception – both about self and about others – was perceptible. In short, the value which each member of staff placed on himself and his colleagues increased. The story has changed.

My experience has been that most staff are much happier doing their work after this kind of intervention. There have, however, been two specific challenges in this respect. Firstly, how does you measure this 'happiness'? Secondly, how do you sustain the change? Happiness can become an acquired behaviour, if we can constantly monitor and emphasise the right kind of stories within organisations. I am not advocating that we should not tell stories about the things which are not yet happening the way we want, but we could end these 'negative' stories by examining what strengths already exist to help change.

I sometimes get feedback that my ideas are too idealistic, but when you have seen the changes and have experienced the happiness which they can bring for yourself and others, then it is difficult to ignore their benefits. **In my opinion, it is the simplicity of the idea that makes it seem outlandish.** We all too often think that happiness is complicated, that it is some kind of Utopian place, where there is no pain and no problems. But I believe that happiness is available here and now, to anyone who seeks it. And the problems and the pain are simply a part of the process. All we need to do is to stop searching so hard, to accept and celebrate our strengths and to find the story which allows us to tap into it.

## The keys

→ **Happiness is not the absence of pain. It is what we do, irrespective of whatever is happening around us. Those who are successful see themselves as being powerful. They believe that they can make things work.**

→ **It is the story we tell ourselves, refusing to accept that we are 'victims'.**

→ **When this story-telling process happens in a large group, the change in perceptions – both about self and each other – is noticeable.**

Dr. Joshi Wasundhara qualified as a paediatrician from TN Medical College and Nair Hospital in Mumbai (India). After working for 10 years in the public health system in Mumbai, as a neonatologist in LTMGH (Sion Hospital), he quit and now dedicates his time to working with SNEHA, an NGO of which he is a founding member. 'It addresses our need to reach out beyond the walls of the hospital, preventing the completely unnecessary admission of mothers and newborns into the intensive care, and to work directly with women and children for their health.'

*'Not getting what you want is sometimes a wonderful stroke of luck.'*

# The butterfly questions

'Happiness is like a butterfly: if you chase after it, it will fly away, but if you stay still it will come and alight on your shoulder.' We hear nonsense like this all the time. But how many times in your life has a butterfly landed on your shoulder? There is a reason why it shouldn't: human beings don't have any nectar. **Sergiu Baltatescu** unmasks three other butterfly questions: and suggests that the ideas currently circulating may prove to be wrong.

## Yes or no?

→ **Happiness never lasts?**

The idea of happiness as a temporary state (some call it a *peak experience*), which is achieved in seconds and may disappear just as quickly, is a conception held by many people. There is also a proverb which says: 'Happiness never lasts'. But I don't really agree. While momentary feelings of supreme joy do exist, happiness is different. It has a more continuous nature. It varies with our achievements and failures, and we can nourish it by accumulating bases for our future development. That is why I prefer

to speak in terms of the sustainability of happiness. Just as we are beginning to under-stand the need to use the earth resources responsibly, in order to preserve our collective future well-being, so we should individually invest in our long-term personal happiness by avoiding short-term benefits which may prove to be damaging in time. Use and abuse of drugs, self-deception and material greed are all examples of unsustainable behaviour for happiness. In contrast, continuous efforts towards personal improvement, a preoccupation with cultural and spiritual fulfilment, taking care of our family and friends and altruistic behaviour in general are the sustainable fuels that can help to maintain our chances of long-term happiness. The bases of sustainable happiness can also be laid down through social behaviour, by avoiding damaging social emotions such as xenophobia, religious intolerance and compulsory consumption.

→ **Are we programmed to be unhappy?**

Do you agree with the idea that we cannot escape our biologically determined happiness, and that sometimes we are simply 'programmed' to be unhappy? In fact, quite the opposite is true. Watching my daughter during the very early years of her development, I was amazed by the way in which she looked to extract the joy from every experience. It struck me that we are indeed programmed – but to be happy, not unhappy. Sometimes, however, we confuse the object of this basic and positive drive with the fulfilment of our momentary desires, the things which we consider, at a certain point in our life, will bring us satisfaction. This way of thinking may prove truly detrimental to our happiness. Happiness is one of our goals in life, perhaps our highest goal, but we often change our view on the means of achieving it. A wise man once said: 'Remember that not getting what you want is sometimes a wonderful stroke of luck'. Moreover, while the feeling of joy and its physiological responses are universally human, the ways of acknowledging, feeling and expressing that joy are very different. The only thing that is written into our genes is a broad, general predisposition towards happiness: the concrete realisation of this happiness will differ considerably from one person to another. In other words, whenever we feel trapped on our journey towards happiness, and perhaps despair of ever finding it, we should remember that we are persons with very specific values, tastes and options. We should cherish our inner nature – a nature that is meaningful, creative and open to new things – and realise that it is often the steep and rugged pathway, rather than the paved road, which brings us to happiness.

→ **Is happiness purely individual?**

The concept that happiness is purely individual is very common in our psychological and utilitarian era. However, by studying the history of well-being, I came to the conclusion that –, on the contrary – happiness is a communal experience; it is socially constructed by groups, societies and civilisations. Starting with our early childhood, we acquire the external criteria by which we will interpret our life and which help us to generate satisfaction in that life. For example, in some societies children learn that competitive achievement is the key to happiness: the 'winner takes it all' mentality. In other cultures, the road to happiness means serving others and living in harmony with them. We also learn – but we are not always aware of it – a certain way to feel and express happiness. Each group and society develops its own 'rules of feeling', the way we recognize, interpret and even trigger our emotions. These rules may urge us to feel happy in some situations (for example, on our wedding day), but will restrain our feelings of joy in other less appropriate circumstances (for example, at a funeral). As members of societies, we are also influenced by public moods which develop as a result of social events. We feel happy when our national team wins the World Cup, while we feel sad when a much-respected leader dies prematurely. In this manner, our happiness is dependent in many different ways on the happiness of our groups and societies. This understanding should encourage us to participate in society, in order to contribute to the common good, from which we will benefit in turn. Research has shown that poor people in rich societies may be better off than average-to-rich people in poor societies, simply because they benefit from the economic and social infrastructure created by national wealth: roads, the health system, freedom and cultural opportunities. In a developed and ordered society the public mood is generally optimistic, which inevitably has a degree of positive influence on the members of that society. But the reverse is also true: it is difficult to be happy while being a member of an unhappy group or society. Far from being purely individual, happiness is therefore the common property of us all and can be achieved and developed by socially-oriented policies at both the individual and collective levels.

## The keys

→ **Positive individual and social behaviour make our happiness sustainable.**
→ **We are programmed to be happy, but the way in which we achieve this happiness is largely dependent on our own creativity.**
→ **We are dependent on the happiness of others. Altruism is crucial for our own happiness.**

Sergiu Baltatescu is a sociologist and associated professor at the Department of Sociology and Social Work at the University of Oradea (Romania). While heading towards a career in computer sciences, he became fascinated by the rapid social changes taking place in Romania after the fall of communism in 1989. He became a sociologist focused on cultural change and quality of life, writing his doctoral thesis on 'Happiness in the social context of post-communist Romania'. He has studied happiness in group contexts (adolescents, gender, minorities, immigrants) and has investigated variable factors of subjective well-being relating to national identity, social trust, public mood, feelings of justice and social exclusion.

## 'We lived with 24 people of 4 generations under one roof.'

# Family ties

The number of joint families has decreased significantly in recent times. In the shadow of the Himalayas, **Dev Raj Paudel** has been living under the same roof with twenty-four people of four generations. He has learned the lessons of life from his grandmother: a lady who never saw a classroom but whose leadership was never questioned. The impact of family ties on happiness.

## All under granny's roof

Although it is indeed an almost unique case, the idea of a family consisting of four generations, all living under a same roof in today's modern era, is a matter of surprise for outsiders. But living in a joint family has been a true source of inspiration for me: sharing a common residence, partaking of food cooked in the same kitchen, following the same religion and sharing common property. Today, as I look back, I truly feel blessed and privileged to have had such a granny. I spent more than thirty years of my life with her. And in those years, I undoubtedly learnt some of the most important lessons of my life. Those years also brought me some of my best moments and happiest experiences, the memories of which I still cherish. With her beside us, life was simply amazing. She was 91 years of age, when she finally left us last year.

Originally, we lived in a village characterized by darkness and illiteracy. It was so remote that it took nearly a day of brisk walking to reach the city. Schools were rare back then, but my granny felt that my father and my uncles should go and study. Often, there were heated arguments about whether or not to allocate some of our scarce money to their schooling. But her unwavering determination and her conviction made her sons the first children in the entire village to complete their high school education. Later on, I was the first individual from the entire village to secure first division status at high school level. Even today, I still marvel at the fact that she could have understood the significance of education and its advantages, when she herself had no schooling of any kind (like the entire village). How did she know? Whom did she take as an example?

Despite being illiterate, she never failed to keep harmony in the family. This was no easy task, since for many years no fewer than twenty-four of us lived in the same house. Twenty-four different individuals with different backgrounds, different attitudes and different priorities. Yet her success was no fluke. The pivotal element that kept our spirits high and inspired us to adhere to the family hierarchy was the foundation and the leadership underlying our family structure. She taught us to share, to compromise, to help, to live together and respect others' freedom. This must have set our values and cemented our relations right from the beginning. To outsider, it might seem inevitable that some members of the family must make sacrifices for the survival of the collective family spirit. But this was not the case. **The ultimate outcome was a win-win scenario for everyone in the family.**

Which characteristics made her so successful in her role as family leader? Justice and ethics. A sense of justice was in my granny's blood. No one ever accused her of being biased or of having favourites. She treated all her children and grandchildren the same, no matter who stepped out of line or violated the family rules. A joint family existence is only possible with this kind of impartial leadership. She used to teach us about morality while sitting around the fire after dinner. She did her best to educate her offspring with evidence-based examples. My granny left no stone unturned to keep our family together throughout her life. She succeeded magnificently – and she proved with pride that a joint family is the best way to live.

## The keys

→ **Joint families show the importance of learning to share things.**
→ **Harmony is based on fair and inspiring leadership.**
→ **The basic elements in family ties are justice and ethics.**

Dr. Dev Raj Paudel is founder and Director of the Capital College and Research Center in Kathmandu (Nepal). The college is affiliated with Tribhuvan University, Nepal. He has double masters in Sociology and Forestry. His research interests are in the field of natural resources management, sociology and appreciative inquiry (linked to positive psychology).

# *The dawn of love*

Anastasia White's life reads like the story of South Africa. Born in a white family; at the age of 15, she became an anti-apartheid activist in the black armed wing of the ANC. After Nelson Mandela's release, she became a peace campaigner and helped the country through the struggle towards reconciliation by working on the themes of respect and forgiveness. Now Dr. **Anastasia M Bukashe** tells her daughter about the pot of gold at the end of the rainbow.

## At the end of the rainbow

It is early in the morning and I sit waiting for the dawn to come. It is a subtle time, a time of whispered possibilities. I have read somewhere that 'hope is the bird that feels the light, and sings while the dawn is still dark'. And as I wait for the first glimmers of day there they are, the birds, singing their melodies to the hopeful promises of the new dawn. This feels like a metaphor for my life: waiting for the possibility of happiness, hoping that what I have heard and read about its existence is true, feeling her presence in my heart. There is a freshness to the morning, a freshness which signals new beginnings and a renewed confidence that life does indeed go on, regardless of who we are or what has gone before. Yes, dawn is a subtle time: the birds, the coolness of the night slowly warming and the almost imperceptible fingers of light beginning to touch the sky. And then she is there, the sun, a glowing ball of fire, popping her head shyly over the horizon to greet the world.

Happiness: so hard to define or pin down, but so blindingly clear when she is present in our lives. She can seep slowly into our consciousness like the breaking dawn or blaze into our lives like the noon day sun. She is the source of vitality and life; she for whom we seek,

yet whose very existence we so often question. This, indeed, is the paradox. Happiness is so central to our being, yet also so elusive, almost like a phantom. At least, this has been true for me. **I am one of those people for whom happiness is the pot of gold at the end of the rainbow, but when I finally get there, I find that there is no pot.** It is ironic that I should be asked to write about happiness, an irony that leads my friends to laugh and wonder what I might possibly have to say. They are right. When I look at my life, it is hard to grasp what I could possibly know about happiness. Yet perhaps to know an absence of something is also to know its presence. Or let me put it another way: perhaps I have had to find her in strange and unfamiliar places.

One thing I do understand is the relationship between happiness and love. These two are inextricably bound together in mutual relationship, and only come alive when they meet. This notion of relationship is also central to quantum mechanics, where the quest to isolate the building blocks of the universe has astounded physicists with what seems to be only a half answer. In an attempt to deconstruct matter and identify the smallest element of the cosmos, they have only found celestial symbiosis. This centrality of relationship is captured in the ancient wisdom of Africa, known as *Ubuntu*. Put simply, *ubuntu* means that my humanity is dependent on your humanity. Even better: **people are people because of other people.** I exist because you exist.

Love has been the subject of many different forms of art throughout the ages. It has also been the quest of individual lives, the topic of countless conversations, and the cornerstone of all spiritual traditions. Love evokes images of wholeness, passion, completeness, success, pain, suffering, longing. Love is the gauntlet of emotions run to the point of breathlessness, the prize so worth the effort, when finally won. It is fitting that love and happiness are soul-mates, for one is as elusive as the other. Once found, we are complete. Yet to hold on to this completeness, we grasp our love and our happiness so tightly, that we strangle them into lifeless shells. Why?. Why are these two life forces inseparable? And why, once found, are they so hard to keep?

In my experience, part of the problem lies with our preconceived ideas about what love is and what will make us happy. Years of research into the human psyche have shown that these ideas are formed in the first years of life. This formative period sees the creation of a set of neurological pathways and determines a pattern of brain development which stays with us for the rest of our days. And although its still possible to change these things, it requires substantial effort and a great deal of loving care from others. These preconceived ideas also result in a set of expectations, which become our guide in our quest for happiness and love, telling us which direction to take and with whom we should make the journey with.

**This guide is often a liar, who leads us down the narrow paths of self-destruction** and onward into the inauthentic existence of unresolved childhood dilemmas. I have learnt the hard way that this guide is not to be trusted. And so I now have a new guide: I follow is the dawn. The quiet, subtle voice of possibility which knows our inner truths and their longing to be fulfilled. The quiet, subtle voice which is drowned out by the rigours of life and social conditioning. The quiet, subtle voice which is sometimes so hard to hear. But once heard, you must listen to it closely, allowing it to speak its truth about who you really are and what will make you happy.

To find this voice, and with it the treasure of all life, requires a journey into what mystics describe as the 'dark night of the soul'. A shattering of ego boundaries, the loss of all we understand to be true, a severing of who we are and what we know. A place of nothingness which is quite rightly called night, because there are no answers and nowhere to go. A place of waiting, where only patience and the passage of time can bring the answers you seek. And this is the secret that I have found there: the true treasure lies within. The love we seek is the ability to love ourselves, and the happiness which this brings endures all the ravages of life. Once we find this core, we are filled with warmth and light. It is the sun, who subtly and gently dawns in our lives and spreads its radiance in order to encompass our entire being.

As the tentative light of happiness dawns in my life, I wonder if there is not an easier way. As I watch my daughter grow, I pray that this might be true. That for her the night will not be so dark or so long, or perhaps not even necessary at all. But I also pray that whatever her path may be, she will persevere with her journey – for now I know that there really is a pot of gold at the end of that rainbow.

## The keys

→ **There is a strong relationship between happiness and love. These two are inextricably bound together in mutual relationship and only come alive when they meet.**

→ **Preconceived ideas create a set of expectations, which become our guide in our quest for happiness and love. But this guide is often a liar. Try to follow the subtle voice of the dawn, with its promise of possibility.**

→ **The true treasure lies within. The love we seek is the ability to love ourselves and the happiness this brings endures all the ravages of life.**

Dr. Anastasia M Bukashe (born Anastasia White) is a South African, born into a family of activists during the anti-apartheid struggle. In this context, she was active in the student movement during the 1980s, while still at high-school. At the age of 15 she was recruited into the armed wing of the African National Congress – Mkonto we Sizwe (Spear of the Nation) and given military training inside the country. By 1990 South Africa had entered a period of negotiated transition to democracy, which led to the suspension of the armed struggle. However, the national negotiation process was beset by violent clashes between political movements and the state at community level. Anastasia worked as a mediator and violence monitor in an attempt to keep open a breathing space in which the negotiations could proceed, despite the continuing loss of life on the ground.

In 1994, Anastasia worked for the Independent Electoral Commission, which was formed to manage the first democratic elections in the country. After 1994 she was seconded to the newly formed Ministry of Safety and Security, to work on creating and implementing new legislation for policing. This work included facilitating reconciliation between police and members of the community who had been adversaries during the struggle.

In 1998, Anastasia began her doctoral studies at Case Western Reserve University in Cleveland, Ohio, USA. Her dissertation work was focused on creating new frameworks for intervention in ethnic, religious and political conflicts, using three comparative cases: Nigeria, South Africa and Israel/Palestine. This work aimed at integrating lessons learned from her personal experience as a participant in conflict, with her professional role as a mediator. She returned to South Africa in 2004 and now heads up the non-profit-making Wilgespruit Fellowship Centre. She continues to work and teach both nationally and internationally, with a specific focus on peace-building.

*'The five key aspects in determining the quality of life of the elderly are health, family, economic situation, social network and leisure activities.'*

# *Happy old people*

People aged 80 and older are the fastest growing section of the population in many countries. Globally, this age group will grow by 233 percent between 2008 and 2040, while the total population will only increase by 33 percent during the same period. In some industrialized countries nearly 20% of the population will be older than 65 in 2020. What effects will this explosion have on their happiness? **Fermina Rojo-Perez** and **Gloria Fernandez-Mayoralas** report from Spain.

## Ageing and quality of life

People live and age at home. This is where they have spent their lives; this is where they have their memories; this is where they want to grow old. Even if they decline as they get older – perhaps because of failing health, a reduced family and social network or a fall in income – the elderly wish to continue living in their home or the home of family members to whom they are closest in emotional terms. Very seldom do they choose to live in a residential home. 17 % of the Spanish population is older than 65 and 98% of them are ageing at home.

Over the last few decades we have been studying this elderly population in terms of their living conditions as part of a quality of life study, which specifically takes their points of view into account. Scientifically, there is no general consensus on what is understood by the term 'quality of life', nor by the term 'happiness'. Nevertheless, this latter measurement is used, together with satisfaction, as an indicator for gaining insight into the position of our ageing population at the beginning of the 21st century.

Quality of life is a concept that can be related to different areas. In other words, it is multidimensional. When the elderly are asked about the most important aspects of their life, the first five they mention are health, family, economic situation, social network and leisure activities. They also mention six further aspects, albeit to a lesser degree: emotional well-being, values and attitudes, religiosity, residential environment, social support and employment situation.

In a general model based on subjective well-being or the level of satisfaction with regard to each of the above aspects, the most important determinants are seen to be: total monthly income, the local community social network (neighbours), general state of health, the family network, place of residence, physical appearance or perceived age and type of cohabitation. Only if the persons questioned declare themselves to be 'very satisfied' in respect of a specific aspect can this be directly related to general quality of life, i.e. being very satisfied is the only satisfaction category that actually increases their quality of life. This is the only way to understand the apparent discrepancy between the relatively low average satisfaction with income declared by the elderly and its effect on their quality of life. In this economic context, the elderly population seeks to focus concern on the need for society to make greater efforts to invest in pensions, health and housing.

A significant part of the over-65 population enjoys relatively good health and functionality, in particular the 'younger' old men and people of a higher social class, who are generally in a best state of health. Functional ability varies according to gender, depending on whether household chores are considered. Men show a lower level of capacity when these types of activities are considered, but not because of any physical disability. It is more a question of the socio-cultural role assigned to women in carrying them out.

Living with one's relatives, (albeit in households with relatively few members) and the network of relationships built around this institution make the family a source of great satisfaction with life for the elderly. **The family is valued not only from the perspective of the emotional bond between family members, but also as a mutual assistance network in case of need.** In fact, it is the primary source of support and care for dependent elderly people. Another key element in the elderly person's social network is their relations with the neighbours in their residential environment. Great importance is attached to this network, which can supplement or even replace the traditional friendship network.

The house, which is the heart of the individual's residential environment, is another factor that determines an elderly person's quality of life. Objectively speaking, this house, which was probably bought many years ago when they were young and in a different stage of their life, may have become unsuitable for their current circumstances, even if the elderly say they are highly satisfied with it. In this respect, new policies will be required to mitigate this unsuitability, possibly through a system of home improvements. Residential mobility is not really an option, since most older people are not interested in moving or can no longer afford it.

This, then, is a scientific summary of the main aspects and conditions affecting the quality of life of the elderly population. From the perspective of the welfare state, this group requires specific action plans from social and political institutions to promote the process of ageing in situ (i.e., at home). However, the needs of elderly people are still poorly catered for in terms of support and care for the most vulnerable, in carrying out their everyday activities within the community. We would therefore like to call on public policy-makers to consider 'ageing in situ' in conjunction with 'quality of life', since poorer living conditions in the community could result in unwanted institutionalisation.

## The keys

→ **Most important aspects of life for older people are health, family, economic situation, social network and leisure activities. The highest levels of satisfaction are expressed in relation to family and social networks, and the residential environment.**

→ **The elderly wish to continue living in their own 'homes' or in the home of family members to whom they are most closely attached, which again underlining the importance of family, neighbours and their own house.**

→ **Our ageing population requires specific action plans from social and political institutions in order to promote ageing in situ.**

Fermina Rojo-Perez and Gloria Fernandez-Mayoralas, both PhD graduates in Geography, are scientific researchers attached to the Research Group on Ageing (RGA) at the Spanish National Research Council (CSIC) in Madrid (Spain). They are involved in a multidisciplinary, longitudinal research of ageing in Spain, targeted to analyse the determinants of ageing across the life span. Their focus is on quality of life in old age.

# *Minute by minute*

People all over the world fill in a diary of exactly
what they do and how they feel: minute by minute.
The Centre for Time Use Research in Oxford analyses
these data. **Jonathan Gershuny** and **Kimberly Fisher**
know exactly which activities we enjoy.

## Daily utility

University of Oxford reader Michael Argyle told his students in the 1990s: 'If you want to
be happy for a day, get drunk; for a year, get married; for a lifetime, get a garden.' Cultural
sensitivities may lead to variations in this prescription, but the different sorts of 'happiness'
associated with different time scales hint at the multiple layers of perception of the quality
of lived experience. We should use different words for the different strands of meaning:
for a day – utility; for a month (perhaps a year) – happiness; for longer – contentment.
Here we intend to focus on utility, the enjoyment people experience during activities.

Our research uses structured 1-day diaries from random samples of people in different
countries throughout a year and covering all days of the week. We persuade diarists to
record what they are doing, whether they did anything else at the same time, who they
were with, and where they were along a time line that shows the number of minutes each
activity takes. Diaries facilitate research into many topics, from how women and men

IF YOU WANT

TO BE HAPPY

FOR A DAY,

GET DRUNK;

FOR A YEAR,

GET MARRIED;

FOR A LIFETIME,

GET A GARDEN.

share paid work and unpaid housework, to changes in the work-life balance and changes in what people do alone and what they do with which other people.

We compared data in the USA and the UK. Comparing with recent data in France gives similar results. People most enjoy out-of-home leisure. **Though people spend a lot of time watching TV, they do not value this activity as highly as other free time activities.** People generally enjoy leisure more than paid work. Unsurprisingly, people rank house-work (and commuting and the chauffeuring elements of transport) lowest. People feel more pleased to have more time doing activities they enjoy, but only up to a point. Past that point, more minutes of the same activity can make people feel less content (at similar rates in the UK and the USA). As the total time in an activity increases, so the utility of leisure drops off more sharply than the utility of other activities.

Women and men enjoy or dislike most activities at similar levels, with some notable exceptions. Women enjoy in-home leisure more and childcare less than men. The latter is explained by the fact that women do the majority of the less pleasant and more routine aspects of childcare, while men in the USA and the UK mostly restrict themselves to more interactive childcare (reading stories, playing sports, helping with homework). All parents find interactive forms of childcare more satisfying than routine care.

Diary studies collected over the decades reveal how people's daily routines change. Knowing how people feel about what they do reveals how people's satisfaction with their routines also changes. If more time in conversation with family members shifts from home to the car, for example, people are less happy.

We can add up diary-based estimates of the total utility derived over a fixed period from the range of activities undertaken by a representative sample of the population – multi-plying time in activities by their associated enjoyment scores – to produce National Utility Accounts (which the leading authors in this field, Alan Krueger and Daniel Kahneman, call National Time Accounts). Overall, **utility totals have not changed significantly over recent history.** Does this mean that happiness has also remained largely constant in recent times? This is far from clear. Activities associated with the day-to-day helping of tetchy teenagers to get them through their school exams may be largely disagreeable – but we might feel happiness once the exams are over, and longer-term contentment that we helped our children through a significant time in their lives.

Total reported utility tells only part of the story. Since the 1960s, women in both the UK and the USA have steadily cut back their time in low-utility unpaid work and their high-utility sleep time, and replaced this time with marginally higher-utility paid work and lower-utility time watching TV. There is no evident process through which these various shifts in utility necessarily balance each other. Current research aims to better explain how changes in activity patterns and utility relate to people's well-being.

Government policies and business strategies can sometimes both help the economy grow and make people happier, but some policies that help the economy come at the price of making life less pleasant. To understand the full impact of policies on quality of life, policy-makers need measures of people's utility and happiness, as well as of their daily activity patterns alongside more traditional economic measures. People need to remind elected and business leaders that well-being, not just money, matters.

## The keys

→ **The different sorts of 'happiness' associated with different time scales hint at the multiple layers of perception of the quality of lived experience: for a day – utility; for a month (perhaps a year) – happiness; for longer – contentment.**

→ **People most enjoy out-of-home leisure and rank housework lowest. But as the total time in an activity increases, the utility of leisure drops off more sharply than the utility of other activities.**

→ **People need to remind elected and business leaders that well-being, not just money, matters.**

Both authors work for the Centre for Time Use Research (CTUR), based at the University of Oxford (United Kingdom). CTUR creates and manages the Multinational Time Use Study (MTUS), the largest cross-time and cross-national database of time-diary survey data. Jonathan Gershuny is a professor of sociology, a Fellow of the British Academy, CTUR Director, and former president of the International Association for Time Use Research (IATUR). Kimberly Fisher is the co-ordinator of the MTUS and the CTUR web resources.

*'We must learn to use pessimism as a recipe for cheerfulness.'*

# A good life

'Individually, we need to strive for a good life, not for a happy life. Collectively, we need to strive for a just society, not for a happy society. Only if we are lucky will all this striving make our lives, and hence our societies, happier than they would otherwise have been. But there is no guarantee.' **Philippe Van Parijs** asks himself: Why not? And does it matter?

## A welcome by-product

What would make our societies more just? What would make them happier? Are the two not intimately connected? In several ways, they are. For example, making our societies more just involves granting everyone basic material security. This should help to remove much of the anguish that plagues the lives of those now condemned to a precarious existence. Making our societies more just also involves getting rid of blatantly unfair privileges. This should help to alleviate the resentment, the indignation and the anger that often mars the lives of those who do not share in them.

And yet, there is no guarantee that making our societies as just as possible will make them as happy as possible. Greater justice may demand that we take from more advantaged people some of the things that they are used to (and will badly miss), and transfer this 'wealth' (in whatever form) to other people who are objectively less advantaged yet happier, because of having adjusted their wants to their modest condition. Greater justice also requires that opportunities be equalised. But as documented by sociological studies from Samuel Stouffer's *American Soldier* (1949) onwards, giving more opportunities for upward mobility to a particular category of people previously deprived of it can unleash a dynamic of relative deprivation that ends up creating more dissatisfaction than before, both in the category in which opportunities have improved and in the ones in which they have worsened.

The general point is that unhappiness is about the gap between what you have and what you want, whereas injustice is about the gap between what you have and what you can fairly claim. There is no general reason to expect that wants and fair claims will necessarily coincide. **It is therefore not surprising that by reducing injustice, as we must, we could also increase unhappiness.**

While therefore making no sense as our collective goal, the idea of achieving maximal happiness might make better sense as the aim of our lives as individuals, albeit within the limits set by fair collective rules. There are two – and only two – ways in which each of us can try to become happier: by moving what we have closer to what we want and by moving what we want closer to what we have. Neither of these two strategies is confined to material goods. Each of them is relevant to our philanthropic ambitions, no less than to our consumerist appetites. Each is relevant to our craving for power, no less than to our romantic desires.

Whichever of these two strategies we consider using, is it right to say that the aim of our lives is to achieve happiness? No, it is not. Our aim should be to have a good life, a life which, after due reflection, we can regard as good by our own standards. **We can probably all think of people we despise, who led or are leading a reasonably happy life**, and of people we admire who are leading or led a pretty miserable one, constantly trying to achieve the unachievable. There is no lack of artists who tortured themselves into the grave, nor of rebels who lost themselves and their families in a vain attempt to oppose situations to which their neighbours happily adjusted. Thus, happiness is not what makes our lives good in terms of conceptual or moral necessity. However, it can often be a factor and sometimes a by-product of our leading a life we can regard as good.

Happiness can help us to lead a good life by making us stronger. Frustration, envy, disappointment, despair, gloom are all debilitating. It is therefore helpful, not just for the sake of making our lives happier, but also for the sake of making them better, to try to manage our psyche in a manner which allows us to navigate away from these feelings. For example, it is wise to escape 'luxury fever', the self-defeating race for ever more lavish material consumption, by adopting more sober tastes which keep us living happily below our means. In the same spirit, **we must learn to transform setbacks into opportunities**. We must learn to forget our failures and our blunders — except in order to learn how

not to repeat them – and must keep looking ahead, instead of wasting our time on pointless regrets. We must learn to view each additional day, especially after a certain age, as yet another of life's undeserved presents. We must learn to accept quietly, as facts of life, the things that we cannot change, including the inevitability of our own death. And we must learn to use pessimism as a recipe for cheerfulness: if we temper our positive expectations and exaggerate our negative predictions, our lives will be filled with pleasant surprises.

In these diverse ways, we can avoid debilitating unhappiness and thereby continue to nurture the hope, the balance and the enthusiasm that we need in order to undertake and pursue the many things, small and big, that make our lives good. Conversely, the goodness of our lives can also contribute to our happiness. If our life is a good life by our own standards, or as good as it can be, then perhaps it is not quite so important that it is not the happiest life it could have been. If we try to make our life as good as possible, this should give us a serenity, a peace of mind that we would otherwise lack. At least, providing certain conditions are met. For us to be able to achieve this sort of happiness, perhaps we need to view the project of our life as a contribution to something that transcends the borders of our own ephemeral person, to a family or a cause, to an organisation or a community, something to which we devote some of our care, some of our efforts, and some of our happy – and less happy – moments. Many of the things that make our lives good will only become evident or come to fruition after we are gone. This, of course, is something that we shall never know. But we can hope. And if we do, we can find happiness. Not because we tried to be happy, but simply as a welcome by-product of doing what we thought we had to do.

## The keys

→ **Individually, we need to strive for a good life, not for a happy life. Collectively, we need to strive for a just society, not for a happy society.**

→ **There are two – and only two – ways in which each of us can try to become happier: by moving what we have closer to what we want and by moving what we want closer to what we have.**

→ **Our aim should be to have a good life, a life which (on reflection) we can regard as good by our own standards. Happiness can be a welcome by-product of this good life.**

Philippe Van Parijs (Hoover Chair in Economic and Social Ethics, UCL, University of Louvain, Belgium) has studied philosophy, law, political economics, sociology and linguistics in Brussels, Louvain, Oxford, Bielefeld and Berkeley. He is a doctor in social sciences and philosophy, and has been a guest professor at universities all over the world. He has published numerous articles and books, his most recent one being: 'Linguistic Justice for Europe and for the World'. He is co-founder and president of the Basic Income Earth Network. For his distinguished scientific research, he has even been honoured by appearing on an official stamp in Belgium.

*'An organization is a miracle to be embraced,*
*rather than a problem to be solved.'*

# *After the tsunami*

'An organisation is a miracle to be embraced, rather than
a problem to be solved.' That is the basic idea of appreciative
inquiry, a development process based on the findings of positive
psychology. **Maulolo T. Amosa** uses this method in helping to
rebuild a small island in the Samoa group, hit by the tsunami.

## The positive way

Of the 181,000 people living in Samoa, 2,500 dwell on a small island called Manono,
which has an area of just 1.1 square miles. This island is unique in many ways, as it proudly
represents itself as one of the very few places which still follows the traditional Samoan
lifestyle. There are no vehicles and no dogs. It only takes about three hours to walk
the perimeter of the island on a narrow footpath. Its people survive mainly on marine
resources, supplemented by a few crops. In 2009, three quarters of the island were ruined
by the tsunami that hit Samoa. Although less than 200 people perished in this natural
disaster, the number of victims was sufficiently high to traumatise the Samoan people,
with their relatively low total population of just less than two hundred thousand.

Five months later, working with the United Nations, we jointly devised a programme for
the whole island of Manono, which aimed at formalising a village plan that would allow
the island to recover from the effect and impact of the tsunami. As expected, the faces we
saw on the first day indicated that there were mixed feelings about our mission. However,
after our first day of interaction with the villagers, using the appreciative inquiry approach,
there were increasing signs of hope, signs which were soon reflected in our dialogue.
The commitment shown by all four villages on the island was testimony to the deep desire
and longing for social and economic resurrection in all aspects of the island's life.

The positive approach was appropriate, since it helped to boost the islander's own self esteem. It also helped to build up morale and a sense of self-motivation among the villagers. Even more important was the fact that the positive method of appreciative inquiry hammers on the message that you need to help yourself rather than relying on whatever assistance is offered by others. In this way, sustainability can be achieved. This method highlights the strengths within yourself, the strengths that need to be activated and utilised.

By the end of our endeavours, a formal village plan was adopted. The most emotional moment was when the island's youth group gave a presentation in which they envisioned Manono as once again becoming a peaceful and harmonious place in which to live.

As we closed the three-day workshop, the women were singing songs to remind them of the happy times before the tidal wave hit the island, but also to express hope for a better future. For us, these were the moments of joy and happiness, as we realised that we had given a little piece of hope to this badly battered island in Samoa.

## The keys

→ **Start a dialogue and create meaning, by exchanging stories of concrete successes.**
→ **Highlight the strengths within every person involved in the organisation.**
→ **Dream your future together and make a plan with priorities; build on the strengths of the people involved.**

Maulolo T. Amosa works for the Ministry of Women, Community and Social Development in Samoa, using the methods of appreciative inquiry.

# Appreciative inquiry

The principles of positive psychology can also be successfully applied to organisations. Appreciative inquiry is a rapidly growing discipline which promotes positive change in business, communities, health care, schools, local governments and other organisations. The basic idea is to build organisations around the things that work, rather than trying to fix what is broken. Instead of focusing on gaps and inadequacies when seeking to improve skills or practices, appreciative inquiry focuses on ways in which existing exceptional performance can be increased and enhanced, once a core of strengths is properly aligned. This opens the door to a universe of new possibilities, since the process doesn't stop when a particular problem is solved, but continues to focus on the question: 'What is the best that we can be?' The approach acknowledges the contribution of individuals, in order to increase trust and organisational alignment. It aims to create meaning by drawing from stories of concrete successes and lends itself to cross-industrial social activities.

The method was originally articulated by two professors in management, David Cooperrider and Suresh Srivastva. It is based on the assumption that organizations change in the way they inquire. When you inquire into problems or difficult situations, you will usually keep finding 'more of the same'. According to appreciative investigation theory, an organisation must try to appreciate what is best in itself – and then it will find 'more and more of what is good'. The methods used should be appreciative, applicable, provocative and collaborative. The cycle focuses on four processes: discover (what works well), dream (of what will work well in future), design (planning and prioritising) and destiny (delivery).

*'More TV = less happiness.*
*So switch off the TV and switch on happiness.'*

# *Affluenza*

Norway is one of the world's leading oil-and-gas nations, with an enviable Gross National Product and a colossal pension fund. But **Reidulf G. Watten** has noticed that Norwegian society seems to be afflicted with 'affluenza', thereby exemplifying *the happiness paradox* – the weak association between happiness, wealth and income, as revealed by studies in various nations all over the world. Happiness is based on more than oil and gas.

## Being, meaning, beauty and ... dignity

*Homo economicus* offers only an incomplete picture of a human being. Using data from the Norwegian Monitor (NM), Ottar Hellevik, a political scientist at the University of Oslo, has presented us with some intriguing evidence about other aspects of Norwegian life and society in recent years. The NM is a unique database, both in terms of its methodological approach (a series of biennial interviews) and its sample size (2,200-4,000 cases per interview). The NM covers the years from 1985 to 2007 and, as an omnibus investigation, addresses a number of areas, including happiness, political behaviour, value orientation, etc. The samples are representative of the population aged 15 years and older.

In the period 1985-2007 there has been a marked increase in the levels of income and material well-being in Norway. However, no parallel increase in the level of happiness has been observed. It would appear that the tendency to give priority to income and material possessions towards the end of the last millennium has had an adverse effect on happiness, although there was a slight increase in the period 2001-2007. Other significant findings and conclusions include:

→ There is no association between happiness and the place where people live, whether it be in a large town, a small town or a rural area.

→ Political values are also of less importance.

→ The level of education and other typical lifestyle factors, such as smoking or drinking, do not add to happiness.

→ Modern materialistic factors, such as the passive consumption of television, have adverse effects. The more time Norwegians spend in front of a television screen, the less happy they are.

→ Some aspects of a person's economic situation enhance happiness, although not the actual level of income itself, but rather the subjective satisfaction which this level of income brings with it.

→ Increased happiness is linked to satisfaction with personal health and fitness.

→ Relational factors within the domains of being and meaning are crucial: satisfaction with our family, friends, and neighbours is a key criterion for happiness.

→ Enjoying our work is more important than the nature and/or importance of that work.

→ Satisfaction with the level of socio-economic equality, confidence in political institutions, trust in other people, and the existence of key social institutions are essential.

→ Existential factors, such as religion and religious activity, are positively related to happiness: the higher the level of activity, the higher the level of happiness.

→ Moderate physical exercise and enjoyment of natural surroundings contribute to our happiness.

→ The greater our level of active participation in aesthetic and cultural activities (such as concerts, art exhibitions, museums, theatre or opera), the happier we are.

→ Our values are also related to our happiness, and the NM has observed interesting changes in the values prevailing in Norwegian society over the last five years. While materialistic values lead to less happiness, idealistic values increase happiness, irrespective of age, gender, social class and economic status. More specifically, the values which encompass socio-emotional relations – being close to other people – are very important.

→ Likewise, the values of altruism, an anti-materialistic attitude, self-realisation and a respect for the law are all positively associated with happiness.

These values strongly suggest that happiness and quality of life are linked to such basic psychological needs as emotional and social attachment. Close personal relations, the ability to enjoy nature and beauty, the opportunity to 'breathe freely', and the availability of social, economic and cultural possibilities for the life-long development of one's human potential all seem to be essential. However, in order to succeed in this development of potential, another factor needs to be added to the list – human dignity. The American philosopher Martha Nussbaum has advocated this point most strongly. She describes ten elements that are necessary for human dignity: life, health, bodily integrity, the possibility of developing human senses, possibilities for thinking and imagining, emotions, practical reasoning, attachment to other humans and other living creatures, self-respect, an ability to play, and the ability to influence one's political and physical environment. I am convinced that our potential for happiness and a better quality of life cannot be fully developed unless there is a greater focus on and a greater respect for human dignity in society.

## The keys

→ **In a rich country, a greater priority on income and material possessions has an adverse effect on happiness. Being and meaning are more important.**

→ **Non-materialistic values are closely linked to happiness: beauty, confidence, trust, socio-emotional relations, etc.**

→ **The potential for happiness cannot be developed without the necessary respect for human dignity.**

Reidulf G. Watten is a professor in general psychology at the Department of Health and Social Science, Psychology studies, Lillehammer University College (Norway). His main research interests are quality of life studies, personality, health psychology, biological psychology and visual perception. But he also enjoys fishing, hunting and singing classical music.

'*The eight domains affecting quality of life are universal for everyone.*'

# Ability in disability

'Orange and yellow are positive colours. Bring those colours into your life. Leave the blue, grey and brown, for those colours will make you depressed. Your life is surrounded by the colour wheel, but let the arrow stop at the positive colours. Let the sun shine in your life!' These words are part of a poem, written by Meagan Ipsen. Professor **Ralph Kober** asks you to read the words again, but this time in the knowledge that the writer is a person with an intellectual disability. There are millions of them. What can we say about their happiness?

## Positive colours

I hope that the realisation that this poem was written by a person with an intellectual disability will make you reconsider any preconceptions that you may have about the abilities of people with such medical conditions.

What do we know about the quality of life for people with intellectual disabilities?

The first thing we need to say is that the basic components of quality of life are universal across all people. However, there may be some variation about the relative value attached to these components across different cultures. In other the words, the positive aspects that lead to a life of quality are the same in China as in the USA, but the importance placed on the different aspects may differ. Secondly, it is important to realise that quality of life consists of both objective (quantitative) and subjective (qualitative) components. The third thing we know is that quality of life is also influenced by both personal (internal) and environmental conditions. Finally, based on these three premises, it is perhaps self-evident that quality of life is a multidimensional construct.

The majority of researchers have come to the conclusion that quality of life consists of the same eight domains for everyone: personal development, self determination, interpersonal relations, social inclusion, rights, emotional well-being, physical well-being and material well-being.

Are there things that we can do to improve the quality of life of people with intellectual disabilities? Most certainly. While there has been widespread research on this matter, I will concentrate on just three factors. Firstly, we could ensure **appropriate housing**. Research into the effect of deinstitutionalisation (i.e., the replacement of large residential institutions, with smaller services that support people with intellectual disabilities within the community) has found this to have a positive influence on overall quality of life. Secondly, we could give people with intellectual disabilities **appropriate employment**. As with non-disabled people, employment increases personal self-esteem and the quality of life of people with intellectual disabilities. For people with mild intellectual disabilities open employment (where the disabled person works in an open environment alongside co-workers without disabilities) results in a higher quality of life than sheltered employment (where the person with a disability mainly works together with other disabled people). It is not yet precisely clear in what way employment increases quality of life. Is it the job per se, or is it increased income, or (most likely) a combination of the two? Irrespective of the answer to this question, the third measure we could take is to **increase income** (or financial support) for people with intellectual disabilities. Research I am currently undertaking appears to indicate that relatively modest increases in the (mostly low) incomes of people with intellectual disabilities can significantly increase their quality of life. In relation to these three possible measures – housing, employment and income – we can already report changes in the public policies of many countries, which have bettered the lives of people with intellectual disabilities. People with such disabilities are no longer being institutionalised, specific programmes have been established to assist them with finding employment, and in some countries people with intellectual disabilities can no longer be paid below the statutory minimum wage.

It would be remiss of me not to mention an exciting new area of quality of life research for people with intellectual disabilities, namely family quality of life. By this I mean the quality of life of the entire family unit, as opposed to the sum of the individual qualities of life of each member of the family. Given the importance of the family unit in the functioning of all societies, it is clear that family quality of life will be extremely important in terms of setting the direction of future disability policy. If a member of a family has an intellectual disability, family dynamics often change from 'normal' interactions amongst the family members to a focus on the individual with a disability. This change in dynamics can have unfortunate consequences on the effective functioning of the family, making it extremely important that we gain an understanding of the quality of life of the family unit. Once we have such an understanding, we can start to explore ways of improving family quality of life: perhaps, for example, through offering support to various members of the family and not just to the individual with the intellectual disability.

Unfortunately, while over the past few decades there have undoubtedly been improvements in the lives of people with intellectual disabilities and their families, research shows that the overall quality of life of the majority of such people and such families is still unacceptably low; often substantially below population averages. Consequently, there is still much to do, and it is incumbent on all of us to ensure that it is done. With the energy and passion of researchers and advocates in this area, I am confident that we will get there – one day.

## The keys

→ **The basic components of quality of life are universal and apply to all people, also for persons with intellectual disabilities.**

→ **We can improve the quality of life for persons with intellectual disabilities by providing them with appropriate housing, open employment and an increase in income.**

→ **Focus should not be on the person with an intellectual disability but on the quality of life of his complete family unit.**

Ralph Kober is an associate professor of management accounting at Monash University in Australia. His research interests cover both the fields of management accounting and quality of life for people with intellectual disabilities. He became involved in quality of life research while completing his PhD and has since published articles in quality of life journals, intellectual disability journals, and accounting journals.

*'I am here for you.'*

# The voice of your parents

Happy children: that is what every parent wants.
And they all want to discover the magic formula that can
guarantee this happiness for their sons and daughters.
Child psychologist **Peter Adriaenssens** has written numerous
books on this subject. His recipe for success? Welcome and accept
the child as it is, and wrap it in a cloak of warm certainty.
Visible happiness is a superstructure built on the unconscious
happiness which flows from the unconditional promise made
by parents to their children: 'I am here for you, wherever you are
and whatever you do.' Your parents' voice is always with you.

## Happy children

Happiness begins from the moment when parents decide that they want to have children,
not from the moment when they discover that they are actually on their way. Parenthood
is happier – and its resultant children are also happier – if the process is a conscious one.
In other words, parents must make a deliberate choice to have children, must wish to
experience the ups and downs of pregnancy together, must welcome with equal joy
the birth of a son or daughter, must look forward to the new life that will gradually grow

and develop its own future. If you can do this, then your children will be something more than just someone to look after you when you are old; or someone to take over the family business in later years; or someone to have that glittering sports career you so dearly wanted for yourself. If you can do this, then you will ensure that your children grow up in an atmosphere of love and contentment, rather than violence or rejection. If we want more happy people, then we need to make greater efforts to inform future parents about the importance of consciously opting for a child. Because as a parent you must be willing to make a lifelong promise to that child: 'I will always be there for you, wherever you are, whatever you do; I will never let you go, you can always count on my love and support.' Unconditionally. In other words, you must make this promise without expecting (let alone insisting) that these feelings are reciprocated. For the child, *having* happiness is the unconditional element in their parents' promise. **And the conscious feeling of *being* happy grows from the unconscious state of *having* happiness.**

Is this naïve? Is this spoiling your child? No, because research has confirmed that children are born completely defenceless at birth. In other words, they are totally dependent on adults.

If a baby is not cared for, it will die. That is the harsh reality of life. Children who are given food but little love develop slowly, are often thin and small for their age. But if a parent cherishes a baby, speaks to it, cuddles it, feeds it, tickles it, laughs with it, then both parent and child will discover the most wonderful of all nature's gifts: true empathy and true attachment between two human beings. This attachment is a kind of human 'glue' – and it sticks a whole lifetime long. This means that your toddler can sit at school, safe in the knowledge that you have not forgotten him. It means that your teenage daughter can call you in the middle of the night if she needs to, and knows that you will always come. It means that your grown-up children can still call you for emergency babysitting duty, when their regular sitter fails to turn up. They all know that you have sworn an oath: 'I have given you life and so I will always be there for you.' Unconditionally.

Researchers are continuing to discover more and more about the neurobiological anchoring of the attachment processes between parents and children, which can have an influence on emotional, intellectual and relational development. If children are abandoned to their fate, or are forced to live in a climate of continual parental stress or partner violence, or have a parent with serious psychological difficulties, parts of their brains will develop with fewer than normal neural networks, when compared with children who are brought up in a loving environment. These deficiencies can later translate into reduced linguistic ability, a reduced ability to recognise and express emotions, a higher likelihood of impulsive, aggressive or hyperactive behaviour, greater difficulty in acquiring maturity, and a reduced capacity to empathise with others, which significantly increases the risk of personality disorders, juvenile delinquency and partner violence.

Happiness is therefore a choice, and it is a hard choice. It is not something romantic, that suddenly overcomes you. It is a gift that you have, a gift that you can give to someone else. **Whoever receives the gift of happiness from their parents will also find it easier in later life to accept the responsibility of passing that gift on to others.** If you choose to have a child, we must dare to say to each other: this child has the right to receive happiness. This can cause some parents to doubt their ability to bring up their children properly, but the very fact that this doubt exists suggests that the current generation of parents will accomplish their task. Doubt is a good attitude for any educator (and parents are educators, too!), who wishes to achieve a true meeting of minds with a child.

We are talking here about the harmonisation of happiness, by removing it from a purely theoretical context and transforming it into a dynamic concept. Theoretical happiness is linear. If your child is loved, lives in a nice house and can pursue its own interests in its free time, then surely it will have everything necessary to become happy? On paper, yes. But let us assume that the child in question is of an anxious disposition (which is the case for one in ten children), who finds it difficult to complete tasks independently, who likes to be cuddled, who enjoys the cosiness of the home environment and who occasionally wants to creep under your blankets in bed at night. And let us further assume that the parents in question have difficulty in doing or accepting these things, perhaps because they have too little time or are too ambitious, working hard to secure their children's future (as they would probably put it). In these circumstances, the child's happiness becomes a kind of stranglehold, something inflexible and preordained, from which it is hard to escape. If this happens, the upbringing of the child is like a train running on a fixed railway line, which must first pass through a number of predetermined stations before arriving at its end destination of happiness. However, there is a serious – and predictable – risk that this train will be de-railed somewhere en route. The human glue between child and parent becomes unstuck, the unshakable attachment dissolves. What the child needs is made-to-measure happiness, not ready-to-wear happiness. There is no single theory of happiness that neatly fits every child. The creation of happiness is a dynamic process between two human beings, which grows through the relationship between father and son, mother and daughter, and so on. The parents possess the wisdom of the adult world, but it is the children who possess the wisdom of the child's world. By being sensitive to each other and to each others' needs, together they can develop a tailor-made happiness that fits everyone – like a glove.

What starts as a specific attachment with parents, will gradually develop into a broader emotional network with family, neighbours, friends at school, teachers and other 'educators'. During the teenage years, peers will assume a prominent place in their lives. Sometimes this can have a healthy effect on the development of young people, but sometimes it can be damaging. Many parents underestimate their influence during this phase of their child's life, and often feel pushed to one side in the emotional maelstrom of rapidly developing adolescence. Appearances are deceptive, however, and your offspring's seeming indifference is purely superficial – providing you have invested enough love and effort in your child's growth from the day of its birth. If your teenager is frightened, lonely or in trouble, he will always know who to turn to first. The human glue will do its work – and he will go looking for his parents.

Happiness is not a series of pleasant moments which you share with your children. These moments are certainly fun, and can add a great deal of pleasure to life. However, happiness is much more than that. It is the quiet contentment which comes from the certain knowledge that there will never be a moment when your child, no matter how old he or she might be, will ever feel truly alone in the world. You know – as Milton Erickson has put it – that they will always hear the voice of their parents, whispering softly in their ear.

## The keys

- → **Parents must consciously choose to have children. This choice must be unconditional. As a result the child is given happiness, which allows it to be happy.**
- → **Parents must wrap their children in a cloak of warm certainty. This will ensure an unbreakable lifelong bond of attachment.**
- → **Attachment to parents will later develop into a broader emotional network. But in times of happiness or times of trouble children will still hear the voice of their parents.**

---

Professor Peter Adriaenssens is child and adolescent psychiatrist and family therapist. He is clinical professor at the Catholic University of Leuven (Belgium) and is founder and director of the Confidential Centre for Child Abuse & Neglect. He has written numerous articles and books on these topics and is a well-known advisor on education.

# *The refrigerator message*

Iceland has often been rated as the happiest country in the world. However, when **Dóra Guðrún Guðmundsdóttir** started her research ten years ago, she could not even find a single study on happiness in her country. Now her results are to be found on all the refrigerators in Iceland. And yes, there are refrigerators in Iceland.

## It's not the easy life that does it…

Whether Iceland is the happiest country in the world may not be the most important question to ask. Finding out which factors predict happiness is much more useful. When I began analysing the data, I found that it did not matter whether you were a boy or a girl, a man or a woman, a pensioner or a teenager. None of these groups was happier than the others. Money didn't seem to matter much, either. In fact, income explained only 1 to 4% of happiness in Iceland. These results may not be surprising to those knowledgeable in the field of happiness studies. However, there is a common belief that money is the key to happiness. When I give lectures I often ask people to guess how much of people's happiness is predicted by their income, and the estimates are always too high. It is actually not unusual for lay people to suggest that income predicts up to 70% of happiness. This misconception is important to correct, in order to avoid people taking ineffective paths in their quest for personal happiness. Of course, some individuals may not seek

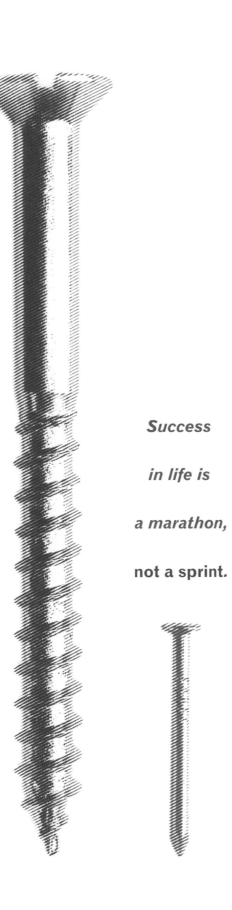

*Success*

*in life is*

*a marathon,*

**not a sprint.**

money for the purpose of gaining happiness. Their goal may simply be to earn more money than the next person. However, they should be properly informed that such an endeavour is not the most effective way towards a happy life.

If monetary income predicts only 4% of happiness, then at least 96% is explained by other factors. According to my (and numerous other) studies, the best predictor for happiness is social relationships. Findings from the Icelandic data demonstrate that living with a partner is more likely to result in a happier life than living alone, and spending time with friends and family also increases happiness. Another important factor for happiness is health, and in particular a person's mental health.

There are many misconceptions about happiness and people are misinformed on this issue by the media, the entertainment world and by commonly accepted 'wisdom'. During my research I came across a study from the 1960's, which suggested that the happiest people would be those who had the easiest lives. This hypothesis was *not* supported by the findings. Those who reported the highest level of happiness had all been through some difficult times in their lives, which they had overcome. It was not the difficulties which made them happy. What mattered most was their attitude towards their adversities, how they coped with them and how they finally triumphed over them.

As a response to these misconceptions, my colleagues and I developed and launched a public campaign for better mental health and greater happiness. We created a simple device in the form of a series of phrases intended to remind people of simple strategies to stay mentally healthy – and so increase their happiness. These phrases were chosen by searching through the research literature for the characteristics of happy and successful people, supported by our own research findings.

The result of this work was the 'Ten Commandments of Mental Health', which I would like to share with you, in the hope that they might help you to enjoy your life even more. They were printed on a refrigerator magnet, so that they could act as a visible reminder in people's daily lives. The Public Health Institute of Iceland sent a magnet to every home in the country as a Christmas gift. This gift was followed up with lectures and a media campaign on the importance of thinking and caring about mental health.

If you ever visit an Icelandic home, I encourage you to go into the kitchen and see if you can find the Ten Commandments of Mental Health. They still have a place on many refrigerator doors.

**The Ten Commandments of Mental Health are:**

→ Think positively

→ Cherish the ones you love

→ Continue learning as long as you live

→ Learn from your mistakes

→ Exercise daily

→ Do not complicate your life unnecessarily

→ Try to understand and encourage those around you

→ Do not give up; success in life is a marathon, not a sprint

→ Discover and nurture your talents

→ Set goals for yourself and pursue your dreams

## The keys

→ **Show people how they overestimate the importance of money. It only predicts 4% of happiness, not the 70% that some people think.**

→ **It is not an 'easy' life that makes us happy. What matters most is our attitude towards adversities and how we cope with them.**

→ **Find easy methods to bring the wisdom of happiness research into the lives of all people. Refrigerator magnets might help!**

Dóra Guðrún Guðmundsdóttir is a psychologist in Reykjavik and has served as the director-general of the Public Health Institute of Iceland. Her main research topics are happiness, mental well-being, and the interplay between mental, physical and social well-being. Her passion lies in translating the results obtained from quality research into everyday language.

# Living in the future

'Engaging in quality of life studies in South Africa has been both rewarding and disappointing,' says Professor Valerie Møller. Over the course of some thirty years she has interviewed many thousands of South Africans from all walks of life about their personal circumstances, hopes and fears.

Our research over the years has been rewarding, in that people from many social strata have been willing to share their experiences. It has also been disappointing, in that so little seems to have changed to meet ordinary people's expectations of the good life. The most exhilarating and humbling moment was without doubt when our research recorded the joy with which South Africans greeted the advent of democracy and new-found political freedom. All South Africans, black and white, registered increased happiness and life satisfaction in the month following the country's first open elections, held in April 1994. Sadly, post-election euphoria did not last, although the goodwill created between all the citizens of the new South Africa contributed to the nation-building effort which followed.
We embarked on quality of life studies in the late 1970s, inspired by the work of pioneers such as Frank Andrews and Angus Campbell. We started by first inquiring into the everyday concerns of ordinary South Africans, who at that time were not often consulted about what would constitute a life of quality. Our first sets of indicators were based on these concerns. To our surprise, every subjective indicator we applied, in both domain-specific and overall life satisfaction assessments, perfectly reflected the unequal socio-economic and political situation in which the different racially classified groupings found themselves. **Black South Africans always scored worst, white South Africans best, with Indian and coloured South Africans somewhere in between.** The reality of apartheid seemed to cast a shadow over all aspects of life, including the most personal: even satisfaction with domains related to the self and the family were significantly lower for black South Africans. A decade and a half later, one month after the first democratic elections were held in April 1994, this pattern was broken for the first time. All South Africans were satisfied and happy at approximately the same level as most people in developed countries. This was the most exciting result any researcher could wish for.

Over the course of the next few decades, we asked people what would make their lives better – a totally unnecessary question according to World Bank economists.

We learned that material factors, the bread-and-butter issues that had been denied to people under apartheid, dominated the wish list now that political freedom had been achieved. Tellingly, the newly elected democratic government, perfectly attuned to the hearts and minds of the people, had chosen 'a better life for all' as its election slogan. However, translating that slogan into reality for over 40 million people would take time.

In those cases where the good life has been achieved, our subjective well-being scores have consistently reflected these improvements. People seem to appreciate the comforts and security of a solid roof over their head, clean water and electricity, and education for their children – things that are taken for granted by many in developed countries. However, in South Africa a higher standard of living may symbolise more than simple material progress. **A good material life is a badge of dignity** for people who in the past have been treated as second-class citizens in their own country.

After 15 years of democracy the good life has not still materialised for many South Africans, who continue to be dissatisfied with their lot, according to our quality of life measures. I have often wondered how the many South Africans who still score so low on our various indicators of personal well-being have managed to keep going. A clue may be another consistent trend we have found in our research. Namely, that the South Africans who are currently dissatisfied with their lives almost always tell us that they expect things to get better. In more recent times, even HIV-positive women contemplating a premature death seem to be capable of imagining a brighter future, if not for themselves then at least for the children they have brought into the world. This is probably the most important lesson that I have learnt while conducting quality of life studies in South Africa. Patience and hope that life will improve, and faith in a 'brighter future' (as many of our respondents put it) have helped to sustain many South Africans through the difficult times. Sometimes I have even speculated whether a more revealing indicator of South African well-being might be *prospective* rather than *present* happiness!

Professor Valerie Møller is head of the Quality of Life Research Programme at the Institute of Social and Economic Research at Rhodes University in Grahamstown, South Africa. She has published several books and is the initiator of the South African Quality of Life Trends Project.

# *A person is no average*

Does happiness mean the same thing for an American businessman and a Japanese nurse? Do the same things make a Swiss retiree and a street child from an Indian slum happy? **Hein Zegers** pays them a visit and just asks them.

**What makes you happy?** I have been asking this question for twenty years in seven languages in more than 100 countries all over the world. Some findings:

→ All over the world, the answer to "what makes you happy" tends to revolve around **other living beings.** Family. Children. Friends. Pets. Neighbours. A smile from a random passer-by. A kiss. Being able to help somebody. Dancing together. Eating together. A pat on the back from a co-worker. Many inhabitants from certain countries are even unable to answer the question "what makes you happy", and automatically start talking about their family or village: for them, "my happiness" overlaps with "our happiness".

→ At first glance, it may look like people do not know what makes them happy. The truth may be somewhat more nuanced: possibly people do know what makes them happy but don't necessarily act that way. A chain smoker may tell you that "good health" makes him happy. A career-focused manager will explain that "leisure time with the family" makes him happy. **People may very well know what makes them happy, yet do something utterly different.**

→ **What makes the average person happy doesn't necessarily make you happy.** Asparagus may be a delicacy for many people, yet this doesn't prove that you like it. The same applies to happiness. A study found for instance that on average, childless couples tend to be happier than couples with children. This does not mean that you will personally be happier without children. A person is no average.

*'Asparagus may be a delicacy for many people,*
*yet this doesn't prove that you like it.'*

**What makes people happy?** After 20 years of research, I still don't know. But I do know what makes Noriko, Jim, Ahmed and Gertrude happy. And that listening to their story makes me happy…

## The keys

→ **Wherever you come from, other people are essential to your happiness.**
→ **Knowing and doing what makes you happy don't necessarily go together.**
→ **Averages from happiness studies may not apply to you.**

Hein Zegers (master in psychology and languages, KULeuven, Belgium) lived, travelled and worked in more than 100 countries in a variety of international jobs. Later in life, he started studying psychology, focusing on positive psychology and the science of happiness. At this moment, he is actively involved in several positive psychology organizations (EvidenceBasedHappiness, Belgische Positieve Psychologie Positive Belge, ENPP, Positieve Psychologie in Uitvoering, IPPA & SIPPA, …).

Graciela Tonon de Toscano

# The key called friendship

During the economical-political-social-national crisis at the beginning of this century, whenever I studied the latest measures of happiness I always noticed the high value people gave to the importance of having friends as a means to increase their quality of life and happiness. As an Argentine, I can understand this. Our country was constructed and our history was written by people who came to Argentina all over the world. They, too, were trying to find a better quality of life, and for them, too, friendship was an important value. Many only arrived here because a friend took their hand, and many only stayed here because other friends gave them shelter in their home.

In Argentina, we meet our friends to feel better. This is as true for children in the kindergarten as for elderly people in their retirement homes. Friendship is one of the more important values of our society. It offers the possibility to share our happiness and to benefit from the support of others when we are suffering. Friendship helps people to feel happier and so it is no exaggeration to say that friendship is one of the crucial keys to happiness.

My father told me that having good friends is one of the most important things in your life. He was right. I feel constant gratitude towards them: their loyalty and affection have always given me faith and courage when things were not going well. Friendship is a unique relation between persons, characterised by loyalty, sincerity, generosity, care and support. This means that it is a relation that persists in time and in space. When you don't have a family, or when your family is far away; when you don't have money, a job or good health, the support of good friends is one of the few possibilities you have to be happy. Friends always give us the hope of a better future.

Graciela Tonon de Toscano is Chairperson of the South America Regional Committee of the International Society for Quality of Life Studies. She works in Argentina as a professor and researcher at the Universidad Palermo, the Universidad Nacional de Lomas de Zamora and the Universidad Nacional de La Matanza. Her main research interests are quality of life and public policies.

# *The movement for happiness*

'Increasingly people ask: "what is progress?" For fifty years we have aimed at higher incomes – and got them. Yet over the same period, there has been no increase in happiness (in Britain or the U.S.), as measured by surveys. And there has been a shocking rise in the number of unhappy and disturbed children. Clearly we have got our priorities wrong and our society needs a radical change of tack.' **Richard Layard** is a specialist on happiness economics, based on modern happiness research. He has recently helped to launch a new international Movement for Happiness.

## The challenge

When we look at what causes differences in happiness between individuals and societies, seven main factors emerge: income; relationships at home; relationships at work (if you have work); relationships in the community; health; personal values; and personal freedom. Income is enormously important to people. But over time, as an advanced society gets richer, its people become no happier. The most important factor in explaining the variation of happiness is the quality of personal relationships. And a key element in any relationship is trust. For many years and in many countries surveys have asked the question 'Do you think that most other people can be trusted?' This is a very interesting question. More trusting people are happier – and so are more trusting societies, like those in Scandinavia.

In Britain and the United States fifty years ago, 60% said 'yes' in answer to this question. Now the figure is down to 30%. That is a measure of what we have lost through the excessive emphasis we have put upon competition between people – all in the name of greater efficiency and wealth-creation. But solidarity and fellow-feeling are also crucial to the enjoyment of life. Competition between organisations is good and necessary, but exaggerated competition between individuals can destroy happiness.

Commitment to a happier society has major implications both for our individual lives and for the construction of public policy. As individuals, we should clearly choose work which we believe is beneficial to others – if it raises the bottom line but brings no serious benefits to society, we should not do it. And we should not by overwork impair the quality of our domestic life. In our private lives, we should take into account all those whose happiness we affect. A good word to describe this aspiration is 'harmony', since it brings out the fact that all parties gain, including ourselves.

If governments seek to promote happiness, does this mean that they will interfere more and more in people's lives? In fact, governments have long sought to promote happiness as one of their objectives. But when I published my book on happiness, one review was headed 'The Happiness Police' and another 'The Bureaucrats of Bliss'. Thus, according to some people, it is perfectly acceptable for private ethics to follow the 'greatest happiness' principle, but not for public policy, because that would lead to the 'Nanny State' or even the 'road to serfdom'. In its extreme form, this argument is absurd. Everyone knows – and the evidence clearly shows – how loss of freedom generates misery: the countries of the former Soviet Union were the least happy countries for which we have evidence – less happy even than the Third World. As we shall see, a happiness-based policy would lead to some new state-sponsored activity – schools would build resilience, parents would be offered more support, there would be more help for mental illness, and so on. The state would also have greater regard to feelings and behaviour, relative to the material and income-generating aspects of life. But it would not necessarily do more things; instead, it would perhaps do different things. It might actually have less regard to some of the material aspects of life – because the detailed regulation of economic life drives many people to distraction, as do reorganisations and other forms of behaviour which bureaucrats gaily initiate with no regard to their impact on happiness. Overall, there is no a priori way to say whether a happiness-oriented state would be more or less active in people's lives.

We do not necessarily need a bigger state – too much regulation reduces happiness. But we do need a different state. If the chief objective of government is really the happiness of the people, we shall require a huge change in government priorities.

**Schools.** Schools must be as much concerned with developing character as with imparting knowledge. Young people must learn to regulate their emotions and behaviour, and must acquire the resilience to withstand adversity. At the same time, they must learn to care for other people. These life skills can be acquired partly through a good school ethos, based strongly on the values of respect and harmonious living. But they also need to be developed through the specific teaching of life skills. This can only be provided through well-trained teachers, who in secondary schools need to be mainly specialists in the subject. One un-surprising finding of recent research illustrates the importance of positivity. If one of our aims for adolescents is to reduce drugs, overeating, smoking, drunkenness and loveless sex, it turns out that the most effective programmes are those that develop positive interests – concentrating on what you should do, rather than what you should not do. This type of finding is a regular feature of happiness research.

**Mental health.** Health, and especially mental health, is vital for happiness. In Britain, mental illness accounts for nearly half of all disability, and the effect of depression on ordinary life is 50% higher than the effect of common chronic physical illnesses like arthritis, angina, asthma and diabetes. Within Britain a record of mental health explains more of today's misery than is explained by family poverty. Mental illness should be taken as seriously as physical illness. In Britain 1 in 10 children and 1 in 6 adults could be diagnosed as suffering from depression, or from an anxiety or conduct disorder. However, only a quarter of these are in treatment, compared with over 90% of people suffering from physical illnesses (which are in many cases less serious).

**Employment.** It is far more important to provide employment for all than it is to raise the long-term rate of economic growth. Young people leaving school need to feel that society wants them, because it offers them meaningful job opportunities.

**Community and equality.** We want a high-trust society in which people have confidence in the good will of their fellow citizens. Research confirms that higher trust and less violence are more common where societies are more equal. And happiness research also confirms that extra money is more valuable to poorer people than to those who already have more. So a healthy community is one in which there is not excessive inequality.

**Environment.** There will be little future happiness in a world beset by droughts, floods and mass migration. There is thus complete congruence between a movement which aims at a more humane society and one which aims at a more harmonious relationship between man and the planet.

**Measurement.** In the end, governments will only take happiness seriously if they also measure it. At a recent OECD Conference on 'What is progress?', Joseph Stiglitz said: 'If you measure the wrong thing, you will do the wrong thing.' How right he is! National governments and local governments need to make regular surveys of the happiness of their people in order to monitor trends, to identify the main pockets of distress, and to have an information base for deepening our understanding of the causes of happiness. And social science should become largely the study of how happiness is determined.

Our society is unnecessarily harsh and it is full of unnecessary suffering. We can surely move onto a higher plateau, with more happiness and less misery. But two things are needed for this to happen. First, we have to agree that this is the objective. And then we have to use all available knowledge and all our spiritual strength to get there.

## Let's move

To improve their personal quality of life, many turn to the burgeoning literature on self-help and to the new science of positive psychology. Policy-makers too sense the need for a change of direction. But much of this activity is sporadic and unco-ordinated. That is why we are creating a Movement for Happiness. The aim is to develop world-wide a group of like-minded people who share common values and can organise themselves in ways that advance their personal happiness and the happiness of the communities where they live. The movement will be based on three principles, to which its supporters will commit themselves. We should each aim to produce more happiness in the world and, above all, to reduce misery. Public policy should have these same objectives, and we should use new knowledge to promote these ends.

This is an ethical movement, based on scientific evidence. It is not about helping people to 'cultivate their garden'; it is about building a society where people care more for each other. That will be good for everybody. For the evidence shows that helping others generally makes you happier, and it certainly makes the others happier.

## The keys

→ **We need a different kind of State, based on trust, solidarity, fellow-feeling and harmony.**

→ **Governments should actively promote happiness: teaching life skills in schools, taking mental illness seriously, providing employment for all, promoting equality, protecting the environment...**

→ **We have to agree that more happiness and less misery is our common objective. And then we have to use all available knowledge and all our spiritual strength to get there.**

Baron Richard Layard is the director of the Well-being Programme at the London School of Economics (United Kingdom). He is an authority on policy-making and happiness economics. He has been advising important policy-makers and organisations throughout the world for many years. Layard graduated in 1967 and has published more than 40 books and numerous articles. His book 'Happiness: lessons from a new science' has been translated into more than 20 languages.

# What we know

After more than 30 years of studying worldwide happiness, **Ruut Veenhoven** is often called 'The Happiness Professor'. He founded the World Database of Happiness, offering the world an updated insight into thousands of studies, surveys and correlational findings on happiness. Answering five questions, he finally summarizes what we know about happiness.

Happiness is a main goal in modern society. Most individuals seek to live a happy life and see much value in happiness. At the same time, support for the moral standpoint that we should aim at greater happiness for a greater number of people is growing. Consequently, happiness is also moving up on the political agenda.

This pursuit of happiness calls for an understanding of conditions for happiness and this in turn requires a systematic study of the subject. The study of happiness has long been a playground for philosophical speculation and this has not resulted in a solid evidence base. During the last decades, survey-research methods introduced by the social sciences have brought a break-through. Dependable measures of happiness have developed, by means of which a significant body of knowledge has evolved. This literature on happiness can be framed within five key-questions that can be ordered as steps in the process for creating greater happiness for a greater number.

## 1   What is 'happiness'?

The word 'happiness' is used in various ways. In the widest sense it is an umbrella term for all that is good. In this meaning it is often used interchangeably with terms like 'well-being' or 'quality of life', and denotes both individual and social welfare. The word is also used in the more specific meaning of 'a subjective appreciation of life' and it is on this meaning that this chapter will concentrate. Happiness is defined as *the degree to which an individual judges the overall quality of his/her own life-as-a-whole favourably*. In other words: how much one likes the life one leads.

## 2 Can happiness be measured?

Since happiness is defined as something we have in mind, it can be measured using questions. A common question is:

**All things considered, how satisfied are you with your life as a whole these days?**

0 / 1 / 2 / 3 / 4 / 5 / 6 / 7 / 8 / 9 / 10

**extremely dissatisfied** ← ——————————— → **extremely satisfied**

Though currently used, these questions are much criticized. Three main objections have been raised: it is doubted that responses to such simple questions reflect a true appreciation of life; there are doubts about the comparability of such ratings across cultures; and it is claimed that subjective appraisals of life are meaningless. These qualms have been discussed elsewhere and rejected by serious studies of Diener, Saris and others. The doubt about the comparability of responses to such questions across cultures has also been disproved in earlier studies of mine.

## 3 How happy are we?

Look at an example. Below is the response to this question in Germany. The most frequently chosen options are 7, 8 and 9 and only 14% score below 5. The average is 7.2. This result implies that most Germans must feel happy most of the time. We can compare this with the results of other countries and construct a global ranking.

**Scheme 1: Happiness in Germany** – Source: European Social Survey 2006

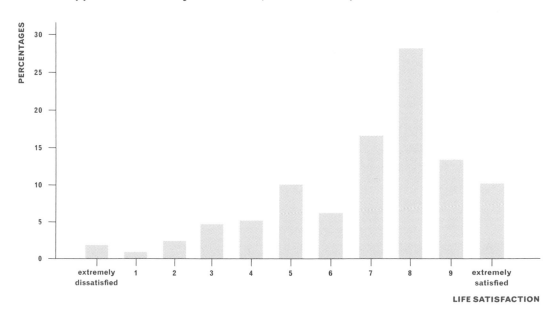

## 4  What causes us to be more or less happy?

Having established that people differ in happiness, the next question is *why*.
Various factors are involved: collective action and individual behaviour, simple
sensory experiences and higher cognition, stable characteristics of the individual
and his environment, as well as freaks of fate. Scheme 2 presents a tentative ordering
of factors and processes in a sequence model.

The model presumes that the judgment of life draws on the *flow-of-life experiences*,
particularly on positive and negative experience. The flow of experiences is a mental
reaction to the *course-of-life events*. This includes major one-time events, such as marriage
or migrations, as well as repetitious mundane events, like getting up in the morning
and doing the dishes. The events that happen in life are partly a matter of good or bad luck,
such as in the case of accidents. The occurrences of life-events also depend on given
conditions and capacities. Traffic accidents are less frequent in well-organized societies
and among attentive persons. Thus, the chances of 'rewarding' and 'aversive' events
are not the same for everybody. This is commonly referred to as *life-chances*.
Present life-chances root in past events and chance-structures, in societal history
as well as individual development.

An example may serve to illustrate this four-step model: A person's life-chances
may be poor because he/she lives in a lawless society, is in a powerless position within
that society, and is personally neither smart nor nice (Step 1). That person will run into
many adverse events. He/she will be robbed, duped, humiliated and excluded (Step 2).
Consequently, that person will frequently feel anxious, angry and lonely (Step 3).
Based on this flow of experience it is reasonable to assume that the person will judge
their life-as-a-whole negatively (Step 4).

**Scheme 2: Evaluation of life: a sequence model of conditions and processes**

| LIFE-CHANCES ⟶ | COURSE OF EVENTS ⟶ | FLOW OF EXPERIENCE ⟶ | EVALUATION OF LIFE |
|---|---|---|---|
| **Quality of society**<br>• Economic welfare<br>• Social equality<br>• Political freedom<br>• Cultural lush<br>• Moral order<br>• Etc. | **Confrontation with:**<br>• Deficit or affluence<br>• Attack or protection<br>• Solitude or company<br>• Humiliation or honour<br>• Routine or challenge<br>• Ugliness or beauty<br>• Etc. | **Experiences of:**<br>• Yearning or satiation<br>• Anxiety or safety<br>• Loneliness or love<br>• Rejection or respect<br>• Dullness<br>  or excitement<br>• Repulsion or rapture<br>• Etc… | Appraisal of<br>average affect<br><br>Comparison<br>with standards<br>of the good life<br><br>Striking an overall<br>balance of life |
| **Social position**<br>• Material property<br>• Political influence<br>• Social prestige<br>• Family bonds<br>• Etc. | | | |
| **Individual abilities**<br>• Physical fitness<br>• Psychic fortitude<br>• Social capability<br>• Intellectual skill<br>• Etc. | | | |
| **Conditions for happiness** | | **Appraisal process** | |

# Quality of society

Why does happiness differ so much across nations? Scheme 3 presents some of the societal qualities which underlie these differences. Many of these factors are part of the 'modernity' syndrome. The more modern the country, the happier its citizens are. This finding will be a surprise to the prophets of doom, who associate modernity with anomie and alienation. Though modernisation may indeed involve problems of this kind, its benefits are clearly greater. The following characteristics of society correlate positively with happiness (in declining order): affluence, economic freedom, urbanisation, schooling, political freedom, civil rights, tolerance of minorities, personal freedom, pluriformity (% of migrants). The highest negative correlation is corruption, followed at some distance by gender inequality and income inequality.

**Scheme 3: Happiness and society** in 146 nations, circa 2006

| CHARACTERISTICS OF SOCIETY | CORRELATION WITH HAPPINESS |
|---|:---:|
| **Affluence** | + .69 |
| **Rule of law** | |
| • Civil rights | + .50 |
| • Corruption | – .69 |
| **Freedom** | |
| • Economical | + .63 |
| • Political | + .53 |
| • Personal | + .41 |
| **Equality** | |
| • Income inequality | – .08 |
| • Gender inequality | – .21 |
| **Pluriformity** | |
| • % Migrants | + .29 |
| • Tolerance of minorities | + .49 |
| **Modernity** | |
| • Schooling | + .56 |
| • Urbanisation | + .58 |

How do you read this scheme?
The maximum is always
+ 1.00 or – 1.00.
The higher the positive number,
the higher the positive relationship.
The lower the negative number,
the lower the negative relationship.
Source: World Database of Happiness
(Veenhoven 2010); (p. 346)

# Social position

Numerous studies all over the world have considered differences in individual happiness within countries. Because most of these studies are inspired by egalitarian social policy, the emphasis is often on social differences, such as differences in income, education and employment. Contrary to expectation, these positional differences bear little relationship to happiness, at least not in a modern affluent society. Together, the positional variables explain no more than 10% of the variance in happiness. The main findings are summarized in Scheme 4.

There is a worldwide positive correlation between happiness and occupational prestige, participation in associations, having a spouse and having friends.

**Scheme 4: Happiness and position in society: summary of research findings**

| | CORRELATION *within* western nations | SIMILARITY OF CORRELATION *across* all nations |
|---|:---:|:---:|
| **Social rank** | | |
| • Income | + | – |
| • Education | ± | – |
| • Occupational prestige | + | + |
| **Social participation** | | |
| • Employment | ± | + |
| • Participation in associations | + | + |
| **Primary network** | | |
| • Spouse | ++ | + |
| • Children | 0 | ? |
| • Friends | + | + |

| | |
|---|---|
| ++ Strongly positive | + Similar correlations |
| + Positive | ± Varying |
| 0 No relationship | – Different correlations |
| – Negative | |
| ? Not yet investigated | ? No data |

Source: World Database of Happiness, collection of correlational findings (Veenhoven 2009); (p. 346)

# Life ability

The strongest correlations are observed at the psychological level; happy people are typically better endowed intellectually than the unhappy. The common variance explained by such variables tends to be around 30%. Some of the main findings are summarized in Scheme 5.

Many of the findings on individual variations in happiness boil down to a difference in *ability to control one's environment*. This pattern seems to be universal.

There is a worldwide positive correlation between happiness and mental health, sociability, physical health, internal control, extraversion and lust acceptance.

**Scheme 5: Happiness and life abilities: summary of research findings**

|  | CORRELATION *within* western nations | SIMILARITY OF CORRELATION *across* all nations |
|---|:---:|:---:|
| **Proficiencies** |  |  |
| • Physical health | + | + |
| • Mental health | ++ | + |
| • IQ | 0 | + |
| **Personality** |  |  |
| • Internal control | + | + |
| • Extraversion | + | + |
| • Conscientiousness | + | ? |
| **Art of living** |  |  |
| • Lust acceptance | + | + |
| • Sociability | ++ | + |

| ++ | Strongly positive | + | Similar correlations |
|---|---|---|---|
| + | Positive | ± | Varying |
| 0 | No relationship | – | Different correlations |
| – | Negative |  |  |
| ? | Not yet investigated | ? | No data |

Source: World Database of Happiness, collection of correlational findings (Veenhoven 2009); (p. 346)

## 5   Is greater happiness possible?

Much of the research on happiness is prompted by the hope of finding ways to create greater happiness for a greater number of people. However, there are several theories about happiness, which imply that the improvement of living conditions will not reduce discontent.

One such theory is that happiness is relative. Another is the theory that happiness is a trait. Both theories have been tested and have been rejected by our research. Another comforting finding is that average happiness can be as high as 8 on a 0-10 scale. If this is possible in these surveyed countries, it should also be possible in other nations.

---

Ruut Veenhoven is emeritus-professor of 'social conditions for human happiness' at the Erasmus University Rotterdam (The Netherlands). He studied sociology and is also accredited in social psychology and social-sexuology. He is often called 'The Happiness Professor' and is respected worldwide for his lifelong research on the subjective quality of life. His major publications are: 'Conditions of Happiness', 'Happiness in Nations' and 'Happy Life-expectancy'. Ruut Veenhoven is founder and director of the Word Database of Happiness and editor of the 'Journal of Happiness Studies'.

# The World Database Of Happiness

Greater happiness for a greater number of people requires better knowledge of the conditions necessary for happiness. Better knowledge in turn requires not only more research, but also better synthesis of the available research findings. Research synthesis requires that the available findings are gathered, selected and described in a uniform way. This preliminary work is time consuming and ill-funded, and given the present scale of the task is impossible for a single researcher to complete in a lifetime. As a result, we risk losing sight of the lessons which this data can teach.

The World Database of Happiness is a tool for dealing with the growing stream of research findings on happiness; both distributional findings (how happy people are) and correlational findings (concomitants of happiness). In its focus on 'findings' the system differs from data-archives that store 'investigations' and from bibliographies that store 'publications'. As yet, there is no established word for this tool for research synthesis. We call it a 'finding catalogue'.

The substantive focus of this database is on subjective enjoyment of one's life-as-a-whole. The database contains five related collections on this matter: 1) The 'bibliography of happiness', which lists some 4,000 publications; 2) a collection of acceptable 'measures of happiness', which contains about 800 variants; 3) the collection of 'happiness in nations' which lists the distributional findings of some 3,000 general population surveys at national level; 4) the collection of 'happiness in groupings', containing the results of some 3,000 studies among particular categories within nations; and 5) the collection of 'correlational findings', which cross-references some 11,000 findings on covariates of happiness.

These collections can be browsed on the internet at
**www.worlddatabaseofhappiness.eur.nl**

# Average happiness in 148 nations 2000-2009

Source: World Database of Happiness, collection Happiness in Nations,
Rank report Average Happiness (Veenhoven 2009).

| | | | | |
|---|---|---|---|---|
| Afghanistan | 4.1 | | Czech Republic | 6.5 |
| Albania | 4.6 | | Denmark | 8.3 |
| Algeria | 5.4 | | Djibouti | 5.7 |
| Andorra | 6.8 | | Dominican Republic | 7.6 |
| Angola | 4.3 | | Ecuador | 6.4 |
| Argentina | 7.3 | | Egypt | 5.7 |
| Armenia | 5.0 | | El Salvador | 6.7 |
| Australia | 7.7 | | Estonia | 5.9 |
| Austria | 7.7 | | Ethiopia | 4.2 |
| Azerbaijan | 5.3 | | Finland | 7.9 |
| Bangladesh | 5.3 | | France | 6.6 |
| Belarus | 5.7 | | Georgia | 4.3 |
| Belgium | 7.3 | | Germany | 7.1 |
| Belize | 6.6 | | Ghana | 5.2 |
| Benin | 3.0 | | Greece | 6.3 |
| Bolivia | 6.5 | | Guatemala | 7.2 |
| Bosnia | 5.8 | | Guinea | 4.5 |
| Botswana | 4.7 | | Guyana | 6.5 |
| Brazil | 7.5 | | Haiti | 3.9 |
| Bulgaria | 4.4 | | Honduras | 7.0 |
| Burkina Faso | 4.4 | | Hong Kong | 6.0 |
| Burundi | 2.9 | | Hungary | 5.5 |
| Cambodia | 4.9 | | Iceland | 8.2 |
| Cameroon | 3.9 | | India | 5.5 |
| Canada | 8.0 | | Indonesia | 6.1 |
| Central African Republic | 4.6 | | Iran | 5.8 |
| Chad | 5.4 | | Iraq | 4.7 |
| Chile | 6.6 | | Ireland | 7.6 |
| China | 6.4 | | Israel | 6.9 |
| Colombia | 7.7 | | Italy | 6.7 |
| Congo-Brazzaville | 3.7 | | Ivory Coast | 4.5 |
| Congo (Kinshasa) | 4.4 | | Jamaica | 6.7 |
| Costa Rica | 8.5 | | Japan | 6.2 |
| Croatia | 6.0 | | Jordan | 6.2 |
| Cyprus | 7.0 | | Kazakhstan | 6.1 |

| | | | | |
|---|---|---|---|---|
| Kenya | 3.4 | | Qatar | 6.8 |
| Kosovo | 5.4 | | Romania | 5.7 |
| Kuwait | 6.6 | | Russia | 5.6 |
| Kyrgezigstan | 5.5 | | Rwanda | 4.3 |
| Laos | 6.2 | | Saudi Arabia | 6.5 |
| Latvia | 5.3 | | Senegal | 4.5 |
| Lebanon | 4.7 | | Serbia | 5.6 |
| Liberia | 4.3 | | Sierra Leone | 3.6 |
| Lithuania | 5.5 | | Singapore | 6.7 |
| Luxembourg | 7.7 | | Slovakia | 5.8 |
| Macedonia | 4.7 | | Slovenia | 6.9 |
| Madagascar | 3.7 | | South Africa | 6.0 |
| Malawi | 4.8 | | South Korea | 6.1 |
| Malaysia | 6.6 | | Spain | 7.3 |
| Mali | 4.7 | | Sri Lanka | 5.1 |
| Malta | 7.1 | | Sudan | 5.0 |
| Mauritania | 5.0 | | Sweden | 7.8 |
| Mexico | 7.9 | | Switzerland | 8.0 |
| Moldova | 4.9 | | Syria | 5.9 |
| Mongolia | 5.7 | | Taiwan | 6.2 |
| Montenegro | 5.2 | | Tajikistan | 5.1 |
| Morocco | 5.3 | | Tanzania | 2.6 |
| Mozambique | 3.8 | | Thailand | 6.6 |
| Namibia | 5.2 | | Togo | 2.6 |
| Nepal | 5.3 | | Trinidad-Tabago | 7.0 |
| Netherlands | 7.6 | | Tunisia | 5.9 |
| New Zealand | 7.5 | | Turkey | 5.8 |
| Nicaragua | 7.1 | | Uganda | 4.5 |
| Niger | 3.8 | | Ukraine | 5.0 |
| Nigeria | 5.7 | | United Arab Emirates | 7.3 |
| Norway | 7.9 | | United Kingdom (Britain) | 7.2 |
| Pakistan | 5.4 | | United States of America (USA) | 7.4 |
| Palestina | 5.0 | | Uruguay | 6.8 |
| Panama | 7.8 | | Uzbekistan | 6.0 |
| Paraguay | 6.9 | | Venezuela | 7.2 |
| Peru | 6.3 | | Vietnam | 6.1 |
| Philippines | 5.5 | | Yemen | 4.8 |
| Poland | 6.3 | | Zambia | 5.0 |
| Portugal | 5.7 | | Zimbabwe | 2.8 |

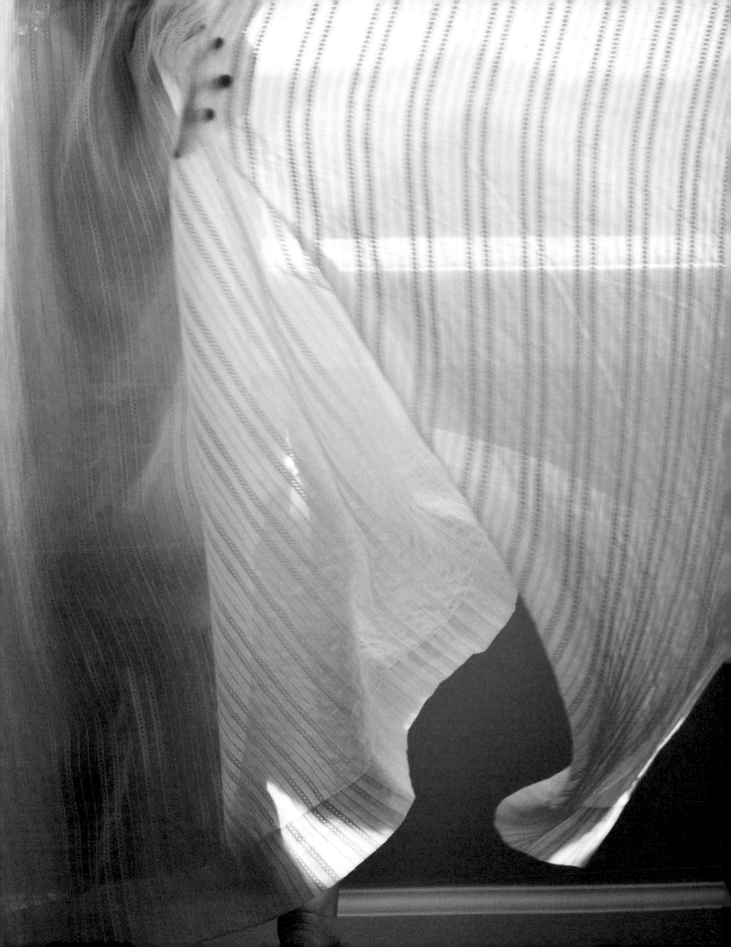

YOU
MAKE ME
HAPP*en*